THE CONNOISSEUR
ILLUSTRATED GUIDES

Furniture

GENERAL EDITOR

David Coombs

THE CONNOISSEUR ILLUSTRATED GUIDES

Furniture

EDWARD JOY

Drawings by Peter Fitzjohn

HEARST BOOKS · NEW YORK

First published 1972
by The Connoisseur
Chestergate House, Vauxhall Bridge Road
London SW1V 1HF

ISBN 0 87851 300 0

Filmset and printed in
Great Britain by
BAS Printers Limited, Wallop, Hampshire
and bound by
G & J Kitcat Ltd
Shand Street, London SE1

Contents

List of Plates

List of Plates

Introduction

This book sets out to describe and illustrate the history of English furniture, from the early medieval period (13th century) until the present day, showing how it has changed in type, form, decoration and construction as it followed the dictates of fashion, employed new materials and adapted itself to the requirements of social life. The social background indeed provides the key to the story, for furniture is above all functional. It is an essential part of the home and its specific purpose is to minister to the many activities—meals, entertainments, recreation, study and so on—and the inactivities— sleep and rest—of domestic life. It thus follows that the study of furniture is a most illuminating guide to the social conventions of the past, giving us, in the words that Horace Walpole (*Anecdotes of Painting in England*, 1762–80) used about the furniture in Hogarth's paintings, 'the history of the manners of the age.'

Changing conventions can alter the usefulness of a piece of furniture or the status accorded to it in the household, or they can bring new pieces into existence as older forms are discarded. Chairs, once reserved for the privileged few, have become commonplace and of great diversity. The chest, one of the most important and essential of medieval pieces, is still with us and still fulfils its original function of storage, but it is of much less significance. One-time status symbols in wealthy households, such as the Tudor court cupboard, the late Stuart cabinet and the Georgian commode, are now collectors' pieces, though some of their functions have continued in other types of furniture. Other pieces, such as the fire screen, which in their day were made with great skill and care, have since been rendered entirely obsolete by changes in household conditions. Many familiar and permanent types of furniture however still remain with us.

Fashionable furniture—that made by the best craftsmen for patrons of wealth and position—is the most susceptible to change. Cottage, country, or vernacular furniture changes least. Vernacular furniture has indeed amazing continuity. It is by definition simple and functional and related directly to basic needs. Some vernacular pieces such as the Windsor chair are recorded throughout the many centuries covered by this book, with only slight modifications of form and none of function. Today special attention is being paid to the intrinsic merits of functional forms, which are particularly suited to machine production. There is thus special point in the study of vernacular furniture, for its simple, utilitarian character, maintained over the centuries by hand skill to serve the needs of primitive communities, has surprising significance for our industrial society.

In the development of English furniture we can see that sensitivity to social change and needs has produced vitality in craftsmanship and a rich variety of forms, while vernacular furniture has made a special contribution to functional design. Both these aspects are examined in detail, with a further note that utilitarian functional forms played an important part in the thinking of those progressive English furniture designers of the 19th century whose work formed the basis of 20th-century design.

Another vital factor in the design of English furniture has been its reaction to foreign influences, mainly from the Continent, but also at times from the Far East. From Europe have come the major techno-logical advances in furniture: the panel and frame construction from Flanders in the 15th century, and with it the emergence of the English joiner; the technique of veneering from France and Holland in the late 17th century, producing the English cabinet-maker; the mechanised production of furniture (and with it new materials) from Germany and Scandinavia in the 20th century, creating the English industrial designer. Europe has always been a free trade area for furniture styles, techniques and forms of decoration—this liberal give-and-take of ideas being in marked contrast to the rigid and bitter protectionist policies which its member-states adopted in the world of commerce. All this has created a steady flow of foreign influences into English furniture-making, to be transmuted into forms suitable for English society. The debt to these influences has always been freely acknowledged. What has not been equally acknowledged is the influence which English craftsmen and designers in their turn have had on foreign furniture.

The French have excelled, under royal and aristocratic patronage, in producing magnificent furniture treated as a field of decoration—furniture which the English upper classes have always admired, acquired or imitated. For exquisite decoration of wood surfaces South Germans have gained universal esteem (so much so that for centuries the French monarchy imported German craftsmen to make furniture). English furniture has its own special place in world furniture for its general simplicity of form, fine craftsmanship and fitness of purpose. Unpretentious yet graceful, showing the beauty of the wood to the full, this furniture has had great appeal to middle classes abroad. Since the late 17th century it has been sent to all parts of the world, making England, with her superb trading position, the largest exporter of furniture in Europe.

It is significant that while foreign furniture styles take their names from rulers, as in France, or from urban and regional centres of craft activity, as in Germany and Italy, England alone has given currency to styles (as distinct from decorative processes) which are named after individual craftsmen.

The earlier part of this book stresses the major developments in foreign furniture which most affected England, where until the late 17th century standards lagged far behind those on the Continent. From that time the story is one of the increasing influence of English furniture overseas. In no area was this more apparent than in America, the first area outside England where her craftsmen settled permanently. The happy relationship between English and American furniture has now some three centuries behind it, and is well worth studying.

THE CONNOISSEUR
ILLUSTRATED GUIDES

Furniture

1
Gothic
to c.1500

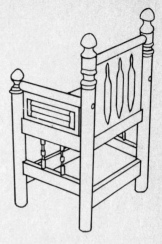

SCANDINAVIAN CHAIR WITH TURNED STRUCTURAL
MEMBERS
*c.*1200

With the collapse of the Roman Empire after the barbarian invasions of the 5th century A.D., the fine furniture developed over the centuries by Graeco-Roman civilisations, and the technical skills which went to making it, were almost entirely swept away in western Europe, although they lingered on in the Byzantine Empire and in Italy. In the West the old traditional craft skills had to be slowly re-learnt, for the primitive conditions of life gave little incentive for the cultivation of comfort and the household arts. Very little of the small amount of furniture that was made in western Europe before c. 1500 has survived. For information about it we have to rely upon illuminated manuscripts, paintings, sculptures and carvings, occasional literary references, and a few inventories. We do know that most of the domestic furniture that was made was almost exclusively used by the ruling classes, who took it round with them in their periodic tours of their territories and estates, and that is why the word for furniture in the main European languages today (English excepted) is the equivalent of 'movables'.

The most important piece of medieval furniture was the chair. It symbolised power and honour and was reserved for important personages. The monarch's throne is an obvious example, but chairs of estate were found in feudal magnates' castles, just as the bishop's throne was to be found in his cathedral (the name of which in fact derives from the Greek word for throne, *cathedra*). The chair illustrated above is Scandinavian and, dating from *c.*1200, is an unusually early survivor. It shows traces of Byzantine influence and is clearly based on stone models. The construction is simple, with turned members. An interesting point is the employment of the mortice-and-tenon joint, a technique which western Europe as a whole did not recover until the 15th century. This chair has primitive arcading, and the flat surfaces are decorated with incised lines. Almost without exception, medieval furniture was painted in bright colours or gilded, both to protect the wood and to add a touch of splendour to interiors.

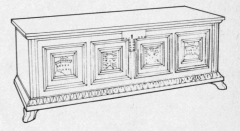

Cassone OF SARCOPHAGUS FORM WITH
RENAISSANCE DECORATION
Italian, late 15th century
(*See also colour photograph 1*)

Cassone, PANELS DECORATED WITH INTARSIA
Italian, late 15th century

The Gothic style never found a secure or happy home in Italy, where the classical tradition lingered. Venice and Genoa were the great maritime trading powers of the Middle Ages, and through commerce were in contact with the cultures of both the Byzantine and Islamic worlds. It is no surprise that in the 15th century Italy, where so many visible relics of ancient civilisation abounded, was the birthplace of the Renaissance, the great classical revival which in time was to sweep across Europe. Wealth through trade promoted a lively urban life in Italy, and the development of a mercantile class; the arts and crafts flourished under the patronage of popes, churchmen, princes, merchants and bankers. Italian furniture was naturally the first in Europe to show the far-reaching changes effected by classicism. This *cassone* (marriage chest) is of classical sarcophagus form, decorated with classical motifs centring in a coat of arms. It dates from the late 15th century.

The *cassone* was the prestige piece of the great Italian houses. Usually two such chests were ordered when a marriage alliance took place between important families, one for the bridegroom and one for the bride. Celebrated artists and craftsmen were commissioned to decorate these pieces with carved, inlaid or painted scenes and motifs. Such was their artistic excellence that collectors have been known to destroy some *cassoni* in order to remove their painted front panels. This example, however, of the late 15th century, has varied forms of decoration: a carved classical repeated decoration across the base, intarsia (inlay or marquetry, often, as here, with perspective views of architecture) on the panels, and interesting carved geometric ornament round the panels, which suggests Islamic influence. (As Islamic craftsmen and artists were forbidden by their religion to represent human and animal figures, their genius was expressed in geometric and natural-istic—arabesque—patterns.) This beautifully proportioned *cassone* was probably made in Lombardy.

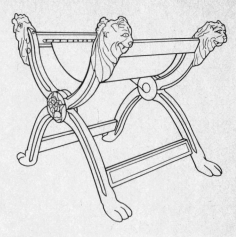

CHEST CARVED WITH GOTHIC FLAMBOYANT
TRACERY
French, late 15th century

FOLDING X-FRAME STOOL OF CLASSICAL ANTECEDENTS
German, c. 1400

While the Renaissance was making its first strides in Italy, the Gothic style continued to flourish in the rest of Europe. This French chest of the late 15th century is exquisitely carved with flamboyant tracery, that beneath the ogee arches being of extraordinary intricacy. The architectural character is further emphasised by the carved columns, complete with crockets, which stand between the panels and at the corners, in imitation of the buttresses on Gothic churches. The differences between this chest and the Italian *cassone* just examined are well worth detailed study. There was a notable increase in the production of French furniture in the closing part of the 15th century. This was to restore the amenities of life at the successful conclusion of the Hundred Years' War with England. There was also abundance of timber, as great stretches of woodland, which had encroached on farming land during the war, were cleared. But despite the excellence of French craftsmanship, there was as yet no sign of the Renaissance.

With the chair traditionally established as the seat of the privileged, stools and benches were used by persons of lower rank. The stool was the commonest form of seat, and was in fact the usual term for any kind of seat for a single person. There were, however, several kinds of stool in use, and one variety, the folding X-stool, had a more exalted function. This type had a long history behind it; counterparts have been traced to ancient Egypt and China, as well as to ancient Rome, where it was the magistrate's seat (*sella curulis*) and was made to fold up for easy transport in his chariot (or *currus*, whence also the modern name of *curule*). Fine examples, like that of 14th century date illustrated above, were reserved for persons of rank, hence the terminal carved decoration of lion's heads and paws, and the rosettes at the intersection of the members. Such stools, which later became of fixed construction, with high backs, and could not be folded, are usually known as X-chairs.

STOOL WITH TRESTLE ENDS
English, 15th century

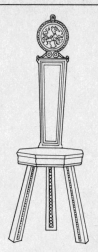

THREE-LEGGED STOOL (*sgabello*) WITH BACK
Italian, *c*.1490

A very common type of stool was three-legged, the legs (turned or cut) being socketed into rough circular tops, or joined to three seat rails in triangular form, finishing with a rush seat. Though stretchers strengthened the legs below, these tripods were insecure supports, and falling between two stools must have been a common occurrence in the medieval hall, particularly on festive occasions. During the 15th century an improved, more stable type of stool came into use. It had sloped trestle ends tenoned into the rectangular seat, as seen above in the English example. Seat rails or apron pieces were slotted into the end supports (or were nailed to them), or sometimes stretchers, often secured by wedges, were used. Gothic decoration of a simple kind can be seen in the base of each end support and in the seat rails. Sometimes a Romanesque arch could be found in Italian stools of this kind. The same sort of construction and decoration were used on contemporary long benches.

The ceremonial chair, while remaining a rarity because of its prestige value, could nevertheless take diverse forms. Another line of development, however, saw the beginning of the appearance in late medieval times of simple types of chairs, coincident with the arrival of more stable domestic conditions. One progression was *via* the stool. This Italian three-legged chair of *c*.1490, of the type known as a *sgabello*, shows clearly its close relationship with the stool, to which a slender back has been added. It evidences considerable refinement—witness the carved apex, the octagonal seat and the moulded legs. A similar but much cruder type, a triangular-seated stool with one leg continued upwards to form a back, is found in Flanders at about this time. Its peasant origins are unmistakable—an example of a type of furniture working its way upwards. The stool-chair which was to appear in England in the Tudor period was known as the back-stool, a name which precisely defines its origins. All such pieces were made without arms and were therefore never known as chairs by contemporaries.

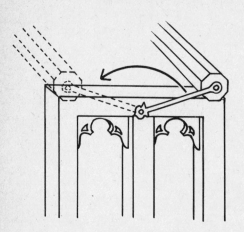

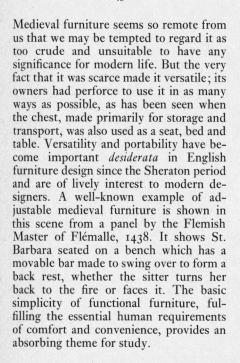

GOTHIC SWING-BACK BENCH; FROM PAINTED FLEMISH
PANEL
1438

OAK CHAIR
Probably oldest surviving English medieval example,
*c.*1250

Medieval furniture seems so remote from us that we may be tempted to regard it as too crude and unsuitable to have any significance for modern life. But the very fact that it was scarce made it versatile; its owners had perforce to use it in as many ways as possible, as has been seen when the chest, made primarily for storage and transport, was also used as a seat, bed and table. Versatility and portability have become important *desiderata* in English furniture design since the Sheraton period and are of lively interest to modern designers. A well-known example of adjustable medieval furniture is shown in this scene from a panel by the Flemish Master of Flémalle, 1438. It shows St. Barbara seated on a bench which has a movable bar made to swing over to form a back rest, whether the sitter turns her back to the fire or faces it. The basic simplicity of functional furniture, fulfilling the essential human requirements of comfort and convenience, provides an absorbing theme for study.

This chair is of special interest as it is probably the oldest surviving English chair of the medieval period. It is in St. Mary's Church, Little Dunmow, Essex, and was made about the middle of the 13th century. Its decoration of simple carved tracery shows the influence of Early English Gothic architecture. It was almost certainly part of a set of choir stalls, but there seems no reason to doubt that similar chairs were used as domestic pieces. The construction points to the development of the chair, or, to be more accurate, one important version of it, from the chest, to which a back and sides have been added. This would seem to be a natural progression from the frequent use of the chest as a seat, and it is unquestionably the basis of the development of the panel-back type of chair which became well established in England in the Tudor period. The chair of *c.*1250 shown here has, of course, undergone much change since it was first made.

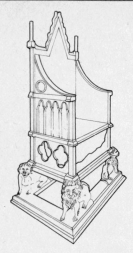

THE CORONATION CHAIR, WESTMINSTER ABBEY
Originally late 13th century, much altered

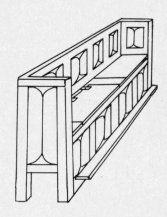

BOX SETTLE WITH HINGED LID, CARVED LINENFOLD
DECORATION
15th century

The ceremonial character of the medieval chair of estate is admirably portrayed in the most famous example in England, the oak Coronation Chair in Westminster Abbey, used at the coronation of English monarchs. Its architectural composition is obvious, with the pedimented gable and two pinnacles at the back, and carved Gothic tracery at the sides. Below the seat, in a shallow platform open at the front and perforated with two pierced quatrefoils at the sides, is the Stone of Scone, brought from Scotland by Edward I in 1296. Imposing as this chair is, it is but a shadow of its former magnificence, for it was originally richly coloured and gilded. The four lions have been added to the base, and the leopards and turrets which once adorned its crest were removed early in the 19th century. The woodwork has been mutilated The original decoration was carried out by the 'king's painter', another reminder that medieval furniture, when it was not covered by costly materials, was brightly coloured, giving it a much different appearance from that indicated by surviving examples.

During the 15th century there occurred one of the most important technical advances in the history of furniture, or, to be more accurate, the re-discovery, after some centuries, of a technique known to the ancient world. This was the panel and frame. Its purpose was strictly utilitarian, to prevent timber from splitting, which it was liable to do when rigidly nailed or pegged. A framework was now made of horizontal rails and vertical stiles, secured by the mortise-and-tenon joint, the mortise being the socket in the stile into which the tenon, the corresponding projection on the rail, was fitted and fastened by pegs. Into this framework, which was grooved on the inside, was fitted the panel, which was tapered on all sides and was thus allowed sufficient room to move to obviate warping. The box settle shown above is taken from a 15th-century German manuscript, and illustrates how a long piece of furniture is built up of a number of panels and how neatness and precision have to be achieved by the craftsman.

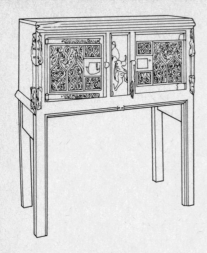

DRESSER CARVED WITH GOTHIC TRACERY; PANELLED
CONSTRUCTION
French, late 15th century

'PRINCE ARTHUR'S CUPBOARD'. DOORS PIERCED WITH
GOTHIC CARVING
c.1500

However utilitarian the object of panelling, its effect was to make furniture altogether better proportioned, lighter in appearance and stronger. Panelled furniture had to be carefully designed; measurements had to be exact and the joints had to be scrupulously executed. A new, more skilled craftsman took over from the carpenter who had been responsible for earlier furniture. This was the joiner, the maker of joined ('joynt') furniture, panelled walls, and doors. This French dresser of the 15th century is a beautiful little specimen (it is about 3½ feet high, just over 3 feet long and 1½ feet wide) with panelled doors decorated with delicate Gothic tracery. The central carved figure has been mutilated. The dresser was originally a table on trestles on which meat was dressed before being served. Later, while the already prepared meal was served from it, it was used to display fine plate and valuables, and so was given special decorative treatment.

The panel and frame technique reached England from Flanders, where a prosperous merchant class had greatly promoted the domestic crafts. So many 'Flaunders chests' were imported into England that their trade was banned for a time in the late 15th century. One of the best known survivors of the early development of English panelled furniture is 'Prince Arthur's Cupboard' of c.1500, so called because it came from a part of Shropshire with connections with Arthur, Prince of Wales, son of Henry VII. This cupboard has pierced doors, which probably indicate that it was used to store food; such types, known as livery cupboards, were used for storing the rations delivered to retainers in large households. The carvings include ornament interpreted by some observers to represent feathers (the Prince of Wales's emblem) and the letter 'A' (for 'Arthur'). The cupboard was apparently covered at one time with vermilion paint, faint traces of which can still be seen.

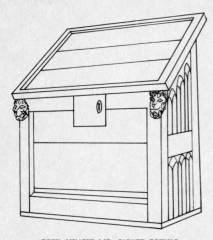

DESK, HINGED LID, CARVED GOTHIC
DECORATION AT SIDES
English, late 15th century

'TUB' CHAIR, PANELLED FRONT AND BACK CARVED WITH
GOTHIC TRACERY
Spanish, 15th century

In the 15th century, in many parts of Europe—including England—the rise of a merchant class, the slow and growing demand for domestic comfort, and the gradual decay of feudalism all promoted wider interest in furniture. Its mobile, nomadic character was slowly lost and it was being made more and more to stay in one part of the house, to become 'dormant', like the table of Chaucer's franklin which 'stood in his hall alway'. There remained, of course, pieces of furniture which were portable in the sense of being moved about the house. Such were medieval writing desks, which were shallow boxes with sloping lids, made to rest on any convenient flat surface. The desk shown here, however, is a larger one; it has a hinged top so that books and documents can be stored inside. It is English, and the carved Perpendicular arcading indicates a date in the late 15th century. Its use was spreading from colleges and schools to merchants' counting houses, and increasingly for the heavy books coming from the newly invented printing presses.

Yet another type of medieval chair is illustrated by this Spanish example of the 15th century, made of walnut. This is the tub chair, which was widely distributed throughout Europe. Its derivation is obvious, for medieval manuscripts often illustrate the type, and more primitive examples were made by cutting away parts of a large barrel. This Spanish chair is a very sophisticated example, with its panelled construction, profuse Gothic carving, and, below the seat, the central coat of arms. Gothic represents only one facet of Spain's cultural inheritance. Until the conquest of Granada in 1492 by Ferdinand and Isabella there had been a long history of the occupation of Spain by the Moors, and the latter left behind many valuable relics of their craftsmanship. Spain absorbed much of the attractive Islamic decorative approach, particularly the geometric patterning already noted on the Italian *cassone* (p. 17). Thus while the chair shows Spanish versions of the Gothic, we shall shortly see the effect of Islamic influence.

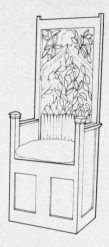

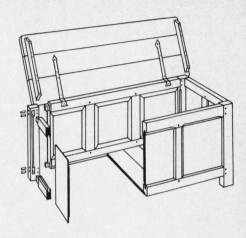

CEREMONIAL CHAIR WITH ELABORATE GOTHIC CARVING
Portuguese, *c*.1470

DIAGRAM OF PANEL AND FRAME CONSTRUCTION

The richness of Portugal's cultural heritage is perhaps only partly appreciated in England, in spite of the long political and commercial ties between the two countries (for Portugal is England's oldest ally). This heritage stems from several sources: Moorish (the Moors occupied Portugal from the 8th to the 13th centuries); Gothic; oriental (through contacts with the East in the epic period of overseas expansion); and classical, through the Renaissance, which in Portugal owed a great deal to the work of immigrant artists and craftsmen. The Portuguese have always shown a flair for lively decoration, and this elaborately carved ceremonial chair is an excellent example of their interpretation of the Gothic in the late 15th century. It was made *c*.1470, and has been traditionally known as the throne of D. Alfonso V.

The evidence so far considered, particularly in the references to French and Italian pieces, shows how much English furniture, for most of the medieval period, lagged behind continental standards in constructional and decorative techniques. Until the 15th century the wooden framework of even the best furniture was obviously of much less consideration than the decorative finishes applied by painters, gilders, carvers, turners, coffer-makers (p. 36) and upholders (the name by which upholsterers were known until the 18th century). Against this background the revolutionary impact of the panel and frame technique, when the woodwork of furniture became of prime importance, can be readily gauged, though the new method was inevitably slow in establishing itself and a clear demarcation between the functions of carpenters and their more skilled rivals, the joiners, was not resolved until the 17th century. The diagram here shows the care that was now necessary over dimensions, preparation of timber and jointing.

2 Early Renaissance c.1500-1650

THE CRACKENTHORPE BED, OAK
*c.*1530–40

The birth of the Renaissance in Italy in the later Middle Ages has already been noted. When Charles VIII of France began the Italian Wars with his invasion of Italy in 1494, his army was astonished to see the new buildings of classical form and other evidence of superb new standards in the arts and crafts. It was like entering another world. The unexpected result of the Italian Wars was to bring the Renaissance north across the Alps into the rest of Europe. While all European countries came ultimately under the spell of classical thought and design, each one interpreted the new movement in its own way and in its own time, influenced by its history, cultural traditions, social conditions, freedom from or involvement in wars and civil or religious turmoil, and its distance from the main centre of influence. Difficulties of travel and poor communications during the period of the early Renaissance hampered the spread of ideas, but later there was to be— particularly in and after the 17th century— an extraordinary swift flow of cultural exchanges.

The great bed was the most expensive piece of medieval furniture, owing to the high cost of its rich hangings. That is why it was so often handed down as a precious heirloom. The hangings on early beds completely covered the wooden framework, which consequently was only roughly made. In England, however, in the Tudor period (1485–1603), the frame, made by the joiner, was left uncovered and was now decorated. The tester (canopy) was supported on the panelled headboard and on the two end posts, which stood free of the bedstock (i.e., the frame supporting the mattress). This example, from Crackenthorpe Hall, Westmorland, is exceptionally well preserved and probably dates from the decade 1530–40. The headboard is decorated above with monsters supporting a shield, and below with birds perched on foliage, with flowering trees and the inscription: 'Drede God; Love God; Prayes God'. Inscriptions, initials and dates are often found carved on Tudor furniture.

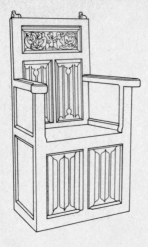

PANEL–BACK ARMCHAIR, OAK
Early Tudor period, *c*.1525–50

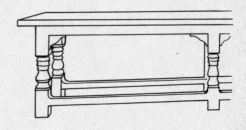

OAK JOINED DINING TABLE
First half of 16th century

The joiner's chair, panelled throughout, was the established type in England in the early Tudor period. This example was probably made *c*.1525–50. 'Panel-back' is a more convenient term for this kind of chair than the former description of 'box-chair'. It has panelled back, sides and seat, resting, without feet, on the solid frame of the base and using the flat rails of the side panels as arms. The front base panels and the lower two on the back use the traditional linenfold decoration (this is a modern term for what was known in France as 'parchment' decoration). The top panel at the back, however, shows attempted Renaissance carving, an indication of an early impact of classical influence which may well have been the work of a foreign craftsman. Henry VIII (1509–47) encouraged Italian craftsmen to work in England, but his efforts to bring the country into the full tide of Renaissance artistic achievements were nullified when direct links with Italy were broken by the Reformation.

In the early Tudor period the long joined table of oak continued to be made on traditional lines in England, and indeed there was little change from medieval times in the time-honoured arrangement of communal eating in the Great Hall. When, for instance, Henry VIII, a would-be Renaissance prince, took over the unfinished Hampton Court Palace from Cardinal Wolsey in 1525, he completed it with a Great Hall in full medieval fashion. The table illustrated here was made in the first half of the 16th century. It is almost 12 feet long, and five of its six legs are turned in baluster style while the sixth, on the rear side, is a plain octagonal post. This last is reminiscent of Gothic decoration, as are the brackets at the top of the legs and the ogee underframing (not visible in the illustration) at the ends. All these indicate the persistence of traditional Gothic forms. This is the type of table that stood on the dais at the end of the hall, for family use.

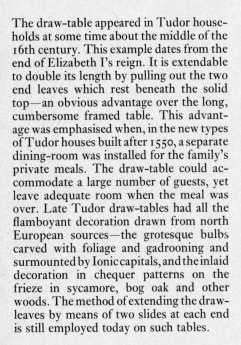

JOINED OAK DRAW-TABLE
c.1600
(*See also colour photograph 3*)

CUPBOARD, OAK AND ASH
From design by Peter Flötner. Nuremberg, dated
1541

The draw-table appeared in Tudor households at some time about the middle of the 16th century. This example dates from the end of Elizabeth I's reign. It is extendable to double its length by pulling out the two end leaves which rest beneath the solid top—an obvious advantage over the long, cumbersome framed table. This advantage was emphasised when, in the new types of Tudor houses built after 1550, a separate dining-room was installed for the family's private meals. The draw-table could accommodate a large number of guests, yet leave adequate room when the meal was over. Late Tudor draw-tables had all the flamboyant decoration drawn from north European sources—the grotesque bulbs carved with foliage and gadrooning and surmounted by Ionic capitals, and the inlaid decoration in chequer patterns on the frieze in sycamore, bog oak and other woods. The method of extending the draw-leaves by means of two slides at each end is still employed today on such tables.

From the point of view of the skilled surface decoration of wood the furniture of south Germany ranks very highly indeed; the abundance of soft wood in that area has encouraged luxuriant carving and flowing tracery which has decorated the frames as well as the panels of cupboards, the chief glory of the southern school. Moreover, the skill freely applied has fostered an imaginative approach, and decorative methods have also included inlay and painting. Germany felt the impact of the Italian Renaissance very early in the 16th century, with the emergence of the 'Little Masters', artists who introduced various classical themes. In some German cities rigid guild regulations kept these new ornamental patterns to rarely-changed traditional forms of furniture, but in the great commercial centres of Augsburg and Nuremberg and in areas where princes and bishops dispensed patronage, there was much more freedom of design and form. This cupboard, dated 1541, made of oak and ash, is based on a design by Peter Flötner of Nuremberg, one of the greatest of the German Renaissance designers.

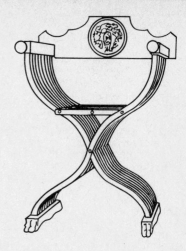

CABINET DECORATED WITH CARVING AND MARQUETRY
South German, first half of 16th century

WALNUT FOLDING STOOL
Italian, *c*.1500

The cupboard overleaf, with the characteristic south German decoration of the frames, on which classical motifs are interwoven with floral frets beneath a formal classical cornice, was made for the wealthy Nuremberg family of Holzschuher. The above cabinet, made in south Germany in the first half of the 16th century, is said to have been based on a design by Holbein and to have been at one time in Whitehall Palace. It formerly belonged to William Beckford of Fonthill. It shows a masterly adaptation of architectural features to furniture. The boxwood carvings of battle scenes are obviously by a craftsman of exceptional merit, but he has not so far been identified. The cabinet rests on a stand which includes inlaid decoration of the Tudor rose and portcullis. This indicates that the stand may have been made in London for the imported cabinet by one of the numerous German craftsmen then working in the capital.

The ancient folding stool or X-chair has already been alluded to (p. 18). It is a 'timeless' piece in the sense that its usefulness, which clearly defines its shape and dimensions, has not been replaced, lost or essentially improved upon. It was given a fresh lease of life at the Renaissance. This Italian example of *c*.1500 is made of walnut and has a number of crossed members. The constructional technique of placing these members close together was known to the ancient Greeks and also formed one variety of the Roman *sella curulis*. The type shown here could be made with or without a back; the back on the present example is detachable. An innovation of the Renaissance is the use of graceful curves of S-form both above and below the crossing. Compare this seat with the English example made over a century later (p. 36). The type remains with us today, in simplified version, in the folding camp stool.

Caquetoire ('GOSSIPING') CHAIR
Early 16th century

FOLDING CHAIR ('GLASTONBURY' TYPE). CARVED OAK
Probably early 17th century

A light type of chair known as a *caquetoire* or 'gossiping' chair (from French *caqueter*, to chatter) appeared in France in the 16th century, intended for ladies' use and so constructed as to be easily moved about. It had a narrow back of a single panel and frame, decorated with Renaissance motifs. Open beneath the arms and seat, it had turned arm supports and legs, and flat arms which curved outwards from the narrow back towards the front. The bowed arms and trapezoidal seat allowed ample room for ladies wearing the fashionable wide costume of the time. The *caquetoire* was in use in early Tudor England. It is uncertain whether such chairs were imported directly from France, made in England by French craftsmen, or brought *via* Scotland, France's traditional ally. They certainly indicate the growing search for comfort and for lighter types of seating furniture to move about at will.

Another type of light chair, even more obviously portable in its conception, was the folding chair, an English example of which, made of oak, is illustrated here. It was in use in late Tudor and early Stuart times. It has, of course, an ancient ancestry, but at the time when the present example was made, probably early in the 17th century, it closely resembled the improved models which were then fashionable in Italy. The arms are hinged by a wooden rod which passes through the top of the legs in front and through the side rails of the seat, to make for easy folding. The decoration of carved Roman arches enclosing a lozenge is typical of the Jacobean period. Since the 19th century such chairs have been called 'Glastonbury' chairs. An example drawn by Henry Shaw and illustrated in *Specimens of Ancient Furniture*, published in 1836, is described as 'the Abbot's chair, Glastonbury', and wrongly dated to Henry VIII's reign—hence the Victorian name for the chair.

BACK STOOL ('FARTHINGALE CHAIR'). OAK,
UPHOLSTERED IN TURKEY WORK
*c.*1625–50

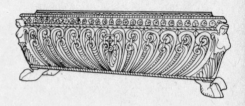

Cassone, CARVED WALNUT
Italian, mid-16th century

Shortly after 1550 appeared in England the first chair without arms—the back stool, to give it its contemporary name. As this implies, this was a stool with its back legs continued upwards to form uprights which were joined by two rails or a panel and given a slightly backward tilt. This oak example is upholstered in Turkey work (i.e., knotted pile on canvas, in imitation of, but quite different from, Turkey carpets) and was probably made *c.*1625–50. It has acquired the modern name of 'farthingale chair', as this version with broad seat is supposed to have been made to accommodate ladies wearing the fashionable hooped farthingale dress. There may be some truth in this, but the name applies to only one version of the back stool, which appeared before the farthingale came into fashion. The back stool may have been made for family use when the dining table was put centrally in private dining-rooms and there was no wall to rest the back against (as there was on the dais in the Great Hall).

English furniture was still far below the best standards reached on the Continent where Italy remained supreme. For some time after 1500 the Italian *cassone* continued to be decorated with great skill in a variety of ways. Painted subjects were fashionable—martial scenes and imperial triumphs particularly in Florence, and religious themes in the north—but gilding, marquetry and intarsia were other favoured media. About 1550, however, these traditional methods gave way to carved decoration, the wood being otherwise untouched except for polishing. The ornament took the form of repetitive patterns, such as those seen on the *cassone* above, which is typical of Florentine work of the later 16th century. This *cassone* is of classical sarcophagus form with lion paw feet. Other *cassoni* had carved scenes of classical history or mythology. Much of the carving showed the influence of Mannerism, the 16th-century Italian movement which, in opposition to rigid classicism, freely used classical forms such as distorted figures and strapwork (later popular in northern Europe).

PANEL-BACK ARMCHAIR, CARVED AND INLAID
Jacobean, c.1600–25

COURT CUPBOARD (THREE-TIERED SIDEBOARD)
DECORATED WITH CARVING, STRAPWORK AND INLAY
Jacobean, c.1600–25

By 1600 the English panel-back chair had undergone subtle changes but, as a close study will reveal, it remained of substantially the same construction (see p. 26). During the first quarter of the 17th century, coinciding very closely with James I's reign (1603–25) the panel-back had shed the panels beneath the arms and seat, thus allowing much more freedom of treatment. The arms, no longer forming the rails of the panelled sides, could be curved for comfort and decoration and given flat, rounded ends. The arm supports, formerly the stiles of the side panels, could now be turned and fluted, as also could the front legs. The panelled back was given ornamental 'head' and 'ear' pieces, which are appendages to exclude draughts and do not form part of the panelled construction. The fashionable inlay in floral and chequered patterns completes this typical Jacobean panel-back chair, which shows only the slightest vestiges of classical Renaissance forms.

One of the new pieces of furniture of Tudor England was the court cupboard. It was used in fashionable circles to display family plate on festive and ceremonial occasions. It was a three-tiered open sideboard—still a cup-board in the medieval sense—and as it occupied a prominent position in the Great Hall or Great Chamber, it acquired all the fashionable forms of decoration. Here we see an example of the early 17th century, very richly ornamented with panels of semi-precious stones, heraldic beasts, strapwork, inlay and classical motifs—a typical mixture of the old and the new in a confused medley of barbaric splendour of Flemish inspiration, inherited from the Tudors. The bottom shelf and feet are modern. The name 'court' is a puzzle, possibly reflecting the grand society for which these pieces were made, possibly referring to their low height (rarely more than 4 feet).

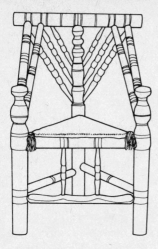

TURNED ('THROWN') CHAIR
First half of 17th century

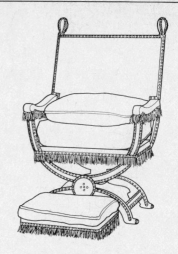

UPHOLSTERED X-FRAME ARMCHAIR
Early 17th century

This English chair is a pertinent reminder of the extraordinary tenacity of vernacular styles and of the fact that while interest is naturally concentrated on outstanding furniture craftsmen and on fashionable styles, in country areas furniture-making continued unhurriedly on time-honoured lines, serving local needs, using local timbers and producing simple, utilitarian pieces. One of the oldest crafts is that of turning. The turned (or 'thrown') chair was composed of members turned on the lathe, which were then socketed into each other. The ornament consisted of patterns worked on the members while they were being turned. This type of chair, intended for cottage use, could be easily made and thus the rate of replacement has been high. Hence the earliest surviving examples, like that illustrated here, are of the 17th century. The 'thrown' chair is the ancestor of the famous Windsor chair, about which more will be said later.

Also of ancient lineage is the X-frame chair, which long remained in fashion in aristocratic circles in England, as this example of c.1625–50, with its matching footstool, shows. It is made of beech and is upholstered in velvet, which has faded from its original crimson. trimmed with 'gallon' (a decorative braid) and fastened with rows of brass-headed nails. This type of chair was made in earlier times by the cofferer who, as his name implies, began by covering coffers and travelling trunks with rich materials, and progressed to covering other pieces of furniture. This chair and footstool belonged to William Juxon, Archbishop of Canterbury who, when Bishop of London, attended Charles I at his execution in 1649. This has given rise to a long-established tradition that it was the chair occupied by Charles at his trial in Westminster Hall, but there is no confirmatory evidence of this story. Beech, though a favourite wood with chair-makers, is very perishable, and such chairs as this have rarely survived.

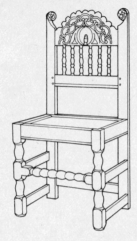

CHAIR, 'YORKSHIRE–DERBYSHIRE' TYPE.
CARVED AND TURNED OAK
*c.*1640

CHEST OF DRAWERS, OAK INLAID WITH CHESTNUT AND
EBONY
Dated 1653
(*See also colour photograph 4*)

The study of regional furniture in England is much neglected. There is evidence that distinct regional characteristics were developed over the centuries, based on local conditions and producing lively versions of vernacular ornament and forms. One distinct type of regional chair is the Yorkshire-Derbyshire variety, associated with those two areas and also with Lancashire. The back was built up in various ways—with two wide flat hoops decorated with carving and pendants, or with an open arcade of turned balusters between two rails, or, as here, with turned balusters set beneath a flat hoop. On some of these chairs made after *c.*1650 the centre of the arched top contains a small carved head with a pointed beard. This is said to have commemorated Charles I after his execution. Hence the name of 'mortuary' chair which has been given to the type with this particular decoration, but the name is a recent one, and there is no evidence that contemporaries ever used this description.

This English chest of drawers, of oak, is dated 1653 on the cartouche inlaid in the drawer in its frieze. It provides an excellent example of the evolution of the chest of drawers from the chest, following the stage in which a drawer or drawers occupied the lower part of the chest while a shallower chest occupied the top part, beneath a hinged top. In this example, there is a shallow drawer in the frieze; below this is a single deep drawer with panelled front; while at the bottom, below the moulding, are three drawers behind the panelled doors. The decoration consists of applied mouldings, inlay of chestnut and ebony and of engraved bone and mother-of-pearl, and split balusters (i.e., turned balusters sawn in half and applied as matching decoration to the framework). The style is strongly Dutch or Flemish in inspiration, and the piece may be the work of a foreign craftsman (cf the Dutch cupboard on p. 39). The date is intriguing, coinciding with Cromwell's puritanical régime, when, in general, markedly decorated furniture was out of favour.

37

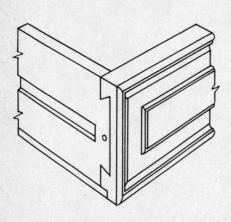

DIAGRAM SHOWING DOVETAIL ON DRAWER
First half of 17th century

CHAIR, EBONY AND ROSEWOOD
North Netherlands, first half of 17th century

With the development of the chest of drawers increasing attention had to be paid to drawer construction. Drawers (known also as 'tills' or 'drawing boxes') had been fitted into travelling coffers and cabinets since *c.*1550, and as they became heavier and larger with the growth in size of case furniture, the problems of fixing their sides to their fronts and of sliding them smoothly in and out of the carcase had to be solved. Early drawers had their parts nailed together, with grooves in their stout oak sides which slid along runners (or bearers) attached to the inside framing. The first dovetails appeared on the sides of drawers in late Tudor furniture. By subsequent standards these dovetails seem very crude, as the accompanying sketch shows. It was not until after 1660 that carcases had horizontal sections between the drawers on which the latter rested and slid, and when this change occurred, dovetails became smaller and thus more numerous.

The 17th century was Holland's 'golden age' when the seven northern provinces of the Spanish Netherlands achieved national unification after their epic struggle with Spain. This chair from the northern Netherlands is made of ebony and rosewood and dates from the first half of the 17th century. Ebony was a comparatively rare wood, and its hardness and strength allowed more slender members than was possible with walnut, the wood normally used for chairs of this calibre. Great attention has been paid to the turned baluster legs. The arcaded back with its filling of small turned balusters appears to have been derived from Italian sources, and versions are known in Spain and England (cf. the Yorkshire-Derbyshire chair, p. 37). Leather upholstery was widely used because of its hard-wearing qualities. It was tacked to the seat rail by large round-headed studs, which made a pleasant decoration and were easily removable when the chair required re-upholstering.

CUPBOARD; CARVED ARCADING
Dutch, c.1650

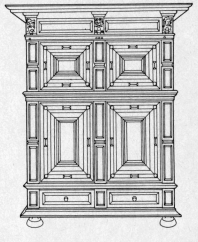

CUPBOARD WITH GEOMETRIC MOULDING
Dutch, c.1640–50

Coinciding with the Dutch Republic's rise as a great maritime, commercial and colonial power came a wonderful flowering of her arts and crafts. Her cabinet-makers were among the most skilled in Europe, and pioneers in such technical processes as veneering and marquetry. As well as importing rare woods, the Dutch brought lacquer from the East to add brilliant effect to furniture. These pioneering processes were to have profound influence after 1650 on France, then on England. But while Holland was thus experiencing unparalleled prosperity, her furniture reflected the comfortable well-being of the rich bourgeoisie rather than, as was the case in Italy, of opulent patrician palaces. Cupboards were particularly favoured Dutch pieces for storing articles of every kind, from household linen to valuables. This Zeeland (i.e., southern) cupboard of c.1650 is made of exotic woods, including ebony. The influence of the classical Renaissance is unmistakable in the round arches complete with keystones.

Solid, well-designed and well-made furniture, using the finest materials, continued to be characteristic of Dutch homes. This Dutch cupboard of c.1640–50 makes effective use of mouldings in relief, the panels and other details being in ebony on an oak carcase. Geometric moulding may have been introduced into the Netherlands by Spanish craftsmen familiar with Arabic decoration. The dramatic contrasts between raised and flat surfaces, and the resulting variations of light and shade, are heightened by the use of these two woods. Though the details are large, they are arranged in a basically simple design. The strongly moulded horizontal sections and the imposing cornice supported on carved human heads are other points of emphasis. Flattened 'bun' feet were usual supports for furniture of this kind, which could be taken apart in several units for easy movement and assemblage. Compare this piece with the English chest of drawers of 1653 (p. 37).

CABINET, VENEERED WITH TORTOISESHELL AND IVORY
Antwerp, first half of 17th century

CENTRE TABLE, WALNUT
Early Baroque style. Italian, dated 1630

While the northern Netherlands gained their independence from Spain, the southern provinces remained under Spanish rule. The latter preserved their great reputation as producers of tapestry and leather of the highest quality, and Antwerp was also famous for splendid cabinets inlaid with fine materials. This Antwerp cabinet of the first half of the 17th century is veneered with tortoiseshell and ivory and is supported on its original stand. The cabinet became the great prestige piece of this century. Its chief purpose was to contain the valuable collections of small curios (or 'curiosities') on which wealthy men spent large sums. It was very useful, in an age when the primitive banking systems offered little real security, and when there were constant threats of catastrophe from war and fire, to have a handy set of valuables to gather up quickly in an emergency. Hence the large numbers of small drawers which were essential features of these cabinets. Antwerp cabinets were so renowned that many were exported to other countries, including England.

Seventeenth century Italy saw the rise of many new wealthy families, partly due, as in Rome, to the lavish patronage of successive popes to their family connections, partly, as in Venice, to the emergence of bankers, and partly, as in Venice again and in Genoa, to the increased number of rich merchants. Rich families, old and new, developed a spirit of emulation which unfortunately encouraged lavish display and thus ostentatious decoration. Tables in particular came in for much attention. This example, a walnut centre table from Piedmont, is dated 1630. The whole of the base and frieze is skilfully carved and there is much elaboration of the three main supports and the turned pendants. Baroque architecture is beginning to influence design. Such furniture in Italy was the work of sculptors who made furniture for state apartments. This table is an early example of their work, for the most famous Italian sculptor-furniture craftsmen, including Brustolon, Parodi and Maragliano, worked in the later part of the century, when ostentation became even more pronounced.

3
Baroque
c.1650-1740

TABLE IN TYPICAL ITALIAN BAROQUE STYLE,
WITH EAGLE SUPPORTS AND MARBLE TOP
*c.*1680–1700

The term Baroque is applied to the architecture of western Europe, and its accompanying arts and crafts, in the 17th and early 18th centuries. In effect a variant of classicism, the style attempted to cultivate a sense of dynamic movement through composition in mass, the use of curvaceous forms and exuberant decoration, and a bold contrasted stress on light and shade. All this was intended to impress the beholder through its powerful forms. Inevitably the interpretation of Baroque varied from country to country. It reached its full significance in England after the Restoration of 1660 in the architectural achievements of Wren, Hawksmoor and Vanbrugh, continuing under the first two Georges (1714–60). In furniture it was characterised by the use of bold curved forms, particularly scrolls, lavish surface decoration and large-scale carving, the ornament derived generally from classical origins. Its final manifestation in English furniture appeared in the designs of William Kent (d.1748).

Baroque architecture was born in Italy and it is no surprise to find that Italian furniture of the late 17th century was greatly influenced by architectural forms. As mentioned opposite, ostentatious display was encouraged by emulation between the many new rich families that appeared during the century. Furniture that was purely decorative, considered as bold, large-scale units, included carved and gilt tables, large carved and gilt thrones, and cabinets decorated with gilding, exotic woods and semi-precious stones. Baroque sculpture inspired the massive carved decoration on furniture—the foliage, scrolls, shells, human figures, *putti* (naked male infants) and eagles. The above table was made in Rome *c.*1680–1700; the supports consist of two eagles with outstretched wings and two scrolls adorned with acanthus leaves, all mounted on a solid base. The heavy marble top was a characteristic Italian feature, but was widely copied throughout Europe.

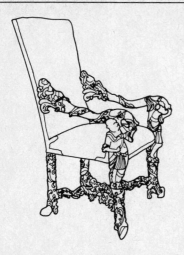

ARMCHAIR CARVED IN RICHLY SCULPTURAL STYLE
BY ANDREA BRUSTOLON
Italian, *c.*1684–96

CENTRE TABLE DECORATED WITH MARQUETRY OF
VARIOUS MATERIALS
South German, dated 1666
(*See also colour photograph 7*)

The greatest craftsman of Italian baroque furniture designed as sculptured compositions was the wood-carver Andrea Brustolon. His chief work was done in Venice and the chair here illustrated was one of a set made from *c.*1684 onwards for a wealthy Venetian family. Arms and legs are carved to represent tree trunks and branches supported by small negro boys; the materials are boxwood and ebony. In addition to marble, Italians used *pietre dure* for table tops and for elaborate case furniture. This was ornamental work, mainly produced in Florence, in semi-precious stones such as agate, jasper, porphyry, etc. *Scagliola*, a composition of plaster and glue incorporating marble fragments in imitation of *pietre dure*, was another Italian product. Venice was also the centre of production of some of the best European japanned furniture (see p. 52). Italian marble work and its imitations, and the excellent Italian carving, as well as the famous upholstery materials, were much admired abroad and influenced the development of the Louis XIV style.

The ruinous Thirty Years' War (1618–48) retarded Germany's progress in the arts and crafts. In the south Munich emerged after 1648 as the dominant new centre of creative activity. A marriage alliance between the ruling houses of Bavaria and Savoy at first brought Italian versions of the Baroque into Germany, but before 1700 French influence became supreme. German pattern-books, based on the designs of Le Pautre, Bérain and Marot, greatly helped in establishing French fashions in interior decoration and furniture among the now powerful aristocracy whose fortunes had risen as those of the cities had declined. This centre table, dated 1666, is an early south German version of Boulle technique. It is decorated with marquetry of brass, tortoiseshell, ebony, pewter and ivory, and was made for Prince Hohenlohe by H. D. Sommer, who, like many other skilled craftsmen working for the aristocracy, had set up his workshop in an area away from restrictive guild regulations.

CUPBOARD OF WALNUT AND EBONY
North German (Hamburg), c.1700

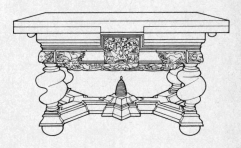

DRAW-TABLE, OAK, OF DANZIG TYPE
c.1700

In contrast to the south, the city-states of northern Germany preserved their powerful status after 1648. Their cultural links were much closer with Holland and Scandinavia than with Italy and France. Conservative taste retained the decorative idiom of the north European Renaissance. The great cupboards, influenced by Dutch examples, many of which were exported to neighbouring countries, became a feature of the furniture development of the chief north German cities, such as Lübeck, Hamburg, Danzig and Bremen. This cupboard (*Schapp*) from Hamburg, made c.1700, is of walnut and ebony and has obvious relationship with the Dutch cupboard illustrated on p. 39. Baroque influence is clear in the boldly shaped and carved moulding on the door and drawer fronts, and in the finely executed detailed carving on the doors and pilasters. Straight cornices were features of Hamburg cupboards; Danzig favoured broken pediments; Lübeck, arched cresting.

This north German oak table of c.1700, of the so-called Danzig type, is another instance of conservative taste in northern Europe. It immediately brings to mind the designs of Vredeman de Vries over a century earlier (p. 34). Extreme massiveness is the keynote—a heavy double top incorporating the draw-leaves, solid underframing relieved by large projecting mouldings, and bulbous legs (which by this date had long been out of fashion in England). Baroque effect is further rendered by the short, thick spiral of the legs, based on the spiral column employed by architects. The frieze by contrast is carved with panels of figures and birds. Examples such as these indicate a preoccupation with ornament rather than with function, as these tables were awkward to sit at. German influence spread into the whole Baltic area, since both Sweden and Denmark (which was at that time united to Norway) had German dynasties.

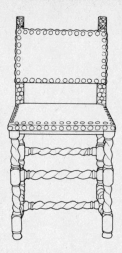

CHAIR DECORATED WITH TURNING IN THE STYLE OF
LOUIS XIII
French, c.1640–50

CARVED AND GILT TABLE IN FRENCH BAROQUE STYLE
Louis XIV, late 17th century

The course of the Renaissance was rudely interrupted in France in the 16th century by the devastating Wars of Religion. With the restoration of order by Henry IV (1589–1610) French crafts revived, mainly under foreign influence. During the minority of Louis XIII (reigned 1610–43) the Queen-Mother, Marie de Médicis, though an Italian, encouraged Flemish artists and craftsmen to work in France. Cardinal Richelieu, Louis' chief minister, established the monarchy on a firm basis and began the policy of developing artistic activity around the person of the king. The rule of his successor, however, the Italian Cardinal Mazarin (d.1661), saw a great influx of Italians into France, where they worked in their ornate style. The furniture of Louis XIII's reign was marked by emphasis on turned decoration. This chair of c.1640–50 has spiral turning and leather upholstery fastened by brass-headed nails. Traces of earlier styles can be seen.

The most brilliant period of the arts and crafts in France began in the reign of Louis XIV (1643–1715), the most powerful monarch in European history, and extended to the end of the 18th century. French decorative arts redounded to the glory of the monarchy, and a centralised organisation for their development was built up regardless of expense. While lavish royal patronage naturally gave every encouragement to the talents of Frenchmen, foreigners of oustanding ability, particularly Italians and Flemings, were also encouraged to work in France. The great organiser was J. B. Colbert (1619–83). In 1662 he set up workshops in the former house of the Gobelins brothers, and from this centre, named in 1667 the *Manufacture Royale des Meubles de la Couronne*, the royal houses were decorated and furnished. Thus a French national style was developed which became the envy and admiration of the rest of Europe, especially after the building of the great palace at Versailles.

CARVED AND GILT SIDE TABLE
Design by Le Pautre, late 17th century

DETAIL OF MARQUETRY IN THE STYLE OF A. C. BOULLE
Late 17th century

The *Manufacture Royale* was placed in the charge of C. Le Brun (1619–90), who provided designs for craftsmen as well as supervising their work. He was responsible for the decoration of Versailles. Showing the utmost skill in co-ordinating all the crafts, and freely adapting the best that foreign craftsmen could offer, he created the French version of the Baroque. Engraved designs of the latest French decorative fashions by Jean Le Pautre (1618–82) were published in the late 17th century and were thus made available for the rest of Europe. Above is shown one of Le Pautre's designs for a carved and gilt side table, and opposite a table clearly adapted from the design. The latter is an exuberant version of Le Brun's Louis XIV style. When in 1685 Louis foolishly revoked the Edict of Nantes, which had granted toleration to the Huguenots, thousands of these Protestants, including some of France's finest craftsmen, fled abroad, taking their highly developed skills with them.

Meanwhile the craft of veneering in ebony had been introduced into France from the Low Countries under Marie de Médicis. Thus began the custom in France of giving the title of *ébéniste* to the most skilled practitioners of this craft (the English equivalent is 'cabinet-maker'). The most famous *ébéniste* of Louis XIV's reign is A. C. Boulle (1642–1732) who in 1672, when he was already described by Colbert to the king as the most skilled craftsman in Paris, was granted workshops in the Louvre and the privilege of working in both metal and wood—a combination of crafts forbidden by guild regulations. For the rest of his long life Boulle furnished the royal palaces, particularly Versailles. His name is inseparably connected with his special form of marquetry, which he perfected but did not invent. Above is seen a detailed section of marquetry on a cabinet of the Boulle type; see also first illustration overleaf.

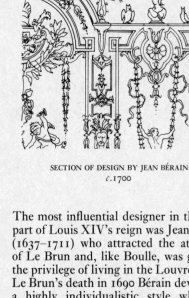

WRITING TABLE DECORATED WITH MARQUETRY IN THE
STYLE OF BOULLE
French, Louis XIV

SECTION OF DESIGN BY JEAN BÉRAIN
c.1700

Boulle's furniture reached its zenith from 1694, onwards when the Gobelins Manufactory was temporarily closed owing to financial difficulties. His marquetry was prepared by cutting out the designs on one or more thin layers of tortoiseshell and brass glued together. With the resulting ornaments two types of marquetry were formed, *première-partie*, with the pattern in brass on a tortoiseshell ground, and *contre-partie*, with the pattern in tortoiseshell on a brass ground. Other materials, such as copper, mother-of-pearl, stained horn and pewter were also used, and were normally applied on a surface of oak. The brass was often finely engraved, and bronze gilt mounts were added, originally to protect the corners and other vulnerable parts of marquetry, later as additional decoration (handles, hinges, etc.). Ebony was used for those parts of the surface not covered by Boulle marquetry (see previous page, right hand column).

The most influential designer in the later part of Louis XIV's reign was Jean Bérain (1637–1711) who attracted the attention of Le Brun and, like Boulle, was granted the privilege of living in the Louvre. After Le Brun's death in 1690 Bérain developed a highly individualistic style which is clearly reflected in Boulle's marquetry and marks a reaction to the earlier heavy Baroque of the Louis XIV style. The essential features of the new approach were light-hearted forms of arabesques (based on the grotesques of antiquity) with festoons of draperies and vine leaves, birds, animals, Chinamen and, with touches of fantasy, monkeys burlesquing humans (*singeries*). The above section of a design by Bérain can be compared with the detail from the Boulle cabinet (p. 45). Bérain's designs foreshadowed the Rococo, to be examined in detail in the next main section.

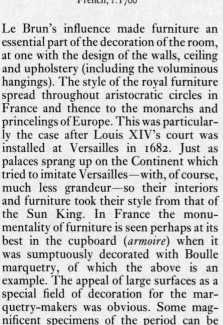

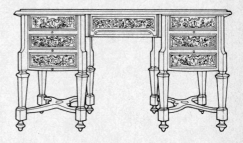

Armoire (CUPBOARD) DECORATED IN THE STYLE OF
BOULLE
French, *c.*1700

WRITING TABLE (BUREAU) IN THE STYLE OF BOULLE
French, *c.*1700

Le Brun's influence made furniture an essential part of the decoration of the room, at one with the design of the walls, ceiling and upholstery (including the voluminous hangings). The style of the royal furniture spread throughout aristocratic circles in France and thence to the monarchs and princelings of Europe. This was particularly the case after Louis XIV's court was installed at Versailles in 1682. Just as palaces sprang up on the Continent which tried to imitate Versailles—with, of course, much less grandeur—so their interiors and furniture took their style from that of the Sun King. In France the monumentality of furniture is seen perhaps at its best in the cupboard (*armoire*) when it was sumptuously decorated with Boulle marquetry, of which the above is an example. The appeal of large surfaces as a special field of decoration for the marquetry-makers was obvious. Some magnificent specimens of the period can be seen in the Wallace Collection, London.

The bureau or writing table was a comparatively new piece of furniture in France in the early years of Louis XIV's reign. It seems to have developed from an early 17th-century writing table supporting a superstructure of drawers. Soon after Louis's accession the drawers were placed beneath the table top, leaving a central knee-hole. The size of these pieces required the support of a number of legs, usually eight, and the above example shows one decorated in the manner of Boulle. The eight legs, of baluster form, are connected by curved stretchers which meet centrally in a flat platform. This underframing was a typical Baroque touch and was to be widely adopted throughout Europe, as a study of the other illustrations of the furniture of this period will clearly show. Indeed, its special character makes it one of the best clues for the identification of furniture of the late 17th century.

BOULLE WRITING TABLE WITH CHARACTERISTIC
CURVED FORMS
French, c.1700
(*See also colour photograph* 6)

CHEST OF DRAWERS (COMMODE) WITH BOULLE
MARQUETRY IN THE MANNER OF BÉRAIN
French, early 18th century

Towards the end of the 17th century French furniture generally began to assume curved forms. This writing table in the manner of Boulle demonstrates this, when it is compared with the previous example. The legs are boldly scrolled, their curves taken up in the stretchers. A central cupboard has been added at the rear of the knee-hole recess, and decorative apron pieces are found beneath the cupboard and the drawer pedestals. The drawer fronts are also shaped, their convex curves contrasting with the concave recesses at each side of the central cupboard. Curved surfaces offer special difficulties for decoration with marquetry, but make a wonderful display of the craftsman's virtuosity. Bureaux, which seem also to have been used as dressing-tables, were sometimes surmounted by a chest of drawers. It will be noted that the marquetry decorates the scrolled legs as well as the stretchers.

The reign of Louis XIV produced the chest of drawers, to which, in its ornamental form, the name of *commode* is generally given. The word commode, however, was not in fashionable use in France until the 18th century, when it was used to describe what had then become the most important piece of furniture produced by the *ébéniste*. This chest of drawers of the early 18th century is decorated with Boulle marquetry, with designs in the manner of Bérain. On this piece the curves are treated with great subtlety. The front is serpentine and, though the shape conceals this from the eye, there are three drawers in the top tier, while the other three tiers contain a single drawer each. The characteristic projecting corner supports are decorated with Boulle marquetry and end on goat's feet. The central repeated ornament of a gilt bronze mask is another typical feature of furniture of this kind; the strikingly ornamental effect of the handles heightens the whole effect. The marquetry is *contre-partie*, i.e. with pattern of tortoiseshell on an engraved brass ground.

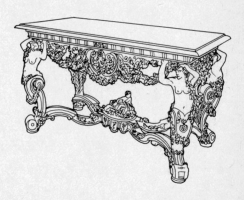

Torchère, CARVED AND GILT, IN FULL BAROQUE TASTE
French, late 17th century

CENTRE TABLE, CARVED AND GILT
Dutch version of the Baroque, *c.*1700

Increasing attention was paid to the lighting in great houses in the second half of the 17th century. The growing use of mirrors, some of great height and in some cases forming the main decoration of the room (as in the famous *Galerie des Glaces* at Versailles) prompted the skilful placing of lights about the house to get maximum reflection from the glass and show up the beauty of the decoration. Candelabra were often placed where required on *torchères* or ornamental stands. This *torchère*, carved and gilt, is a typical Baroque piece, with large-scale carving and effective employment of scrolls, especially for the base. Inevitably the grand effect of such pieces was increased by their gilt decoration. As will be seen, similar pieces were introduced into England about 1700 by Jean Pelletier.

While Dutch middle-class furniture such as the cupboard continued to be made on traditional lines for some decades after 1650, Dutch craftsmen were also showing considerable enterprise in adopting new methods of construction and decoration Japanning, painting and veneering were all used for decoration, and inspiration for ornament was derived from many parts of the world. These processes and designs were absorbed and transmuted by the Dutch and taken up abroad, at this time by the French and then the English; later, in the constant give-and-take of ideas, the Dutch were to be much influenced by the French. The Baroque style reached Holland when her furniture-making techniques were highly developed. Established pieces of furniture, such as the cupboard, were given heavier mouldings and a more pronounced architectural character. On other pieces exuberant carving was employed, as on this table of *c.*1700.

CABINET ON STAND DECORATED WITH PARQUETRY
Dutch, c.1690

ARMCHAIR, WALNUT SPIRALLY TURNED, CANE SEAT AND
BACK
c.1660

By the end of the 17th century the large Dutch cupboards were out of fashion, superseded by the new type of cabinet on stand, with straight, flat front and sides and marquetry decoration. This form of pictorial and geometric veneering is described in more detail later (p. 58). Floral marquetry was obviously inspired by the fine still-life paintings of contemporary Dutch artists, but in the above example the whole emphasis is on the arrangement of small veneers, cut from branches, into an intricate geometric pattern, of the kind known in England as parquetry. Both the construction and decoration of the cabinet required totally new skills, more advanced than any known in Europe since the collapse of the Roman Empire. In the present example, the main wood is acacia, a durable dull-yellow timber with brown markings, but as was usual in intricate work of this kind, many other woods were also used.

With the Restoration of Charles II to the throne in 1660, English furniture came under the full influence of the most progressive developments of continental Europe. This marked the real beginning of the English Renaissance, encouraged by the lavish patronage of the court and aristocracy. They were enthusiastically followed by the landed gentry and merchants, aided by the growing national wealth. At first the inevitable reaction against eleven years of Cromwell's Puritan rule (1649–60) led to much ornate decoration on furniture, until good taste re-asserted itself. English craftsmen, taught the new furniture techniques by immigrant teachers, Flemish, Dutch and French, quickly assimilated what they learnt into a truly national style. The Great Fire of London in 1666, which led to the rebuilding and refurnishing of much of the city, gave craftsmen an unparalleled opportunity to provide up-to-date furniture for the new brick-built, well-lighted houses.

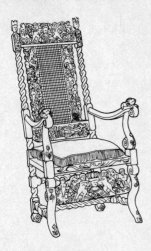

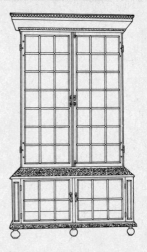

TYPICAL CHARLES II CHAIR; WALNUT WITH CARVING
AND SPIRAL TURNING
*c.*1680

OAK BOOKCASE
Closely resembling type made for Samuel Pepys in
1666

These two chairs illustrate some twenty years' development. The first new types of post-Restoration chairs were strongly influenced by Dutch and French examples (see p. 50). They were made of walnut and had a cane back and seat. The cane, imported from the Far East by the East India Company, gave them a lightness and comfort which readily explains their popularity. The decoration of spiral turning on the uprights, legs and stretchers was done by an inexpensive mechanical process. By 1680, however, these chairs had lost much of their original simplicity, being taken up by the fashionable world. Lavish carving now adorned the wide panels of the back, the cresting and the matching front stretcher. The curved arms and scrolled arm supports and front legs, all added their touches of flamboyancy so expressive of the Carolean age. Walnut was used for the best chairs of this kind, but beech, stained to resemble walnut, was found on cheaper varieties.

Bookcases had been known in England since medieval times, but only in monasteries and colleges. The domestic bookcase had to wait until the invention of printing and the decreasing cost (and size!) of books allowed the educated classes to build up their own collections. The first recorded instance of a domestic bookcase in England is made in the famous diary of Samuel Pepys, which gives us an invaluable survey of the social scene in late 17th-century England. On 23 July, 1666 Pepys writes: 'Comes Simpson, the joiner; and he and I with great pains contriving presses to put my books up in.' Twelve bookcases were subsequently made and were left by Pepys to Magdalene College, Cambridge. The bookcase illustrated above, of oak with carved decoration, is from Dyrham Park, Gloucestershire, and closely resembles those which Simpson made for Pepys. Thereafter the bookcase was to become an accepted part of the equipment of a gentleman's house.

DAY-BED; CARVED WALNUT AND CANE SEAT
c.1670–80

JAPANNED CHAIR FROM HAM HOUSE
Late 17th century

The day-bed, the forerunner of the couch (to be carefully distinguished from the settee, built up from two or three chairs) was a familiar sight in large houses in late Stuart times. In those days of late rising, it was used by gentlemen receiving morning visitors. This example of the later part of Charles II's reign (c.1670–80) has obvious affinities with contemporary chair design. The six legs with paw feet are linked by massive side stretchers, which are heavily carved with scrolls and acanthus leaves and resemble the ornament on chair backs. The cane seat, which gives a certain lightness to the heavy framework, was normally covered by a deep mattress. The back of this day-bed is tilted for comfort and can be adjusted to the angle that best suits the occupant. The basic form of the day-bed remained unchanged until c.1750, though it naturally followed prevailing fashions.

Oriental influences were destined to play an important part in the decoration of English furniture after 1660. One of the most fascinating decorative media from the Far East was lacquer, and many efforts were made in England (and indeed throughout Europe) to imitate this by home-made substitutes. Nothing, however, succeeded in matching the superb colouring and lasting quality of oriental lacquer. This chair from Ham House, Surrey, is an early attempt at imitating lacquer, with the substance known as 'japan', which is here worked in polychrome on a black ground and incorporates oriental motifs. The 1683 inventory of Ham House shows that it then had twelve of these chairs, described as 'back stooles with cane bottoms, japanned'. The cresting has the cypher and coronet of the Duchess of Lauderdale. Ham House is a rare example of a 17th-century house which retains much of the original furniture of the time.

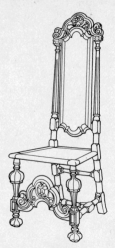

WILLIAM & MARY CHAIR, BEECH, CANE BACK AND SEAT
c.1695

CHAIR, BEECH, JAPANNED GREEN AND GOLD ON RED
Chinese type, c.1710

The accession of William and Mary to the English throne in 1689 had a sobering effect on English furniture. William, a Dutchman, brought over cabinet-makers and decorators from Holland, and through their influence the worst excesses of Carolean decoration began to disappear. This chair of c.1695, of carved and painted beech, well illustrates the changes. The spiral-turned uprights have now been replaced by graceful balusters. The chair backs are taller than those of the Charles II period because the arched crestings, which still match the front stretcher, are fixed above the uprights instead of between them. The cane filling, now of finer mesh, is set in a much simpler frame. Cane is also employed on the seat. After c.1690 front legs began to assume baluster forms or were square and tapering, with various cappings, square, mushroom or pear-shaped. The back had a decidedly backward rake, which imposed a dangerous strain on the uprights immediately above the back seat rail.

Some interesting and far-reaching developments in English chair design occurred in the last decade or so of the 17th century, marking a distinct break from established traditions. The exact origins of these changes are still a matter of discussion, but an influential source seems to have been a new type of chair imported from the East by the East India Company. A version of c.1710 is illustrated above. It is made of beech, japanned green and gold on a red ground. The design is a simple yet skilful arrangement of subtle curves. Beneath the yoke top the two slender uprights enclose a central splat, which is concave at shoulder height for the sitter's comfort. The legs of cabriole form end on hoof-style feet, which do not need stretchers. This was an early form of cabriole. derived from the shape of an animal's leg; later, the knee piece was to become wider and various kinds of terminals were to be used.

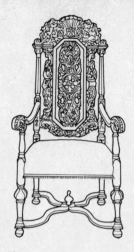

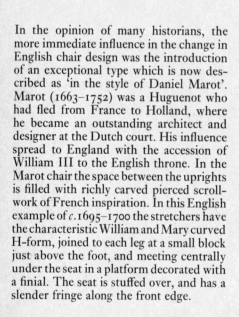

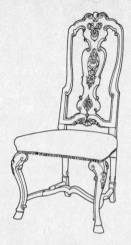

CHAIR 'IN THE STYLE OF DANIEL MAROT'
c.1695–1700

CHAIR, CARVED WALNUT, CURVILINEAR FORM
Similar to set by R. Roberts at Hampton Court,
1717

In the opinion of many historians, the more immediate influence in the change in English chair design was the introduction of an exceptional type which is now described as 'in the style of Daniel Marot'. Marot (1663–1752) was a Huguenot who had fled from France to Holland, where he became an outstanding architect and designer at the Dutch court. His influence spread to England with the accession of William III to the English throne. In the Marot chair the space between the uprights is filled with richly carved pierced scrollwork of French inspiration. In this English example of c.1695–1700 the stretchers have the characteristic William and Mary curved H-form, joined to each leg at a small block just above the foot, and meeting centrally under the seat in a platform decorated with a finial. The seat is stuffed over, and has a slender fringe along the front edge.

Whatever the origin of the new type of chairs, their freedom of form gave great scope to English chair-makers, and here illustrated is a superb walnut example of c.1717. The outline of the back now takes on a hoop form. The central splat, finely carved, is fixed to a cross-rail (or shoe) between the uprights just above seat level. The cabriole legs, finished off with scrolls at the knee pieces, end on hoof feet. This chair employs stretchers, which the cabriole legs did not really require, but instead of four stretchers uniting all the legs, there are two between front and rear legs joined by a single cross stretcher. The stuffed-over seat is covered with velvet. In 1717 a set of 18 chairs similar to this example were supplied to Hampton Court (where some still remain) by George I's chair-maker, Richard Roberts; they were described in the royal accounts as having 'India backs', presumably because of the pierced carving on the splats.

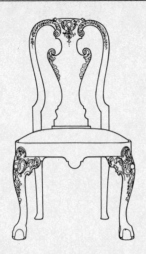

CURVILINEAR CHAIR, WALNUT, SHAPED SPLAT AND
CABRIOLE LEGS
c.1730–5

STATE BEDSTEAD
Very similar to design by Daniel Marot, c.1695

By the early 18th century the curvilinear chair—the name now generally given to this new type to distinguish it from the traditional panel-back and its many variations—assumed the fine proportions which have made it one of the finest chairs ever made in England. This walnut example of c.1725 has a simple elegance which comes from a wonderfully contrived balance of contrasted curves. Note how the hooped back breaks its curves at the hips. The central splat, attached to the rear seat rail by its moulded shoe, has a graceful vase outline, which is 'bended' (i.e., concave) at shoulder level. The cabriole legs, finely carved at the knees, end in the celebrated claw-and-ball feet, a motif of Eastern origin derived from the jewel of Buddha grasped by a dragon's claw. The splat, uprights and seat rails are all decorated with selected walnut veneers. The former description of these chairs as 'Queen Anne' is not accurate, as some of the best examples were made after that queen's reign.

The highly decorative baroque character of Marot's designs was particularly marked in his tapestries, hangings and upholstered furniture. He also pioneered the adaptation of Chinese decoration to European interiors. He is known to have visited England in 1694–6 and again in 1698. His work became widely known through his published designs, first in parts, then in a collected edition in 1702, in which he is described as 'architect to William III, king of Great Britain'. This state bedstead, made for the first Earl of Melville, c.1695, closely resembles Marot's published designs. The pine frame is covered with crimson velvet and white silk. The Earl's cypher in appliqué work is on the headboard. Beds had now increased in height, and the ornamental hangings in this example are typical Baroque features. In other state bedsteads of the time, as at Hampton Court, imposing ostrich plumes were added to increase the height.

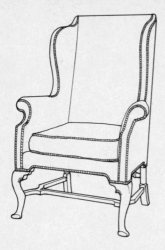

WING ARMCHAIR, WALNUT, UPHOLSTERED IN WOOL
EMBROIDERY
c.1720

THE GLEMHAM SETTEE, UPHOLSTERED WITH TAPESTRY
c.1720

Studied formality was the accepted social convention in the arrangement of furniture in reception rooms, seen in the dignified forms of the chairs of the period, which were always arranged imposingly in rows against the walls. Matters were far different in the intimate family rooms, where relaxation was the rule. In the late 17th century appeared the classic example of the English easy chair, the wing armchair, so called from the protruding wings on the back to exclude draughts. Heavily upholstered, with thick seats and wide arms, these chairs typify the growing search for comfort in furniture in the post-Restoration period. This example, of c.1720, has short cabriole legs ending on pad feet. Stretchers are used owing to the considerable weight of the frame and upholstery, quite apart from that of the occupant. This type of chair, though naturally subject to numerous variations, has established itself in the English domestic interior for three centuries.

Settees, developed from combinations of two or three chairs, were also established in English houses by the end of Queen Anne's reign. They were upholstered in various materials, among which were English tapestries from Soho or Mortlake. This walnut settee, originally at Glemham Hall, Suffolk, was made c.1720, shortly after the marriage of Dudley North to the daughter of Elihu Yale, celebrated as the founder of the university at New Haven, Connecticut. The graceful forms of the cabriole legs, with a simple carved shell on the knees and ending on plain disc feet, prove an admirable foil to the tapestry, which is probably English and has patterns of naturalistic flowers on a rose ground. It now became customary for craftsmen to make matching sets of settees, chairs and stools. Similar to the settees of the late Stuart period were the wide chairs for two people to which the modern name of 'love seats' has been given.

WINDSOR CHAIR OF 'COMB-BACK' TYPE, ELM
First half of 17th century

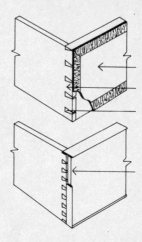

DEVELOPMENT OF DOVETAILS
c.1680–1720

The most celebrated English vernacular chairs are the Windsors or 'stick-backs', whose ancestry, it has been noted, goes back to the turned or 'thrown' chairs of early times (p. 36). This type of chair is still being made in large quantities. The name 'Windsor' is a mystery, for though it was already used to describe such chairs in the early 18th century, there is no special connection between them and the town of Windsor. In fact, they were made in all parts of the country, until their manufacture became centred at High Wycombe, Buckinghamshire, at the beginning of the 19th century. The oldest surviving Windsors date back to the early 1700s. These are of 'comb-back' type, so called from their shaped top rail supported on sticks. Turners used various woods for making Windsors, but usually beech for the sticks, legs and stretchers, elm for the seat, and ash or yew (first steamed or soaked to make the wood pliable) for bentwood sections.

The revolutionary technique which reached England from the Continent after 1660 was that of veneering, the gluing of thin sheets of sawn wood to the flush surface of specially prepared 'carcases' or solid frames. Veneers were sawn to the thickness of about $\frac{1}{16}$ of an inch and were carefully chosen for the figure of the wood. The most fashionable wood until c.1750 was walnut, and particularly attractive figures were 'crotches' taken from the junction of branch and trunk, and burrs, cut from malformations on the trunks and providing an irregular but attractive decoration. Many other woods besides walnut were used for their figuring, among them elm, yew, maple, ash, mulberry and kingwood. 'Oyster pieces', the oval veneers cut from the branches of small trees, especially olive and laburnum, were also in great demand. The preparation of flush surfaces, necessitating the use of dovetails, and the process of veneering could not be done by the joiner, who was now superseded as the craftsman of fashionable furniture.

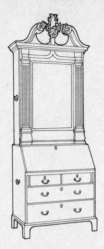

MARQUETRY CABINET ON STAND
Late 17th century
(*See also colour photograph 5*)

BUREAU–CABINET, WALNUT
Inscribed Bennett, London, early 18th century

A prestige item of the late 17th century was the cabinet holding its wealthy owner's collection of 'curiosities'. Such cabinets, mounted on stands, were often decorated with marquetry, which entailed the building up of complicated patterns of floral designs with hundreds of pieces of different veneers, chosen in this instance for their colour and not for their figure. These patterns were applied to the cabinet doors, inside and out, and to the numerous interior drawer fronts. This cabinet-on-stand of *c.*1670 has oyster pieces forming the circles on the outer doors and providing the background for the ovals of marquetry on the drawer fronts. The skilled French craftsmen who pioneered veneering in ebony called themselves, as we have seen, *ébénistes*; their English counterparts, who were able to make a cabinet and decorate it with marquetry, adopted the new name of 'cabinet-makers'. Marquetry in geometric form, made with oyster pieces, was known as parquetry.

The great achievement of English cabinet-makers at their best has been to avoid excess in current fashionable decoration. This bureau-cabinet is an outstanding example of this national characteristic. Made in the early 18th century, it is decorated with walnut burr veneers. The graceful proportions exhibit a masterly control of design. The cresting of the curved broken pediment centres in a trophy, with touches of gilding to balance simplicity of the rest. Fluted pilasters flank the mirror door. The base is finished off with bracket feet. This bureau-cabinet is very unusual in having the maker's name, Samuel Bennett of London, engraved inside the doors. In contrast to France, where craftsmen in the Paris guild had to mark their goods with their registered sign, English craftsmen very rarely marked or stamped their work until the 19th century.

LONG-CASE CLOCK, WALNUT WITH ARABESQUE
MARQUETRY
By Godfrey, London, c.1700

CARD TABLE, ITALIAN WALNUT, FOLDING TOP
c.1700

The golden age of English clock-making began in the late 17th century, when meticulous accuracy in the mechanism of the clock movement (aided by the use of the pendulum and the anchor escapement) was matched by the superb proportions and decoration of the cases. A new form was the long-case clock, known since Victorian times as a 'grandfather' clock, which was made to contain the long pendulum of 39·1 inches, giving a swing of one second. Clock cases were decorated with brilliant examples of marquetry, parquetry and japanning, though some of the most beautiful cases relied on walnut veneers. This example, made by Godfrey of London c.1700, is decorated with arabesque marquetry (p. 66). The domed top, so shaped to contain the bells for striking, is surmounted by brass finials. The clock face also comes in for much decoration, but this never obscures the dial's function of telling the time.

Card-playing, often for very high stakes, was a favourite pastime of the upper classes in England from 1660 onwards (much to the disgust of the diarist John Evelyn, who was very critical of this gambling mania). In spite of the popularity of cards, however, the first tables made specifically for play did not appear until the reign of William and Mary. This example of c.1700 shows that the earliest tables of this kind had six legs, two of which formed a gate to swing out to support the half-oval folding top. There are three drawers in the apron front. The table is made of Italian walnut, a reminder that this timber was often imported from abroad for its fine figure; indeed, the most prized walnut in Europe came from Grenoble in France. It was the dearness of imported walnut which encouraged its use as a veneer, though the process of sawing the wood to produce veneers meant that much of the precious figure was wasted in sawdust.

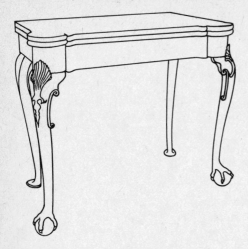

CARD TABLE, WALNUT, CABRIOLE LEGS
c.1720

'SCRIPTOR' (WRITING CABINET) IN BURR WALNUT
From Ham House, c.1675

The introduction of the cabriole leg in the early 18th century added elegance and convenience to card tables, as this walnut example of c.1720 clearly demonstrates. Since the new leg did not require stretchers, there was more leg room for the players, while a glance at the slender cabrioles on the above table, with the carved shell on the knees and the claw-and-ball feet, will confirm their particularly graceful lines. One of the legs is hinged to the framework and swings out to support the flap when it is opened for play; when closed, the table stands out of the way as a side table. As the opened table with one leg extended appeared somewhat ungainly to some observers, an ingenious hinged framework, extending and closing in concertina fashion, and keeping a fixed leg at each corner, came into use c.1715, though it never replaced the extending leg.

There was a notable increase in the number and types of English writing furniture in the last third of the 17th century. Postal services in London were efficiently organised, with several collections and deliveries daily. After the Great Fire of 1666 many London merchants preferred to move out to the new suburbs, instead of returning to their old sites in the city, where they had often lived over their warehouses. Thus they required writing furniture in their new houses for business as well as for personal correspondence. This 'scriptor' on stand is veneered with burr walnut veneers and decorated with carving and with silver mounts. It retains the form of its French prototypes, but with greater compactness and elegance. It figures in the 1679 inventory of the contents of Ham House and is thus a well authenticated piece, made c.1675. 'Scriptore' is its description in the inventory, and is one more anglicised version of the original French name.

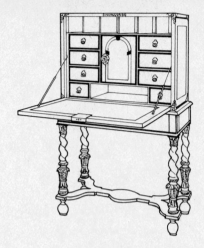

INTERIOR OF 'SCRIPTOR'
From Ham House

CABINET ON STAND, BURR WALNUT AND FLORAL
MARQUETRY
Late 17th century

The fall-front of the Ham House scriptor, when let down and supported on brass rods, reveals a well-arranged interior with a central cupboard flanked by three tiers of small drawers, a row of six pigeon-holes above and, below, an open space with a small drawer at each side. There is also a drawer in the stand which is supported on the spiral turned legs, united by flat stretchers, which are so characteristic of the period. Elegant though this scriptor is, it has the disadvantage that there is little space into which to push papers and documents when it is necessary to close the fall-front. It was this lack of space which gradually put the fall-front type of writing cabinet out of fashion and led to the development of the bureau, in which the sloping top had the convenient space behind to keep papers when it was locked. In addition, the large fall-front, which was fastened at the top, was heavier than the sloping bureau top to handle.

The cabinet on stand retained its fashionable lead until the early 18th century, though by 1700 the stand—not always a reliable support—was in some cases being replaced by a chest of drawers. The finest decoration continued to be lavished on these pieces, but a distinct change in the treatment of marquetry became apparent during the reign of William and Mary. The strikingly bright colours employed in Carolean times were now toned down, and preference was shown for browns, buffs and golds. Where floral marquetry of the former kind was used it tended to be in the form of smaller panels, as in this example of the late 17th century, which is mainly decorated with attractive burr walnut veneers. The cabinet was now taller than previously; the stand contained a deeper drawer in the frieze, and legs were shorter and sturdier, though often of attractive baluster form.

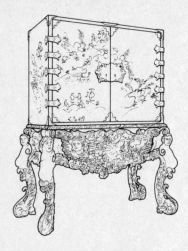

JAPANNED CABINET ON SILVERED STAND
c.1675–1700

CHEST OF DRAWERS, WALNUT VENEERS AND MARQUETRY
PANELS
c.1675–1700

In 1688 Stalker and Parker published their *Treatise of Japanning and Varnishing*, a practical handbook of methods of japanning, gilding and painting 'for the splendour and preservation of our furniture'. It was an immediate success, prompting enthusiastic amateurs everywhere to try their hand at japanning their furniture, and spurring professional japanners on to produce more versions of oriental pieces to compete with imported lacquer. This late 17th-century cabinet has japanned decoration on its doors and interior drawer fronts which resemble designs in Stalker and Parker's manual. The wide gilt-brass hinges and large keyplates are imitations of oriental fitments. The stand is English, of carved and silvered wood in full Baroque style, perhaps the closest approach in English furniture ornament to Continental examples in this style. Most japanned furniture of this period has disappeared, and only exceptional examples have survived.

The evolution of the chest of drawers from the chest has already been noted. By 1700, as this example of the last quarter of the 17th century demonstrates, the chest of drawers in its familiar modern form had arrived. Here the pine carcase is veneered with walnut; the drawer fronts and the top have the early form of floral marquetry in oval panels, the flowers set on an ebony ground. The intervening spaces are filled with oyster pieces. The drawer fronts are cross-banded, i.e., have an outer edging of veneers forming a kind of frame. The carcase between the drawers is decorated with an applied moulding of half-round section. The base is a later addition; the present bracket feet have replaced the original ball or 'bun' feet. This is a well-proportioned piece, attractively decorated, and a good example of the distinct advances made in furniture design after 1660. The chest of drawers as finally developed has kept its form, with due deference to fashion demands, to the present day.

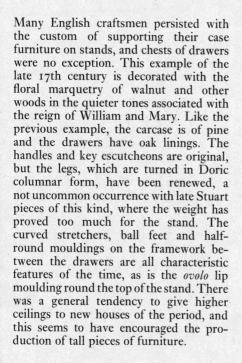

CHEST OF DRAWERS ON STAND, WALNUT, MARQUETRY
DECORATION
Late 17th century

CHEST OF DRAWERS ON STAND WITH CABRIOLE LEGS,
WALNUT
c.1720

Many English craftsmen persisted with the custom of supporting their case furniture on stands, and chests of drawers were no exception. This example of the late 17th century is decorated with the floral marquetry of walnut and other woods in the quieter tones associated with the reign of William and Mary. Like the previous example, the carcase is of pine and the drawers have oak linings. The handles and key escutcheons are original, but the legs, which are turned in Doric columnar form, have been renewed, a not uncommon occurrence with late Stuart pieces of this kind, where the weight has proved too much for the stand. The curved stretchers, ball feet and half-round mouldings on the framework between the drawers are all characteristic features of the time, as is the *ovolo* lip moulding round the top of the stand. There was a general tendency to give higher ceilings to new houses of the period, and this seems to have encouraged the production of tall pieces of furniture.

This walnut chest of drawers on stand of c.1720 was made perhaps a quarter of a century after the previous example. It is an impressive illustration of the fine craftsmanship of the late walnut period, when marquetry went out of fashion and full effect was obtained from the beauty of walnut veneers. The cabriole legs have carved shell ornament on the knees and claw-and-ball feet on which, with a touch of refinement, the claws are made of ivory. The stand has one long and two short drawers and a curved apron which continues the line of the cabrioles. The front corners of the upper stage have been chamfered (i.e., smoothed off where the two surfaces meet) and have carved and fluted (i.e., grooved) quarter columns with Corinthian capitals. The drawer fronts provide an early example of cock beading, a decorative projecting moulding on the edge of the drawers. This was to become the favourite moulding on Georgian drawers.

CHEST OF DRAWERS ('BACHELOR'S CHEST'), WALNUT
VENEER
c.1700–25

TALLBOY, WALNUT VENEER
c.1720–30

Contemporary with chests of drawers on stands were the smaller kinds without stands. This chest of drawers, dating from the first quarter of the 18th century, is another fine example of a simple, functional piece of English furniture made attractive by its good lines and unpretentious but skilful decoration. Carefully matched walnut veneers now replaced elaborate marquetry. The bracket foot, now in general use on case furniture, made a much more satisfactory base than the former ball and bun foot. This chest of drawers has a hinged top which unfolds to rest on the two pull-out slides (or 'lopers'). The main purpose of this opened top was to provide a brushing surface for clothes, but it could be put to other uses—writing, for instance. This type of chest with folding top has been given the name of 'bachelor's chest'; it continued to be made on very much the same lines for the rest of the century, at the end of which, according to Sheraton in 1803, it was described as a 'lobby chest'.

The chest of drawers on stand ultimately developed into the tallboy, as it is now known, or 'chest-on-chest' or 'double chest', as contemporaries called it. This example of c.1720–30 makes a fine field for its walnut veneers which are applied to an oak carcase and have cross-banded borders. It rests on bracket feet and has a concave moulding in the frieze. There is a writing slide at the top of the lower stage. A sunburst design in box and ebony has been inlaid in a recessed semicircle in the centre of the bottom drawer, while the front angles of the upper stage have been chamfered and fluted. The tallboy remained fashionable for most of the 18th century, but its height (5 ft. 10 in. in the present example) made it difficult to get to the top drawers. By c.1800, as Sheraton records, it was going out of fashion.

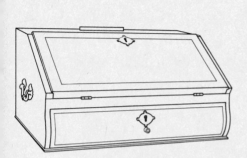

PORTABLE DESK, WALNUT VENEER
Early 18th century

CANDLE STAND, CARVED AND GILT WOOD
Made by Jean Pelletier for Hampton Court, c.1700

The portable desk, whose origins go well back into the medieval period (see p. 23) had a surprisingly long life, in spite of the development of other forms of writing furniture. The small desk, besides being easily movable, had the advantage of being able to be set on any convenient flat surface. It was also of obvious use for travellers. This example of the early 18th century has walnut veneers on oak, burr veneers being used on the sloping top and the drawer front. The interior of the top is fitted with two tiers of drawers, the upper tier also containing three pigeon holes. There are brass handles at each side for carrying. The top and drawer front have cross-banding and an inner feather banding made up of tiny strips of veneer— a fashionable refinement found on drawer fronts of good quality throughout the walnut period.

This carved and gilt candle stand was made c.1700 for Hampton Court Palace by the royal carver and gilder, Jean Pelletier. Almost certainly it is one of the group of stands which are invoiced in the royal accounts and for which Pelletier charged £30 a pair. A brief glance at the torchère illustrated on p. 49 will show its close similarity to Pelletier's work. Like Marot, Pelletier was a Huguenot who had fled to Holland before receiving commissions from William III. Through him, English craftsmen were introduced to the magnificent gilt Baroque furniture of Louis XIV's court. Pelletier also supplied carved and gilt frames for tables, screens and mirrors to the Crown. For the first thirty years or so of the 18th century there was to be a great demand in English palaces and great houses for gilt gesso furniture.

E

SIDE TABLE, CARVED PINE DECORATED WITH GILT
GESSO
Probably by James Moore, c.1714–18

WRITING TABLE VENEERED WITH ARABESQUE
MARQUETRY
Probably by G. Jensen, 1690

Gesso is a composition of whiting and parchment size which is first laid as a paste on the wooden ground in successive layers, then, when dry, given a coating of red or brown clay before the gold leaf is finally applied. One of the earliest English practitioners was James Moore, the partner of John Gumley, both cabinet-makers to the royal family. This side table of c.1714–18 is attributed to Moore on stylistic grounds; it closely resembles furniture which he supplied to Hampton Court (where some of it can still be seen) and which he occasionally stamped with his name. This particular table, however, bears the monogram of Baron Cobham. It is a fine example of Baroque decoration and a witness of the rapid and successful assimilation of even the most advanced French techniques by English carvers and gilders. There are less frequent examples of gesso furniture being silvered. In either case—gilding or silvering—intricate surface patterns were the rule.

While the Frenchman Jean Pelletier was bringing to England the latest French styles in gilt furniture, the Dutchman Gerreit Jensen (anglicised to Garett Johnson) was introducing Boulle marquetry at the English court. Jensen served the royal family over four reigns, from Charles II to Queen Anne. He is the first craftsman known to have decorated furniture in England with marquetry of tortoiseshell, brass and pewter in the manner of Boulle. He also employed arabesque marquetry, as on the writing table illustrated here, which corresponds to an entry in the royal accounts in 1690. This table, of which the stand has been renewed, has a folding top inlaid with crown and cypher. Arabesque marquetry and the closely related 'seaweed' marquetry (a peculiarly English version of this form of decoration) were the English craftsmen's counterpart to metal marquetry, which never established itself as an English craft except for a brief revival period in the early 19th century.

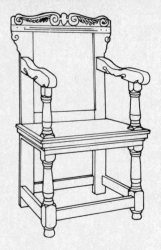

CHAIR, OAK, OF JACOBEAN STYLE
New York, c.1680–1700

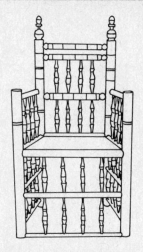

'BREWSTER' ARMCHAIR
Formerly owned by Governor Bradford,
Massachusetts (d.1657)

The earliest pieces of American furniture that have survived all date from the second half of the 17th century. They make a fascinating study, for the first English settlers took with them across the Atlantic the furniture styles of the mother country and these were copied and translated in process of time into American versions. Furniture based on English vernacular types was made for the primitive homes of the early colonists. Later, as towns developed, a more fashionable type of furniture, taken from English middle-class prototypes, was made by American joiners. Remoteness from Europe for long kept the colonists out of touch with up-to-date fashions and skills. This oak chair, like other surviving pieces of the period, recalls Jacobean models (see p. 35) although it was made in New York in the last two decades of the century.

Colonial joiners naturally used their abundant local woods for making the sturdy massive pieces in early Stuart style. Oak, pine, maple, poplar, elm, hickory, ash and others were all employed. As the colonial settlements spread along the eastern seaboard and penetrated into the interior along the river valleys, regional features can be distinguished in the furniture. Some American authorities consider that these differences spring from English regional types. By 1700, however, in the more prosperous urban areas, imports of English furniture and immigrant English craftsmen began to introduce new forms and decoration. Among early American chairs two types from Massachusetts, the 'Brewster' and the 'Carver', named after two prominent members of the colony, the latter a Governor, have become particularly well known.

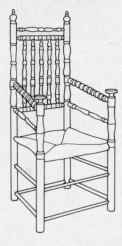

'CARVER' ARMCHAIR
New England, c.1660–1790

'SLAT-BACK' ('LADDER-BACK') ARMCHAIR
New England, c.1680–1710

Both Brewster and Carver chairs have turned spindles and posts, like the 'thrown' chairs of traditional English form. The Brewster chair is the more elaborate of the two. It has rows of turned spindles in the back, in one or two tiers, beneath the arms, and beneath the seat. The example shown overleaf is a particularly good specimen and belonged to Governor Bradford of Massachusetts, who died in 1657. The Carver chair, basically the same type, has a single row of spindles in the back, but there are none beneath the arms and seat, stretchers taking their place, as the above example from New England shows. There is an obvious relationship between these two chairs, *via* the English 'thrown' chair, to the sturdy Scandinavian chairs of the 12th century which appear among the first illustrations in this book.

Slat-back chairs, of the English 'ladder-back' type, were another early form of American chair made up of turned members. This example from New England, made c.1680–1710, is of oak, maple and ash. The slats were made in various shapes. In this instance touches of refinement are indicated by the cushion on the rush seat, the finely shaped finials on the rear uprights, and the flat cappings of mushroom shape on the arms supports. These cappings can also be seen on the Carver chair already described. As in England, chairs were relatively scarce in 17th-century America and were reserved for privileged persons, while others had to make do with stools, benches or chests. Slat-backs associated with the Delaware River Valley have a distinct series of arched slats, from four to six in number. Almost always, for all these early chairs, the seats were made of rush.

PRESS CUPBOARD
In style of T. Dennis, Massachusetts, c.1660–80

'SUNFLOWER' (OR 'HARTFORD' OR 'CONNECTICUT')
CHEST
Connecticut, late 17th century

Chests and cupboards of various kinds were important pieces of furniture in 17th-century American households. A prominent American joiner, Thomas Dennis of Ipswich, Mass., who was active after 1668, is associated with pieces displaying much carved work, including strapwork, split balusters and bulbous supports, all derived from Jacobean prototypes (themselves, of course, much influenced by Flemish Renaissance decoration). The press cupboard above, of oak, pine and maple, is of this type, showing carved arcading in the lower panels with a leaf design in the columns, *guilloches* (interlaced circles of classical origin) within this arcading, and, on the upper panels, a geometric pattern of lozenge form. The frieze is decorated with carved strapwork. This press cupboard can be dated to the decades 1660–80.

A distinct type of late 17th-century American chest from the Connecticut River Valley is described as a 'sunflower and tulip' chest because of the stylised carved decoration of these flowers on the front panels, as seen on the above example. This floral pattern is characteristically flat and crisp, while other features are the split baluster ornaments which vary in size according to their position. These balusters, like the drawer handles, are of ebonised wood, contrasting with the pine and oak of the carcase. This type of chest is associated with Peter Blin of Wethersfield, Conn., and the present example can be dated to 1675–1700. (Most of the surviving early colonial furniture, it will be noted, comes from New England.) An interesting suggestion is that the sunflower may be a vernacular version of the Tudor rose, possibly derived from East Anglia.

'HADLEY' CHEST
Massachusetts, c.1700

CHEST OF DRAWERS
Probably by T. Dennis, Massachusetts, dated 1678

The towns of Hadley and Hatfield, both on the Connecticut River, were also prominent furniture-making centres in late 17th-century America, and there two joiners, John Allis and Samuel Belding, with their families, made a number of chests with distinctive features. These Hadley chests had the whole of their fronts, panels, rails and stiles, covered with incised flat carving of tulips, vines and leaves of more flowing design than the floral carving on the 'sunflower and tulip' chests. As the above example shows, they lack the split baluster decoration of the latter. Hadley chests were used as dower chests mainly between 1690 and 1710, and are found marked with their owner's initials, a useful pointer to their dating, particularly when the date of the owner's marriage can be verified.

One of the best-known landmarks in the development of American furniture in early colonial days is provided by the chest of drawers illustrated here. It has the date 1678 carved on the bottom drawer, and was probably made by Thomas Dennis for John and Margaret Staniford of Ipswich, Mass. In addition to the carved strapwork on the lower drawer fronts—a distinctive feature of Dennis's work—it has applied split balusters and also painted designs, both geometric, here in red, green and white, and of tendril form, in black. The painted decoration is a rare survivor. Altogether this chest of drawers may well be taken to represent at its best New England craftsmanship in the last quarter of the 17th century, a craftsmanship derived from traditional English oak techniques.

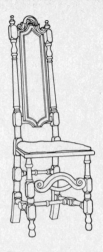

'HIGH CHEST' (CHEST OF DRAWERS ON STAND), MAPLE
American, early 18th century

CHAIR IN WILLIAM AND MARY STYLE, MAPLE
American, c.1700

Significant changes occurred in American furniture styles towards 1700, one likely reason being the influx of immigrant cabinet-makers from London into the prosperous city of Boston. Baroque elements of the William and Mary style began to appear on American furniture; new types, such as the dressing-table, the fully developed chest of drawers and the desk, came into use, and walnut and other woods became fashionable for their attractive figure. Burr (known in America as burl) veneers were in particular favour. This American chest on stand ('high chest') has all the characteristics of the William and Mary period, but was made some time later (cf. p. 63), possibly even in the 1720s. It is decorated with burr maple veneers. The time-lag between English and American styles gradually narrowed when the growing stream of governors, officials, merchants, etc., and their families took up-to-date English furniture of good quality to the colonies, and when a regular export trade in furniture from England was developed.

With the advent of the William and Mary style the traditional types of American chairs, panel-backs, Brewsters, Carvers and slat-backs practically disappeared from the fashionable world, though they continued to be made (as was the case with old English types) in rural areas. Chairs began to take on the tall, slender aspect of English chairs; scrollwork appeared on cresting and front stretchers and sometimes on the front legs, and shapely baluster uprights flanked the central back panel. This example of c.1700 is made of maple. It shows that cane from the East was used on the back and seat. These single chairs (known in America as 'side chairs') were made in increasing numbers; so were completely upholstered wing armchairs on the English model, introduced for bedrooms. Thus it is clear that the American version of the Baroque was well established in the first quarter of the 18th century.

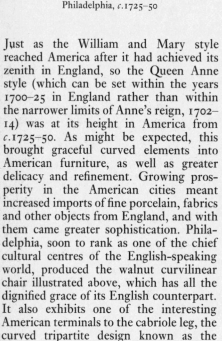

WALNUT CHAIR IN QUEEN ANNE STYLE
Philadelphia, c.1725-50

'HIGHBOY' (TALLBOY), MAPLE AND WHITE PINE,
JAPANNED
Boston, c.1735

Just as the William and Mary style reached America after it had achieved its zenith in England, so the Queen Anne style (which can be set within the years 1700-25 in England rather than within the narrower limits of Anne's reign, 1702-14) was at its height in America from c.1725-50. As might be expected, this brought graceful curved elements into American furniture, as well as greater delicacy and refinement. Growing prosperity in the American cities meant increased imports of fine porcelain, fabrics and other objects from England, and with them came greater sophistication. Philadelphia, soon to rank as one of the chief cultural centres of the English-speaking world, produced the walnut curvilinear chair illustrated above, which has all the dignified grace of its English counterpart. It also exhibits one of the interesting American terminals to the cabriole leg, the curved tripartite design known as the trifid.

Perhaps no piece more fittingly represents the growing sophistication of American taste under the first two Georges than this highboy or chest of drawers on stand, made in Boston c.1735 of maple and pine. The broken curved pediment with its central and flanking finials, the balanced effect between the centrally placed upper and lower carved shells, and the general light proportions of the whole piece, proclaim it as one of the masterpieces of the American Queen Anne style. Moreover, it is decorated with japanning. Stalker and Parker's *Treatise of Japanning* of 1688 (see p. 62) had an eager following in the colonies. The oriental designs in this instance have been painted on maple and deal. Boston was a pioneer centre of japanned decoration, and one of the leading japanners was Thomas Johnson, to whom the decoration of the above piece is attributed. Johnson's printed trade card, similar to those issued by London makers, has survived.

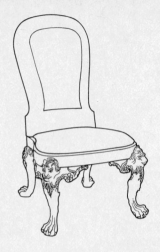

CHAIR, CARVED MAHOGANY WITH LION MASK ON KNEES
c.1725–30

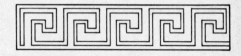

GREEK KEY PATTERN, MUCH FAVOURED BY
WILLIAM KENT

In the second quarter of the 18th century English furniture design began to be influenced by a new wood—mahogany. The first substantial shipments, in increasing quantities, came from the West Indies, particularly from the Spanish colony of San Domingo, hence its early name of 'Spanish wood'. This variety was dark in colour, heavy and close-grained, with relatively little figure. It was hard to work, but gradually its superb qualities were revealed. Its metallic strength enabled it to be carved into crisper forms than was possible with other woods. It first reached England when there was a reaction against veneering and marquetry in favour of a return to work in the solid. This chair of 1725–30 shows typical early mahogany carving; the cabriole legs have lion masks on the knees, and realistic paw feet. This is sometimes known as the 'lion period', as these lion motifs were so popular, but eagles' heads, cabochons (oval, gem-like ornaments) and human masks were also often used.

The most brilliant period of English Baroque furniture occurred in the 1730s and 1740s. This late fling drew its inspiration mainly from Italy, though French influence was still strong. The chief figure was William Kent (1685–1748), architect, artist, landscape-gardener and furniture-designer, who has a special place in English furniture history as the first English architect to treat furniture as an integral part of interior decoration. Kent's career is a good illustration of the pattern of patronage in Georgian England. He was a young artist studying in Italy when he met there Lord Burlington, who befriended him and became his life-long patron. From 1720 until his death Kent was to display an amazing versatility as a designer in many fields. Burlington, a distinguished amateur architect, sponsored a revival of Palladianism, the severely correct version of the classical style of the 16th-century Italian architect, Palladio, which had been briefly introduced into England a century earlier by Inigo Jones.

ARMCHAIR, CARVED AND GILT
After design by William Kent, early 18th century

CONSOLE TABLE, CARVED AND GILT; MARBLE TOP
After design by Henry Flitcroft, c.1735

Burlington was the leader of a rich and influential group of noble patrons, and through this circle Kent was commissioned to build and decorate a number of houses, including Chiswick House for Burlington, Holkham for the Earl of Leicester, and Houghton for Sir Robert Walpole. But while exteriors conformed to the 'chaste' and balanced Palladian principles, Kent's interiors were based on those he had seen in the great houses in Italy. His furniture— bookcases, chests, chairs, library tables, pier glasses (i.e., mirrors gracing the walls between windows), 'marble tables' (i.e., side tables with tops of Italian marble), console tables, and 'terms and bustos', or pedestals mounting busts—were distinguished by elaborate carving of large-scale ornament, often in mahogany 'parcel' (i.e., partly) gilt. Typical motifs were human masks and figures, rich festoons or swags of flowers, leaves and fruit, lion heads, the

Vitruvian scroll or wave pattern, and the Greek key (p. 73).

The chair shown above left is practically identical with a set of armchairs which Kent designed for Burlington's villa at Chiswick, and is very typical of his Baroque approach. The pine framework is carved and gilt in the Italian manner with scrolls, shell and scales. The cresting and the crossed front legs are decorated with large acanthus scrolls. A repeated bell-shaped flower is carved on the uprights and front legs, and a foliate motif on the arms and arm supports. The cut velvet brocade, displaying a floral design of crimson and green on a light ground, is original. It was made at the Spitalfields manufactory which was established by Huguenot refugees after 1685. These craftsmen had brought their advanced skills of silk-weaving to London, with enormous improvement in the quality of high-grade upholstery materials now available in England.

MIRROR, MAHOGANY, WITH BROKEN PEDIMENT
c.1745

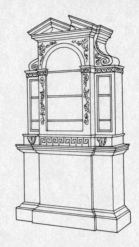

MAHOGANY CHINA CABINET OF ARCHITECTURAL FORM
In the style of William Kent, c.1750

Very typical also of Kent's style were his long side tables with marble tops, their scroll legs linked by enormous swags. Furniture of this kind was considered primarily as architectural features. The smaller console table, for instance, which stood against the wall supported on two bracket legs or on a spread eagle, became very fashionable, but as it was never intended to be moved, its purpose was almost purely decorative. The example seen opposite follows a design by Kent's contemporary, the architect Henry Flitcroft. Mirrors, too, with their matching pier tables, were made to conform to the plan of the room. These mirrors were given a decidedly architectural appearance, as in the above example, the mahogany frame of which has a carved Vitruvian scroll. Horace Walpole described Kent's furniture as 'immeasurably ponderous', but it was perfectly in keeping with the interiors for which it was designed. In smaller houses its influence promoted for a time the addition of architectural elements—pediments, pilasters, etc.—to case furniture.

The Kentian tradition is well summed up in the architectural character of this china cabinet, of carved mahogany and mahogany veneer, which was made at about the time of Kent's death. The broken pediment above the central arched door, the scrolled brackets flanking this arch, the Greek key pattern and acanthus decorating the drawer fronts beneath the glazed cupboards, and the general proportions of the piece, all denote an architectural composition. The pilasters with their floral pendants alone betray signs of a change; they introduce Rococo elements into the essentially Baroque piece. Such furniture illustrates the limits of Kent's influence, for it is conceived in architectural terms more appropriate for stone than for timber. It lacks the practical touches of a cabinet-maker's design, and it is very significant that England's 'golden age' of furniture was to come in the second half of the 18th century when the pattern books of practising craftsmen were all-important.

4
Rococo
c.1730-65

COMMODE. OAK VENEERED WITH KINGWOOD
French. Louis XV. Attributed to Cressent.
(*See also colour photograph 10*)

The Rococo is a decorative style which originated in France shortly after 1700, and gets its name from the French rocaille ('rock-work'). In reaction to the massive and ponderous Baroque, the Rococo favoured the use of lively and delicate forms based on nature. The straight line went out of fashion, and curved forms, particularly 'C' and 'S' scrolls, often asymmetrical, are found in endless intricate combinations, mingled with animals, human figures, birds, flowers, foliage, etc., and with occasional Chinese and—in England—Gothic motifs. French Rococo furniture is universally described as 'in the style of Louis XV (1715–74)'. In England the style is inseparably associated with the name of Chippendale, who produced designs in an anglicised version for practically every type of furniture. While lacking the subtlety and virtuosity of the finest French pieces, English Rococo furniture has great appeal for its skilful rendering of curved forms and delicate carving. It was much admired abroad and widely imitated.

The initial phase of the Rococo in France is known as the *Régence* style, which continued to c.1730 and thus considerably outlasted the regency of the Duc d'Orléans (1715–23) from whom it takes its name. The first great interpreter of the new style was the *ébéniste* Charles Cressent (1685–1768), whose furniture marked the transition from Boulle's massive forms and dark colours to more lively designs and lighter colours. Cressent, who began his career as a sculptor, made furniture for the Regent, Louis XV and the aristocracy. The commode became the most decorative of all pieces of French furniture, and the above example, which is confidently attributed to Cressent, displays the bold and vigorous use of ormolu mounts, of cast and gilt bronze and brass, with motifs in advanced Rococo taste, for which he is celebrated. This commode has a double bowed and *bombé* (outward swelling) front and *bombé* sides and is veneered with kingwood.

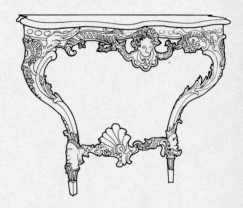

WALL BRACKET
Design by Nicholas Pineau
French, early 18th century

CONSOLE TABLE, GILTWOOD
French, Régence, c.1730

From c.1730 the second phase of the Rococo in France was marked by its development into a light and frivolous form known as *le genre pittoresque*. For this phase two designers, Nicholas Pineau and J. A. Meissonnier, born in Turin, were chiefly responsible. Both men set the fashion for asymmetrical ornament, which was mainly intended for interior decoration. Meissonnier indeed specialised almost entirely in designing small objects and silver, and not much furniture, but his work popularised *rocaille*, the 'rock-work' imitating nature. Pineau became a very fashionable designer in Paris in 1726, and his designs for furniture formed part of his schemes for interiors into which the furniture fitted exactly, even to the point of occupying a set place in the room to conform with the ornament on the wall. Above is illustrated one of Pineau's designs for a bracket to hold candelabra. The commode just described was probably after a design by Pineau.

Another piece of furniture which readily lent itself to Rococo decoration in its most characteristic form was the console table, which has already been mentioned in connection with William Kent and his contemporaries (p. 75). The console table stood against the wall, often beneath a high mirror, as an important decorative feature of state rooms. The above is a typical French example of c.1730. It has two front legs only, skilfully curved outwards at the top and backwards below, to hold the heavy marble top firm against the wall. The stretcher, linking the two supports below, is a very ornamental feature, carved in high relief. The boldly scrolled legs, stretcher and asymmetrically carved frieze, with its central mask, are all gilded. This type of console table, an original French contribution to furniture design, was widely imitated throughout Europe, and examples of the period can be found in many English houses.

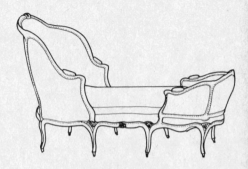

ARMCHAIR, CANE BACK AND SEAT
French, Louis XV

Chaise longue, WALNUT, DAMASK UPHOLSTERY
French, Louis XV, *c*.1760

The Rococo was by no means entirely a matter of brilliantly conceived and daring forms carried out by craftsmen of consummate skill. Curved shapes brought the notion of flexibility of form into furniture design, and as lines became more fluid, seating furniture was adapted to the contours of the body, to introduce a new concept of comfort. Simpler kinds of chairs had cane backs and seats, as in this example, in which the curves of the back, of the arms, which are set back along the seat rail, of the cabriole legs and of the front seat rail all established s ch distinctive outlines that in England, as elsewhere, this type was simply known as a 'French chair'. It was much admired and copied in the Chippendale era. Grander chairs of this kind had carved Rococo ornament on their frames and were upholstered with expensive materials such as brocade, damask and tapestry.

The development of smaller rooms in new or modernised great houses in France—inevitably copied throughout the Continent—encouraged the creation of new types of furniture in astonishing variety to fit these intimate surroundings. French craftsmen experimented with many different kinds of seats, some of which, adapted to the needs of conversation, were made to be freely movable. These were the *sièges courants*, in contrast to the more imposing *sièges meublants* which stood formally against the wall. It is impossible to enumerate all these varieties here, but two kinds became further established European types—the *bergère*, a deep, wide armchair with closed upholstered sides, in some cases with wings like the English easy chair (p. 56), and the *chaise longue*, graceful in form and comfortably yet elegantly upholstered, as in the example shown above, of *c*.1760. The *chaise longue* was sometimes made in two separate parts, the end being an armchair of *bergère* type, and the whole known as a *duchesse brisée*.

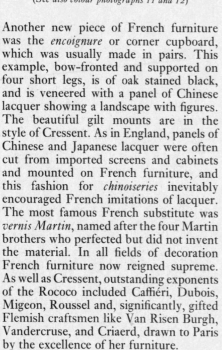

Encoignure, STAINED BLACK, VENEERED WITH LACQUER
French, Louis XV, in the style of Cressent
(*See also colour photographs 11 and 12*)

WARDROBE, CARVED OAK
German (Aachen), *c.*1750
(*See also colour photographs 8 and 9*)

Another new piece of French furniture was the *encoignure* or corner cupboard, which was usually made in pairs. This example, bow-fronted and supported on four short legs, is of oak stained black, and is veneered with a panel of Chinese lacquer showing a landscape with figures. The beautiful gilt mounts are in the style of Cressent. As in England, panels of Chinese and Japanese lacquer were often cut from imported screens and cabinets and mounted on French furniture, and this fashion for *chinoiseries* inevitably encouraged French imitations of lacquer. The most famous French substitute was *vernis Martin*, named after the four Martin brothers who perfected but did not invent the material. In all fields of decoration French furniture now reigned supreme. As well as Cressent, outstanding exponents of the Rococo included Caffiéri, Dubois, Migeon, Roussel and, significantly, gifted Flemish craftsmen like Van Risen Burgh, Vandercruse, and Criaerd, drawn to Paris by the excellence of her furniture.

French furniture fashions spread widely among European ruling classes; and in many foreign countries furniture was made which was a close copy of French prototypes, or which grafted Rococo curves and decoration on to traditional forms. But there was also a potent and growing influence from another quarter—England, whose well-made, well-mannered, unpretentious furniture made a great appeal to middle-class taste and was exported in increasing quantities to many overseas markets. All the time, of course, vernacular furniture in all countries continued to be made with only minor concessions to prevailing changes in fashion. Thus many factors were at work influencing the design of furniture on the Continent, among them the degree of foreign influence, the extent and direction of patronage, the ease or difficulty of trade and communications, and a host of political, social and economic considerations peculiar to each country.

CABINET ON CHEST OF DRAWERS, BURR WALNUT VENEER
Dutch, c.1750

COMMODE, PAINTED DECORATION
Venetian, c.1750

Overleaf and above are examples of Rococo influence on a German wardrobe and a Dutch cabinet on chest of drawers, both of c.1750, which retain their traditional forms in all essential respects and are both superbly made. The German two-door wardrobe has adopted a curved profile centring in an asymmetrical scroll, but it proclaims the Rococo taste most clearly in the exquisite carving in low relief on the doors. This carving, so expressive of Germany's genius in furniture decoration, fully equalled the best that could be produced in France. The Dutch cabinet stresses outline more than decoration, with its serpentine cornice and *bombé* shape. Rococo decoration can be seen in the carved motifs on pediment and apron and in the scrolled moulding, broken by carved foliate ornament, on the door panels. Typical of Dutch treatment is the decoration of burr walnut veneers which are applied to both front and sides, a sign of craftsmanship of the highest order.

The Rococo was very influential in Italy, where in the continued desire for splendour which had marked the production of Baroque furniture (p. 41), the new style was eagerly adopted by the carver-cabinet-makers, who produced some very intricate pieces of furniture for state apartments. In many instances, indeed, the showiness of this state furniture bordered on the frivolous. In Venice, the established tradition of painting and japanning furniture quickly absorbed the potentialities of the Rococo. The Venetian commode of c.1750 illustrated here shows how Italian craftsmen were prepared to go a stage further than the French. The *bombé* commode of the *ébénistes* is here translated into a bulging, high-breasted outline. The painted decoration known in Italy as *lacca* (which also included japanning) exhibits a typical love of lively forms, which here develops into a riot of asymmetrical floral patterns.

CHAIR
Design by De La Cour, *c*.1745

CONSOLE TABLE
Design by Matthias Lock, English, 1746

The introduction of the *genre pittoresque* into England was mainly accomplished through the French engraver Hubert Gravelot, who taught design at the St. Martin's Lane Academy, London. This Academy had been founded in 1735 by the English artist William Hogarth, and it is very significant that it was situated in the heart of the most fashionable furniture-making area of London. Gravelot provided designs for cabinet-makers and it seems very likely that leading members of the furniture trade, including Chippendale, learned to draw at the Academy. Centred round Hogarth and Gravelot, a group of artists and designers began to challenge the Palladianism of Burlington and Kent and turn to the Rococo. Another Frenchman working in England, De La Cour, published eight books of *rocaille* ornament between 1741–7. These included (*c*.1745) engravings of chairs which, though strongly Baroque in form, gave hints of the Rococo in the interlaced bands on their backs.

The Rococo began to affect English furniture design in the 1740s. In 1740 Batty Langley included, without any acknowledgment, six designs for tables by Pineau in his *Treasury of Designs*, a builder's manual in which furniture plays only a small part. The true pioneer of furniture designs in Rococo taste was Matthias Lock, a carver and draughtsman, who from 1740 onwards published a number of small books of *rocaille* decoration. The sketch for a console table above is taken from his *Six Tables*, 1746. Two of Lock's design books were published in collaboration with Henry Copland. Though Lock's designs were principally intended as carvers' pieces—mirrors, girandoles (wall lights), clock cases, etc., as well as console tables—and thus had only limited application to general furniture, they expressed with obvious understanding much of the liveliness of the Rococo and were not mere imitation, for certain purely English additions, such as scenes from Aesop's fables and from English rural life, appear in his *girandoles*.

F

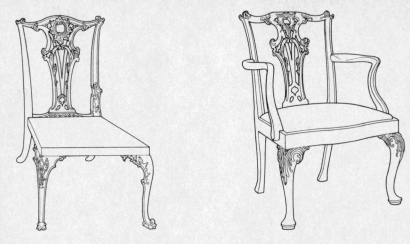

MAHOGANY CHAIR
The design (left) from Plate XII in Chippendale's *Director* (1754) was
obviously the inspiration for the armchair (right), *c.*1755

Lock's designs were only preliminaries. The creator of the English version of Rococo furniture, the man whose interpretation has given his own name as a universally acknowledged label to the style, is Thomas Chippendale (1718–79), the most famous of all English cabinet-makers. His fame rests on his pattern book, *The Gentleman and Cabinet-Maker's Director*, first published in 1754 with 161 plates and notes, then followed by a second edition, virtually a reprint of the first, in 1755, and by a third and final edition, enlarged to 200 plates, in 1762. The *Director* had the distinction of being the most detailed publication devoted entirely to furniture ever printed, and the first to be issued by a cabinet-maker. It has made Chippendale's name a household word. In doing so it has obscured, until recently, the achievements of distinguished contemporaries, for, unlike them, Chippendale, although he served wealthy patrons and made some fine furniture, never received a royal appointment.

It is essential to remember that the *Director* was intended, as its title indicates, to be a guide to the latest furniture styles, for the benefit of craftsmen and of patrons who wished to furnish their houses. Both tradesmen and men of position, some titled, appear among the list of 310 subscribers printed in the first edition. Chippendale's designs were thus available for any interested party to imitate or adapt. Formerly it was considered that surviving furniture of the period which is based on *Director* designs must have been made by Chippendale. Nobody would accept that conclusion today. No piece of furniture is now credited to Chippendale unless there is definite documentary or most convincing stylistic evidence. Above are shown a design from the *Director* (1754, plate XII) and a chair which is clearly based on it, yet there is no real evidence to connect the latter with Chippendale, whose authenticated furniture at present amounts to very little.

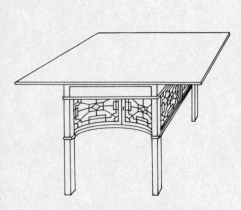

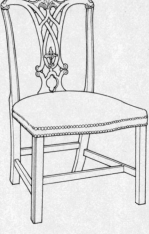

BREAKFAST TABLE
Design, Plate XXXIII, in Chippendale's *Director*
(1754)

CHAIR, CARVED MAHOGANY
English, *c.*1760

Chippendale was born in Otley, Yorkshire, in 1718 and migrated to London, where his presence is confirmed by his marriage certificate in 1748. Of the first thirty years of his life nothing definite is known except these two facts. In 1754 his workshop was situated in St. Martin's Lane, then the centre of London's fashionable cabinet-making industry—proof that he was making a success of his career. Various bills, letters, etc., connect him with a considerable number of houses and distinguished clients, but only occasionally is there any substantial information about him. Documentary evidence concerning his furnishing of Nostell Priory, Harewood House, Burton Constable—all in Yorkshire—Mersham-le-Hatch, Kent, Dumfries House, Ayrshire, Paxton House, Berwickshire, and two houses owned by Sir Lawrence Dundas, has led to the positive identification of some of his furniture. Most of this evidence, however, covers Chippendale's later years, when he was working in the neo-classical style.

Chair designs occupy a prominent place in the *Director*. The third edition of 1762 has 25 plates of chairs and other seats to a total of 60 designs. These include designs simply labelled 'chairs' or 'chair backs' which were versions of the Rococo, and others designated French, Gothic, Chinese, 'ribband-back', hall and garden chairs. Some designs have a strange appearance, as they have two different front legs and uprights and alternative forms of decoration. These differences were intended as a guide 'for the greater choice' of prospective buyers and craftsmen, and are shown on other pieces of furniture in the *Director*. The typical rococo chair associated with Chippendale, and one that in numerous variations has become world-famous, has a 'cupid's bow' cresting rail, outward-curving uprights, and a pierced and carved splat with interlaced C and S scrolls. However varied the theme—English, American and foreign, examples of which will be noted—the Chippendale stamp is unmistakable.

CHAIR, 'RIBBAND-BACK'
Resembling design, Plate XVI, in Chippendale's
Director (1754), English, *c*.1755

ARMCHAIR, MAHOGANY
Based on design, Plate XXII, in Chippendale's
Director (1762), English, *c*.1760

The variety of leg designs suggested for chairs in the *Director* left much scope for personal choice. Front legs might be straight, with or without stretchers (their re-introduction was a question of appearance, not of function, for mahogany legs were strong enough without them), or of slender cabriole form ending on varied kinds of feet among which the 'French scroll' (outward-turning) and 'knurl foot' (inward-turning) were prominent. The claw-and-ball foot was now going out of favour. A more extravagant version of Rococo decoration is seen in the 'ribband-back' chairs which had their backs carved in the form of interlaced flowing ribbons. Their cabriole legs were also fancifully carved. Only three designs for this type were shown in the *Director*. They were no doubt a concession to those among the English upper classes who wanted their furniture to follow French taste as closely as possible.

Ten designs in the *Director* (1762 edition) were labelled simply 'French chairs' and these were modelled mainly on the much admired French type whose Rococo curves had done so much to advance comfort in seating furniture (p. 78). Chippendale's versions were upholstered armchairs, two with plain backs, the other eight with carved scrollwork on their curved frames, arms, arm supports, seat rails and slender cabriole legs. According to Chippendale's notes in the *Director*, some of these chairs were 'intended to be open below the Back', i.e., were given a space between the back and the rear seat rail, a refinement, the notes add, 'which makes them very light'. In closer imitation of the French counterparts, the frames of these chairs were often gilded. Such French chairs long remained fashionable in England. Chippendale imported chairs of this type from France, for in 1769 he was fined by the Customs for under-declaring the value of 60 unfinished French chair frames which he had imported *via* Calais.

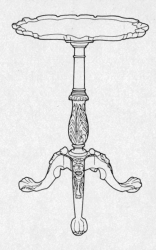

TEA TABLE, CARVED MAHOGANY
English, c.1750–75

CLAW-TABLE (TABLE ON TRIPOD STAND). MAHOGANY
English, c.1750–75

One important contribution to furniture design which the English can rightly claim to have pioneered is the making of furniture for tea drinking. Tea had been introduced to England in the 17th century by the East India Company. It had at first been drunk in public tea-gardens, but when these became too popular and crowded, the well-to-do took to drinking it in their own houses. Taking tea was an informal occasion, and the necessary furniture was brought in and cleared away by the servants. Such furniture, light and portable, included some of the most charming pieces made by Georgian cabinet-makers. Chippendale named tea tables 'china tables' because of the precious tea things which stood on them, protected by a tiny fretted gallery. His designs showed straight legs, but other contemporary examples had dainty cabriole legs with claw-and-ball feet and carved decoration on the knees.

Other tea furniture illustrated in the *Director* included tea-kettle stands. Two of these were square, of box-like form. The other was a 'claw-table', to give it its contemporary name, the pillar-and-claw type which had a tripod base and a shaft supporting a circular top with tiny fretted gallery. Other tables of this kind had tops with scalloped ('pie-crust') edges, grooved and carved, instead of the gallery. These circular tops were hinged to a square 'cage' at the head of the shaft so that they could be tilted up and placed out of the way against the wall. Tea, an expensive item, though its price gradually dropped as more was drunk, was kept in tea caddies enclosing two or three containers for different kinds of tea. The tea caddies illustrated in the *Director* were called 'tea chests', and as this name implies, they were like miniature shaped chests, with scrolled feet and sides, carved rococo ornament and handles of brass or silver.

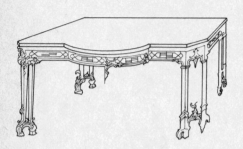

SIDEBOARD TABLE
Design, Plate XL., in Chippendale's *Director* (1754)

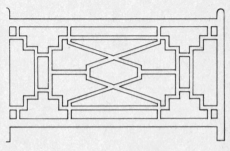

'CHINESE RAILING'
Design, Plate CXCVII, in Chippendale's *Director* (1762)

There has been considerable controversy about Chippendale's personal responsibility for the designs in the *Director*. Did he do them himself or did he employ professional artists to do them for him? In his preface to the *Director* Chippendale says that the designs are his own—'I frankly confess, that in executing many of the Drawings, my Pencil has but faintly copied out those Images that my Fancy suggested'—and his signature appears on the plates. Two American experts, Fiske Kimball and Edna Donnell, however, have argued that Chippendale employed Lock and Copland, the two pioneers of the Rococo in England (p. 81) to do the designs for him. Though Lock and Chippendale seem to have collaborated for a time, close examination of all the evidence now convincingly gives Chippendale full credit for his own designs. It seems that leading cabinet-makers designed their furniture independently to a great extent, even when they were co-operating with architect-designers—a point to be examined further in connection with Robert Adam.

Though the designs in the *Director* were predominantly versions of the Rococo (which the title page described as 'the modern taste'), there were also two subordinate styles, the Chinese and the Gothic, both of which had their fashionable following. There was a resurgence of interest in *chinoiseries* in the 1740s following the translation into English in 1736 of a widely-read travel book on China by the Frenchman Du Halde, and Chinese designs appeared in pattern books published in the early 1750s in England by Matthew Darly and W. and J. Halfpenny. This revival was ridiculed by many contemporaries, and certainly some Chinese designs are bizarre in the extreme, but this fanciful interpretation produced at the same time many charmingly whimsical effects. What has become known as 'Chinese Chippendale' includes two distinct decorative elements, one geometrical frets and latticework (illustrated in the *Director* as 'frets' and 'Chinese railings'), the other a diversity of oriental motifs.

PIER GLASS FRAME
Part of design, Plate CLXIX, in Chippendale's
Director (1762)

CHAIR, CARVED MAHOGANY, CHINESE LATTICEWORK
English. *c.*1760

These motifs embraced decorative features drawn from contemporary pattern books—mandarins and other figures in Chinese costume, pagodas, long-necked birds, bells, bullrushes, icicles, etc. They blended easily with the Rococo, particularly on furniture with ornamental frames such as mirrors, pier glasses, chimney pieces and girandoles. These were usually gilded and were among the most expensive pieces of the time, especially if they included large mirrors. Their prominent position on the wall naturally made them objects of special treatment. They were found in Chinese rooms, particularly bedrooms, with imported hand-painted Chinese wallpaper and English japanned furniture decorated with Chinese scenes and frets. The above illustration of a section of a *Director* design for a mirror shows how well Chinese figures fit into the swirling curves and scrolls of the Rococo; one can note a pagoda cresting, a Chinese figure, icicles and a bird.

The 'Chinese chairs' shown in the *Director* have latticework in varied patterns in their backs and under their arms. The top rails are either straight or slightly curved, one example of the latter having a pagoda crest. The front legs in every case are straight, a common feature in all furniture in the Chinese taste. These legs are plain or decorated with lattice ornament which is pierced or carved in low relief (the latter being known as 'card-cut'). Decorated legs sometimes have a fret-cut bracket in the angle with the front seat rail. If stretchers are employed, they too are pierced or carved in the same fashion. The notes in the *Director* recommend that these chairs as 'very proper for a Lady's Dressing-Room, especially if it is hung with India [i.e. Chinese] paper'. The seats can be either made of cane, or can be upholstered and fastened with brass nails.

BED, JAPANNED AND GILT WOOD IN CHINESE TASTE
English, c.1754

CHAIR, CARVED MAHOGANY IN GOTHIC TASTE
English, c.1760

Probably the most famous piece of Chinese furniture of this period is the bed formerly in the Chinese Bedroom at Badminton, Gloucestershire, and now in the Victoria and Albert Museum. This is a magnificent example of the fanciful, uninhibited exploitation of oriental motifs. The pagoda-shaped roof supports, within a fretted gallery, a vase filled with gilt-metal acanthus leaves, while its corners have each a carved and gilt scroll surmounted by a winged dragon. The back of the bed is filled with a large-scale Chinese railing. The whole framework is japanned, with gilt enrichments. For many years this bed has been attributed to Chippendale, but it is now known to have been designed, with its matching chairs, by his gifted contemporary, John Linnell, and probably made by the firm run by William Linnell, John's father. John Linnell's album of drawings (also in the Victoria and Albert Museum) includes the designs for the bed and chairs.

In contrast to both the Rococo and the Chinese, the Gothic style of the *Director*'s furniture was entirely English in origin and application. The source of inspiration was Horace Walpole, son of Sir Robert Walpole, who between 1750 and 1755 transformed his house at Strawberry Hill, Twickenham, into 'a little Gothic castle'. Walpole's voluminous correspondence, which throws such a vivid light on Georgian society, reveals how he developed his highly personal interpretation of the 'Gothick' by decorating his house with Gothic tracery modelled on medieval masterpieces and installing furniture to match. Walpole's tastes were copied by his friends and others, and it says much for Chippendale's business acumen that he sensed so quickly the interest in the style among the well-to-do. Some purists derided 'Strawberry Hill Gothic' as frippery, but the delicately carved crockets, finials, pointed arches, cusps and other features again blended smoothly with the Rococo.

COMMODE
Pen and wash drawing by Chippendale, *c.*1760

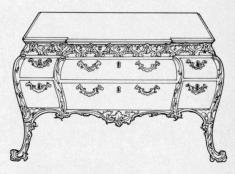

COMMODE
Design, Plate LXV, in Chippendale's *Director*
(1762)

The 'French Commode Table', or simply 'Commode Table', was the name in the *Director* for the ornamental side table with drawers which was inspired by the French commode. English craftsmen at this stage did not attempt to emulate the masterpieces of the *ébénistes*, with their exuberant curves, marquetry of exotic woods and ormolu mounts. Mahogany remained their principal wood, serpentine fronts and curved sides were favoured instead of continuous curves, and the *bombé* shape was rarely employed. Rococo carved ornament, often of acanthus leaves, appeared on the frieze, curved end supports and apron, and as moulding on cupboard doors. Ornate gilt-metal handles were much in favour. The arrangement of drawers and cupboards in commodes was done in various ways: the drawers extended the full width, or shorter ones flanked a central cupboard or were centrally placed and flanked by cupboards, or the whole front of drawers was enclosed by two doors.

The design of the 'French Commode Table' illustrated above is taken from plate LXV in the 1762 edition of the *Director* (it was also in the first edition) and is dated 1753. A fine commode of carved mahogany, which very closely resembles this design and was obviously based on it, was made for Captain Townshend of Raynham, Norfolk, about 1760. It has since been sold and is now in the Philadelphia Museum of Art. It is sometimes considered that a piece of furniture that is based directly on a design in the *Director* points to Chippendale as the maker, on the grounds that other cabinetmakers did not make exact copies of his designs. There may be more substance in such an argument, in the absence of further evidence, if the original owner is known to have been a subscriber to the *Director*, though many critics reject this suggestion, again, as unconvincing. In the case of this Townshend commode, however, there is no evidence of any kind.

COMMODE, JAPANNED DECORATION
English, c.1755

CHEST OF DRAWERS, MAHOGANY
English, c.1750–75

Some commodes were japanned, as they were intended for bedrooms in the Chinese taste. Illustrated above is a commode from the Chinese Bedroom at Badminton, already referred to as the source of the famous Chinese bed (p. 88). It is japanned in gold on a black ground with Chinese landscapes. The central section, serpentine in shape, is of break-front form, i.e. juts forward from the wings. Chinese frets of various kinds figure in the gallery on top, in the latticework doors enclosing the two side sections (each of which has three drawers) and as painted decoration along the base. Recently published evidence proves that this commode, like the Chinese bed, was made for Badminton by the firm of William Linnell, possibly from a design by his son, John. It can no longer, as it was formerly, be attributed to Chippendale—an attribution based on the fact that the Duke of Beaufort, owner of Badminton, subscribed to the *Director*.

'Chest of drawers' does not appear among the list of contents printed on the title page of all three editions of the *Director*. The first edition uses the term for four designs, but only one is retained in the third edition. This solitary chest of drawers is actually a tallboy enclosed by doors in both its stages. It seems that the advent into fashion of the French commode was, temporarily at least, making the name 'chest of drawers' out-of-date. Nevertheless the mid-18th-century cabinet-makers compromised with 'commode chest of drawers', and an example of c.1760 is illustrated above. Made of mahogany, it shows distinct Rococo influence in its serpentine front, the carved and fluted angle-trusses, and the decorated apron between the bracket feet. There is a pull-out slide below the cornice. 'Chest of drawers' (a contemporary term in the 17th century) came back into use and did not, as it threatened to do, yield to another name.

LIBRARY BOOKCASE, IN GOTHIC TASTE
Design, Plate XCVII, Chippendale's *Director* (1762)

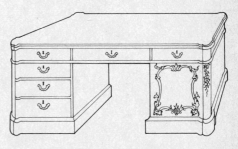

LIBRARY TABLE
Design, Plate LXXXI, in Chippendale's *Director* (1754)

A great deal of attention was paid in the *Director* to library furniture, in the general development of which English designers have played a prominent part. In the 1762 edition Chippendale has designs for no less than 14 bookcases, adding their exact measurements and, in most cases, detailed drawings of the profiles of their mouldings. They vary considerably in size, the largest being 15 feet long. The break-front type, with recessed wings flanking the centre, was evidently very fashionable. Various kinds of pediments, triangular, arched, broken and swan-necked, emphasise their architectural character. In every case the bases are solid, or formed of cupboards with doors. Mahogany was pre-eminently favoured for all library furniture. The shape of the glazing bars and the carved decoration on the doors and pediment reflected the particular style that was favoured—Gothic, for instance, by a fret of Gothic tracery across the top and by arched glazing bars.

Library tables were often of monumental size and were again evidently in great demand, for the six designs of these tables in the *1754 Director* were increased to 11 in the 1762 edition. They are of open pedestal type, the pedestals equipped with drawers or a cupboard with shelves. The kneehole, the recessed centre, has a drawer above. Card-cut frets on the frieze and pilasters, and carved mouldings on the doors display the style—Rococo, Chinese or Gothic—of the owner's preference. One of the masterpieces of English furniture, and a rare authenticated piece by Chippendale in the Rococo taste, is the library table which he supplied to Nostell Priory, Yorkshire, in 1767 for £72. 10s. It is superbly carved, but is a late example of the Rococo, for it already shows evidence of the neo-classical style. This library table is described in detail in Chippendale's bill to Sir Rowland Winn, and is still in the library where it was first sent.

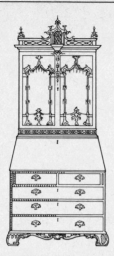

DESK AND BOOKCASE
Design, Plate LXXX, in Chippendale's *Director* (1754)

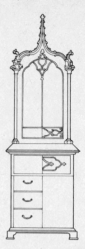

LADY'S DESK
Design in *Household Furniture in Genteel Taste* (2nd edn.), attributed to Ince and Mayhew, *c.*1760

Another writing piece, the bureau-book-case, was known in Chippendale's time as a 'desk and bookcase'. The lower stage, the desk or bureau, always had a sloping top, and was either a chest of drawers, with or without doors, or a 'frame' of two drawers on cabriole legs, a form very reminiscent of the stand of the late Stuart period (p. 63). Decoration of the pediments, glazing bars, cupboard doors and apron was carried out in carved ornament to interpret the prevailing tastes. All the desks and bookcases in the *Director* have their doors glazed with mirror glass, a very expensive treatment. A 'dressing chest and bookcase' in the *Director* is a variant and has a knee-hole desk beneath. This piece was intended for writing letters in the bedroom. To judge from surviving examples of the bureau-bookcase types of this period, mirror doors seem to have been too costly for most owners, and solid wooden doors were made instead to enclose the shelves.

The success of the *Director* was infectious, and a number of other pattern books were published in England in the 1760s which, though inferior to Chippendale's, helped to promulgate the Rococo, Chinese and Gothic styles. In 1760 the 'Society of Upholsterers' (about which nothing is known) published *Household Furniture in Genteel Taste for the Year 1760*. This had a third edition in 1763, and included drawings by Chippendale, Ince & Mayhew, Manwaring and Johnson, but it was of no particular merit. Obviously based on the *Director*, but with fewer designs and more ornate decoration, was the *Universal System of Household Furniture* issued by the successful cabinet-makers William Ince and John Mayhew, first in parts in 1759 onwards, then in one volume, probably in 1762 or early 1763. The text was in both English and French, presumably to attract foreign clients. Robert Manwaring published 100 designs for chairs in 1765 in his *The Cabinet and Chair-Maker's Real Friend and Companion*.

Girandole
Plate LI in Thomas Johnson's *Designs*, published 1758

LIBRARY TABLE, CARVED MAHOGANY
English, attributed to William Vile, *c*.1740–50

A few pieces of furniture have been recorded which follow closely some of the designs in both the *Universal System* and the *Real Friend*, but in Manwaring's case his chairs rarely display real understanding of the Rococo. For the fullest and final expression of the latter, outstripping Chippendale's restrained treatment, we must turn to Thomas Johnson, a carver and designer of London. He published *Twelve Girandoles* in 1755 and *One Hundred and Fifty New Designs* in 1761, the latter being the second edition of a series previously issued in monthly parts. Johnson's designs are for carvers' pieces such as frames, candlestands, tables, etc. His approach is very lively and imaginative, with much employment of human figures and animals amid naturalistic compositions in which asymmetrical patterns are often more daring than those of the French. With Johnson the Rococo in England reached its climax; by 1765 it was on the wane and was being supplanted by the neo-classical style.

Supreme among the English cabinet-makers working in the Rococo style was William Vile, the partner of John Cobb, both royal craftsmen, of St. Martin's Lane. These two were employed by George III in the early years of his reign, after having served him when he was Prince of Wales. The carved decoration on pieces known to have been supplied by Vile is perhaps the finest ever found on English furniture and surpasses that on the best furniture from Chippendale's shop in this period. Identified pieces by Vile have finely carved pendants and large applied carved oval mouldings with clasps of acanthus. A lion's or satyr's mask with pendants from the mouth is another favourite motif. These oval, wreath-like mouldings were, however, used by other makers, so caution is necessary about attributions, but there is no question that Vile's documented work has a superb quality and individuality of design that are unmatched. Only recently has research rescued it from obscurity.

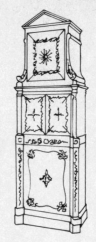

BOOKCASE, CARVED MAHOGANY
English, made by William Vile for Queen Charlotte
in 1762

MEDAL CABINET, MAHOGANY
Altered by William Vile for George III in 1761

Several masterpieces by Vile are fully authenticated by the Lord Chamberlain's accounts and are still in royal ownership. A mahogany bureau-bookcase made in 1761 for Queen Charlotte has a *bombé* base, the apron of which is beautifully carved in Rococo style. The upper stage has straight sides and is fronted with delicate carved latticework in Chinese fashion. A jewel cabinet also made in 1761 for the Queen is of mahogany veneered with exotic woods including padouk, tulip, amboyna and rosewood, and has its doors and top inlaid with ivory. The frame and cabriole legs with their scroll feet are carved in Rococo taste. A famous break-front mahogany bookcase made by Vile in 1762 for the Queen is of classical design, but the superlative carving on the cupboard doors of the base and on the entablature, which is supported on four carved columns with Corinthian capitals, is again fully Rococo. Many consider that this is Vile's supreme achievement.

It was customary at the death of a monarch for some of the royal possessions to be given to distinguished state servants. In this way some pieces of furniture originally made for the crown have passed into other hands and occasionally, through subsequent sales, into museums. This has been the story behind the 'grand medal case' which Vile made as a single piece for George III when he was Prince of Wales and later, in 1761, altered for him by detaching its two cabinet wings. These cabinets were given to the Duke of Wellington; one is now in the Victoria and Albert Museum, the other in the Metropolitan Museum, New York. Each cabinet is in three stages and each stage is decorated with crisply carved Rococo mouldings. On the lowest (and largest) stage the moulding is simplified and has carved foliage at the corners, one of Vile's favourite motifs. Vile died in 1767. His partner Cobb continued in business (though not in the royal service), and his furniture in neoclassical style will be examined later.

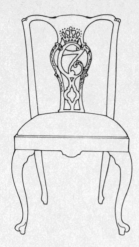

CHAIR, BEECH
Incorporating cypher of Christian VII, Danish,
1767–8

CHAIR, BEECH
Adapted from English type, Norwegian, c.1750

Already by 1750 exports of English furniture, highly regarded for its intrinsically sound qualities and reasonable price, were reaching world-wide markets. We have seen how English traditional furniture styles were carried across the Atlantic by the early colonists, and it was natural that the demand for furniture from England should be sustained by all English settlers overseas, e.g., in the West Indies. Foreign demand for English furniture was nurtured through trade. Cultural ties were close where trade was well established, and furniture was regularly exported to old customers like Holland, Flanders, Germany, Italy, Denmark and Norway (then a joint kingdom), Portugal and Spain. These were outstanding examples—there were many more. Official trade figures disclose the increasing value of the exports, but these are by no means the total, for they do not include the many pieces of furniture bought in England and taken out as the private possessions of visitors, sea captains, merchants and others.

Admiration abroad for English furniture led to much imitation of English styles and techniques by foreign craftsmen, sometimes as close copies, sometimes as English mannerisms incorporated in their own traditional furniture (just as English craftsmen assimilated foreign influences). The English certainly had much to teach to foreigners. Two of Europe's greatest craftsmen, Abraham Roentgen of Germany and Georg Haupt of Sweden, completed their training in London. Sweden is an interesting case, for she was devoted to French fashions and imported far less English furniture than her neighbours, yet 'English chair-maker' was a title adopted by Swedish craftsmen. David Roentgen, Abraham's son, called himself 'English cabinet-maker', and the same title was used by craftsmen in Holland, Germany and Denmark. In Holland from 1711 to 1762 the craftsman's test piece for admission to the guild at The Hague took the form of an 'English cabinet'. In many parts of the world it is sometimes very difficult to distinguish between English and native work.

CHAIR, BEECH
In Chippendale style, Norwegian, end of 18th century

CHAIR, ROSEWOOD
Adaptation of Chippendale style, Portuguese, c.1760

English furniture was very popular in Norway, a country with which England had a flourishing import trade in timber. A colony of Norwegian merchants was established in London near the timber yards on the Thames, and ever since the late 17th century, when Norwegian timber helped to rebuild London after the Great Fire, these merchants took back home with them furniture and other products of English craftsmanship. Norway lacked a landed aristocracy of any importance and her tastes were largely dictated by her dominant merchant class. The English curvilinear chair had a particular appeal to Norwegians. In the Chippendale period the carved shell and foliage ornament on these chairs was given a large-scale *rocaille* form, but otherwise the shape of the chair was not affected. It was some time before the typical Chippendale chair was introduced. The above example is a Norwegian chair made at the end of the century, long after the Rococo had gone out of fashion in England.

In Southern Europe Portugal, England's oldest ally and close trading partner, particularly since the Methuen Treaty of 1703, developed a great fondness for English furniture in the Chippendale style. There is even a tradition in Portugal that Chippendale visited the country, so closely does some Portuguese furniture follow his designs, but no evidence of this visit has come to light. The *Director* was doubtless available in Portugal, and there were plenty of imported English pieces to copy. Portuguese furniture was often made of rosewood (from Portugal's colony, Brazil), and like mahogany it had great strength. Thus Portuguese chairs have crisply pierced and scrolled splats, but the carving tends to be shallower than on English chairs, the cresting rail is deeper and the cabriole legs are joined by stretchers. A strange survival by English standards was the Portuguese custom of pegging tenon joints, e.g., at the junction of seat rails and uprights.

PLATE I

1 (*above*). Casket, painted and gilt wood with relief decoration in gesso. Italian (Florentine), *c*.1400.

2 (*right*). Cabinet, ebony with carved and gilt decoration. French, 16th century.

3 (*below*). Draw-table, bench and pair of carved stools, oak. English; table and stools, *c*.1600, bench, *c*.1650.

PLATE II

4. Chest of Drawers (detail), oak inlaid with chestnut and ebony, decorated with bone and mother-of-pearl. English, dated 1653.

5. Floral marquetry (detail) of various woods on box top. English, late 17th century.

6 (*below*). Dressing-table, pine veneered with marquetry of brass, ebony, tortoiseshell, etc. in the manner of Boulle. French, c.1700.

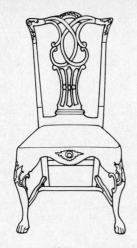

CHAIR, CARVED AND GILT DECORATION
Spanish, *c*.1750–60

TEA TABLE, VENEERED WALNUT, BOMBÉ DRAWER
Dutch, *c*.1750

At first sight it would seem strange to find English furniture in Spain, and Spanish furniture based on English models, in view of the long history of warfare between the two countries. Besides, Spain had her own well-developed furniture traditions, as has been seen, and was also much influenced by Italy and France. The *vargueno* (p. 33) indeed had disappeared, to be replaced by the French commode. Nevertheless, much English furniture was exported to Spain. Giles Grendey of Clerkenwell, London, sent fine japanned seating furniture there *c*.1740, and fine English clocks can still be seen today in many Spanish churches. Spanish chair design was clearly influenced by the Chippendale style. Their splats took on scrolled and curved forms beneath a 'cupid's bow' cresting. But the richly carved ornament remained Spanish in inspiration and was also often gilded. The cabriole leg with claw-and-ball foot was retained, together with stretchers, as in Portugal.

It is impossible here to examine in detail all the markets to which English furniture was exported, from the West Indies, where the rich planters sought the latest fashions from home, to the shores of the Baltic, or to gauge the influence abroad of that furniture and of English pattern books. In Italy English types of furniture, such as the bureau-bookcase, are known to have been copied, and English pattern books inspired much of the Italian furniture made for smaller houses. In Holland, where tea-drinking was introduced, as in England, from the Far East, tea tables based on English models were in fashion with, in true Dutch style, a *bombé* form adopted for the frieze. A great deal of furniture went to Gibraltar, which became a distributing centre for the whole Mediterranean area. English influence on overseas furniture is indeed a vast subject, which is only now being studied in depth. American furniture, however, has been well documented and well repays further consideration.

'SAMPLE CHAIR'
Attributed to Benjamin Randolph, Philadelphia,
c.1765–80

ARMCHAIR, MAHOGANY, 'MARLBOROUGH' LEG
Boston, c.1765–70

As already noted (p. 67), English furniture styles were closely followed in the American colonies, with, however, continued development of regional features in the main American cities as well as in rural areas. There was an inevitable time-lag, and thus English and American styles overlapped. Palladian architecture enjoyed a considerable vogue in the colonies and much furniture there carried architectural features longer than was the case in England. The Chippendale (or 'New French') style affected American furniture mainly in the period 1760–80, inspired by English pattern books and sustained by the imports of English furniture and the immigration of English craftsmen. Americans often ordered furniture direct from London or commissioned friends or merchants to bring pieces back for them. In 1757 George Washington ordered a 'dozen strong chairs, of about 15 shillings apiece' from London as his own American chairs were 'too weak for common sitting'.

From c.1760, curved forms, 'cupid's bow' cresting and the widespread use of cabriole legs and claw-and-ball feet were features of the best American chairs, with carved mahogany as the principal medium. In Philadelphia the trade card of c.1770 of Benjamin Randolph, a leading cabinet-maker, displays designs of Rococo furniture in the London fashion of a decade earlier. Philadelphia chairs are outstanding for their profuse Rococo carving on the front seat rail, cresting and uprights. Attributed to Benjamin Randolph are six famous 'sample chairs' (i.e., samples of the maker's skill) which have the most elaborate carving known on American furniture of the time, including rare examples of 'hairy paw' and 'French scroll' feet. Some American chairs have straight 'Marlborough' legs which are associated with Thomas Affleck who emigrated from London to Philadelphia in 1763. The name 'Marlborough', current in England but of obscure origin, referred to a leg of square or square-tapering form, with or without plinth feet, and often with chamfered inside edge.

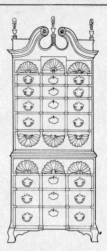

HIGH CHEST OF DRAWERS, MAHOGANY
Philadelphia, c.1765–80

CHEST-ON-CHEST, MAHOGANY, BLOCKFRONT
By Goddard-Townsend, Newport, R.I., c.1765–70

Philadelphia is also distinguished for the production of splendid high chests of drawers, perhaps the best expressions of the interpretation of the Chippendale style on case furniture in that city. Above is shown one of the most famous examples, the mahogany Turner Van Pelt highboy. Its maker has not been positively identified, though the name Randolph is often associated with it. It can be dated to the period 1765–80. Rococo carving of very high quality is seen on the cabriole legs and claw-and-ball feet, the shell and foliage on the central bottom drawer, the scrolls on the apron, the delicate surface ornament below the broken pediment and the crowning pierced asymmetrical device. The 'flame' finials are also features of Philadelphia case furniture. Very similar refined Rococo carving is found on a number of Philadelphia dressing-tables on which the apron, cabriole legs and central bottom drawer are specially ornamented.

At this time appeared one of the most distinctive of American contributions to furniture design, the blockfront. This affected the whole range of case furniture —chests of drawers, dressing-tables, chests-on-chests, secretaries, desks, etc. The fronts of drawers and cabinets were so shaped that the centres were recessed and the ends curved outwards, in both instances in a flattened bulge. This blocking was a feature of New England furniture and is particularly connected with the town of Newport, Rhode Island, and with its inter-related families of Goddard and Townsend, Quaker craftsmen, who worked for many important clients. As the above Goddard-Townsend chest-on-chest shows, shells were often carved at the top of the blocks, two convex and one concave. This shaping was employed on furniture by Boulle (p. 48) and had considerable influence on German and Dutch furniture but very little on English. Blockfront furniture, with local modifications, is found in other parts of New England.

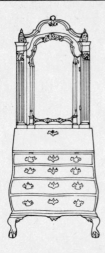

DESK AND BOOKCASE, MAHOGANY
Attributed to John Cogswell, Boston
c.1770–80

WINDSOR CHAIR, 'BOW–BACK', CARVED AND TURNED
YEW
In 'Gothick' taste, English, c.1750

Another special feature of American furniture, also found in New England, but in this case centred in Boston, Massachusetts, is the *bombé* form on chests of drawers and bureaux. The best work in this form is associated with John Cogswell, who is first recorded in Boston in 1769 and whose furniture thus covers the later phase of American Chippendale. It is distinguished for its finely carved detail as well as for its *bombé* shape, as seen in the above desk and bookcase which is attributed to him and is dated 1770–80. The bookcase has a mirror door which is flanked by Ionic pilasters, a fashionable decoration on Boston furniture. The arched pediment and mirror mouldings are Baroque in inspiration, but Rococo touches appear in the carved ornament above the mirror and pediment, and on the apron. This *bombé* form may well derive from Dutch cabinets and explains the use of claw-and-ball feet instead of bracket feet. Other bookcases of Cogswell attribution have solid doors with curved panel outlines.

About 1750 the 'hoop'- or 'bow'-back Windsor chair came into use in England. Its curved frame is now more familiar than the 'comb'-back, though it did not supersede the latter. Sometimes two stays were fixed from the top of the hoop to a small platform ('bobtail') at the back of the seat to give extra strength. These inexpensive and serviceable chairs were great favourites in cottages, farmhouses, tea gardens, inns, etc., and they were also found in smaller town houses and in the servants' quarters and kitchens of large houses. Mahogany Windsors are known to have been supplied to the royal family. Windsors were often used out of doors, in which case they were painted or stained, usually green. Modifications to the design occurred when efforts were made to assimilate fashionable changes such as the cabriole leg which, however, was not always happily united with the clean functional lines of the chair. On the example above, Gothic decoration is achieved by substituting a series of splats for the sticks and piercing them with appropriate tracery.

WINDSOR CHAIR, 'COMB-BACK'
Philadelphia, c.1770

ARMCHAIR, CARVED AND GILT
Made by Chippendale to Adam's design, 1764–5
(*See also colour photograph 13*)

Windsor chairs were introduced into the American colonies about 1725. As in England, by c.1760 the comb- and bow-back types were the most popular, sometimes found combined into a single piece. They were found in all types of houses and in public buildings, a celebrated example of the latter being the State House, Philadelphia, where members of the Continental Congress in 1778 sat on Windsor armchairs. The main centre of production, but by no means the only one, was Philadelphia. Particularly favoured woods for these chairs were pine for the seat, as it could be easily shaped, hickory, maple, birch and ash for the turned members, and ash and hickory for bent parts. When compared with their English counterparts, American Windsors tend to have thicker seats, more widely splayed legs and thinner sticks. They were much less influenced by fashionable additions such as cabriole legs and decorated splats.

The carved and gilt armchair illustrated above is of particular interest. Recent research has shown that it was supplied by Chippendale in 1765 for the London home, 19 Arlington Street, of Sir Lawrence Dundas. It was part of a suite of eight armchairs and four sofas which were designed by Robert Adam in 1764 and charged for in 1765. The designs are still preserved in the Soane Museum, London. Chippendale's bill for the eight armchairs, described as 'exceeding Richly Carv'd in the Antick manner', amounted to £160, and for the four sofas to £216. 'Antick' is Chippendale's term for 'classical', and refers to the carved winged sphinxes, anthemions (stylised honeysuckle) and arabesques on the chair frames, mingled with Rococo scrolls. This suite thus not only proves that Chippendale worked at times from designs by Adam, but also provides a valuable record of the transition from Rococo to Neo-Classical—from, that is, the style associated with Chippendale to that associated with Adam.

5
Early
Neo-classical
c.1765-90

PATERA AND FESTOONS OF HUSKS
R. and J. Adam, *Works in Architecture*, 1773–1822

Neo-classicism is the style which, in reaction against the Rococo, marked a return to classical forms, and became the last great phase of the classical movement that began with the Renaissance. Neo-classical furniture falls into two main periods. The first, c.1765–90, which is associated in England with Robert Adam and in France with Louis XVI, produced a light and delicate interpretation of classical decoration, in which a revival of marquetry played an important part. The second, ending c.1830 but persisting in 'sub-classical' forms until c.1850, was based on a stricter and more literal execution of classical forms and decoration. This phase reached its climax in France in Napoleon's Empire style, which was disseminated throughout Europe by his conquests, but England developed her own version in the Regency style. It was during the earlier period of neo-classicism that the furniture of English cabinet-makers can be said to have rivalled that of the French ébénistes.

During the 18th century scholars were much occupied with the study of the styles of antiquity, and through their researches an increasing amount of accurate information became available for artists, architects and designers. Archaeological excavations at the sites of Herculaneum and Pompeii, the two Roman cities which had been buried by the eruption of Vesuvius in 79 A.D., yielded important evidence which was published in detail in the 1760s. In 1762 James Stuart and Nicholas Revett, after study in Greece, published the *Antiquities of Athens*, which gained Stuart the nickname of 'Athenian'. Such discoveries provoked a great debate throughout Europe as to the relative superiority of Greek or Roman styles. Later in the century, in the 1790s, the Greek Revival began and was at its peak in Europe in the 1820s and 1830s. By that time considerably more information was also available about ancient Egypt, and Egyptian motifs were fashionable in the early 19th century.

ANTHEMION OR HONEYSUCKLE
R. and J. Adam

CLASSICAL LEAF ORNAMENT
R. and J. Adam

There has been involved and sometimes acrimonious debate concerning the origin of neo-classical furniture. Were its design and decoration largely the inspiration of Robert Adam, or were the French responsible? It is impossible here to detail all the arguments on both sides—the issue must remain inconclusive until more decisive evidence appears. It does seem, however, that the French were active in the 1750s in sponsoring the study of antique remains, and the first designs of neo-classical furniture may well have been made by French artists. In 1763 'Greek taste' (*le goût grec*) was said to be all the rage in Paris. On the other hand, some of the earliest surviving pieces of furniture in truly recognisable neo-classical style are English. Whatever the origin, it is beyond all doubt that once the new style got under way, it developed in England, under Adam's influence, into a highly individual style, mainly independent of the French, though, as was the custom of the time, occasionally borrowing from them.

It was during the late Georgian period that English craftsmanship reached its peak of achievement. This is, by common consent, the 'golden age' of English furniture. Perhaps the key reason for this high standard lies in the special relationship between patron and craftsman. The upper classes who dictated taste were discerning and cultured patrons, reared in the classical tradition and taught to regard a competent working knowledge of the arts, architecture and crafts as an essential part of every gentleman's education. After university, their training was completed in a practical way by the grand tour, of three or four years' duration, to France and Italy, to study the buildings of antiquity and of the Renaissance and to bring back pictures, statues and furniture. These objects can be seen today in many of the great houses which were built during the century in classical style, and which were regarded as 'temples of art' to house their owners' collections.

CLASSICAL PATERA
R. and J. Adam

COMMODE; BOMBÉ FORM AND FLORAL MARQUETRY
By Pierre Langlois, 1764, for Croome Court

English craftsmen attained supreme standards of hand skill, which were combined with thorough training in design. It has already been noted that Chippendale and his contemporaries were able when necessary to design their furniture independently. At this time unity of design was achieved in architecture, interior decoration and furnishings to a degree unknown before. England's world-wide trade brought the finest available timbers into the workshops of fashionable cabinet-makers. In addition to mahogany, satinwood now became in great demand, to be rivalled later by rosewood, calamander, amboyna, zebra wood and others from the East and West Indies. Ormolu, the fire-gilt metal previously imported from France, was manufactured in England in the early 1760s by Matthew Boulton in the famous Soho Works, Birmingham. When marquetry was revived in the 1760s, after being out of fashion for half a century, the decoration was usually of light-coloured woods in a ground of mahogany, satinwood and harewood veneers.

In the transition from the Rococo this marquetry revival was first seen in the furniture of Pierre Langlois, an important but somewhat mysterious figure of French extraction, whose work is now the centre of much interest. From his workshop in Tottenham Court Road, London, came a number of outstanding pieces which have only in recent years been identified. His masterpieces are commodes with marquetry decoration, first in the French manner of floral sprays, then incorporating neo-classical motifs, made in the relatively short period of 1759–66. Langlois worked for the Duke of Bedford at Woburn Abbey and for other distinguished patrons. He used elaborate gilt mounts and *bombé* forms of French inspiration, but preferred wood tops for his commodes instead of the marble ones customary in France, except in the case of two commodes at Woburn Abbey which have tops of *pietre dure*. This is a form of mosaic work consisting of hard stones and marble fragments inlaid into a surface and highly polished.

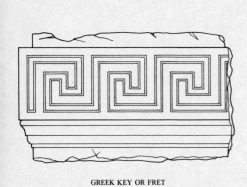

GREEK KEY OR FRET
R. and J. Adam

CLASSICAL URN
R. and J. Adam

Robert Adam (1728–92) was born in Scotland, the second of the four sons of William Adam, a leading Scottish architect. After study at Edinburgh University, and practical experience in his father's office, Robert took over the family business with his brother John on the death of William Adam in 1748. He completed projects on which his father had been engaged, undertook commissions on his own, then, from 1754 to 1758, went on the grand tour abroad. He made only a short stay in France, and spent most of his time in Italy, during which he crossed over to the Dalmatian coast to make measured drawings of the ruins of the palace of the Emperor Diocletian at Spalatro (modern Split), the results of which were published in 1764. In Italy Adam made an intensive study of ancient sites and met many of the leading artists, architects and designers of the time. On completing the tour, early in 1758, Adam set up practice in London with his brothers.

Adam began his career in London at an opportune time. Rococo was on the wane and the accession of the young George III in 1760, at the height of Britain's success in the Seven Years' War (1756–63), was an excellent opportunity to introduce a new style. For decoration Adam employed a wide range of classical motifs, including festoons of husks, paterae, vases, anthemions, shells, medallions, palm leaves, running frets, rams' and satyrs' heads, etc., all applied in a characteristically delicate fashion. Adam's tastes were definitely Roman and he was particularly fond of the grotesques with which Raphael had decorated the loggias of the Vatican and the Villa Madama in Rome, and which were based on early Christian decoration in the catacombs. In the *Works in Architecture of Robert and James Adam*, the first volume of which was published in 1773, the nature of these decorative forms is explained. The new approach provided what Sir John Soane described many years later as the 'electric power' of the revolution in taste.

CLASSICAL ROMAN GRIFFIN OR FABULOUS MONSTER
R. and J. Adam

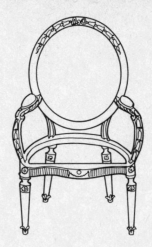

CHIPPENDALE'S DESIGN FOR A NEO-CLASSICAL CHAIR
c.1775, Burton Constable, Yorks.

'Grotesque' is described as the 'beautiful light style of ornament used by the ancient Romans in the decoration of their palaces, baths and villas . . . by far the most perfect that has ever appeared for inside decorations'. Such ornaments were brightly coloured and fanciful, providing a 'gay and elegant mode capable of inimitable beauties'. The development of the Adam style is clearly observable in the famous collection of over 9,000 drawings bought by Sir John Soane after Adam's death and now in the Soane Museum. They include several hundred furniture designs, but actually few of these refer to pieces as finally executed. At one time it was assumed that the drawings for the latter must have been made by Adam and sent to cabinet-makers for execution and not returned to him, for it was considered that only Adam himself could have been responsible for the designs of furniture that fitted so admirably into his general schemes of decoration, in which everything conformed to a unified design.

But it has been pointed out that Georgian cabinet-makers were trained to be independent designers, and the view is no longer acceptable that Adam designed all the furniture in his houses. The Soane Museum drawings indicate that he designed the pieces that were essentially part of the wall decoration—mirrors, side tables, sideboards, pedestals, window seats, some chairs, etc.—for which, as architect, he was responsible. For the rest of the furniture, with but few exceptions, the cabinet-makers undertook the commissions themselves. This does not rule out, of course, collaboration and discussion between architect and craftsmen, and does not in any way detract from Adam's all-pervasive influence, but it does give the craftsmen their due credit. John Linnell, Samuel Norman, and above all, Thomas Chippendale, provided furniture for Adam's houses, and unless an Adam design for a piece definitely survives, the authorship of the design must be credited to the maker concerned.

SIDEBOARD TABLE
Kedleston Hall, Derbyshire, from Adam design
dated 1762

WINDOW STOOL, MAHOGANY
From Adam design, 1764–5. Croome Court

Well-defined phases can be seen in the development of Adam's furniture style. His first major commission, in 1759–60, was for the furnishing and decoration of Kedleston, Derbyshire, for Sir Nathaniel Curzon (later Lord Scarsdale). Until c.1764 his designs remained frankly experimental. 'Athenian' Stuart had already designed furniture of classical inspiration for Spencer House, London, and in fact had also provided designs for Kedleston before Adam took over. In 1762 Adam, in one of his first efforts as a furniture designer, designed well-known sideboard tables at Kedleston which, with straight legs of square section and with classical ornament, were of neo-classical form seemingly inspired by Stuart's drawings. But for other furniture of this period made for further commissions, Adam's designs were retrospective, retaining traces of Kent's Baroque and of the Rococo. To this particular period belongs the chair made by Chippendale to Adam's design of 1764 for Sir Lawrence Dundas (p. 101).

As Adam's commissions increased, including work at Osterley Park House, Syon House and Kenwood, all in Middlesex, his furniture designs became more strictly neo-classical by 1768. Straight tapered legs, one of the chief features of the style, were now an accepted part of his designs, exemplified in the fine side tables designed for Syon House in 1765. These have the four front legs arranged in pairs, separated by a wide central gap, and are decorated with classical motifs in carved and gilt wood. Perhaps the first completely neo-classical piece of seat furniture in England is the window stool made c.1764–5 to Adam's design for Croome Court, Worcestershire. At this time there was a certain amount of influence from France when war ended in 1763, but its extent has not yet been fully gauged. Not only was ornament on classical lines now developed in Adam's designs, but classical forms of furniture, such as the lyre-back chair and pedestals and urns were introduced. Painted or gilded decoration was favoured.

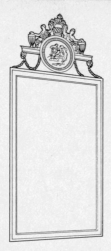

PIER GLASS, PAINTED BLACK WITH GILT ORNAMENT
Adam design, 1775. Osterley

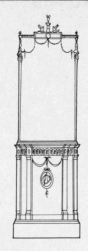

MIRROR AND COMMODE
Designed by Adam, 1778

Adam's furniture style probably reached maturity in the years between 1769 and 1777. He undertook commissions in all parts of the country and the furniture of this time includes some of the greatest masterpieces of English cabinet-making. In addition to the furniture at Osterley and Syon House, where Adam's work was spread over many years, there are superb pieces in his style at Harewood House, Nostell Priory and other great houses. Adam's own designs included some notable compositions such as wall mirrors and matching side tables, and sideboards made up of side tables flanked by pedestal-cupboards bearing urns. Also, ranked among the finest of their kind, are semi-circular commodes, of which the pair at Osterley of c.1775 (p. 116) are outstanding examples. These are decorated with marquetry which Adam himself used only rarely, though it was often employed to a superb standard by cabinet-makers. By this time, delicacy of ornament matched delicacy of form.

From c.1777 until his death in 1792 Adam's style gradually lost its maturity and inventiveness, to become increasingly repetitive and perhaps somewhat insipid. At Osterley the decline in quality was described in 1785 as 'gingerbread and sippets of embroidery' by Horace Walpole, who had been an admirer of Adam's earlier work. Adam now had many competitors, once his style was established; the disastrous War of American Independence (1775–83) curtailed spending in the fashionable world; and there was increasing challenge from supporters of the more literal version of classicism, who considered that Adam's highly personal interpretation was far removed from the purity of antiquity. For a study of the development of Adam's style there is no better method than a visit to Osterley (now administered by the Victoria and Albert Museum), for visitors are taken through the rooms in the order in which Adam decorated them.

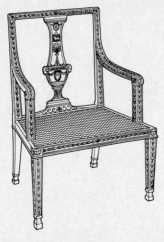

ARMCHAIR; IN ETRUSCAN TASTE
Designed by Adam, 1776. Osterley

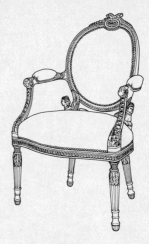

ARMCHAIR; CARVED AND GILT
Adam design, 1777. Osterley

Adam invented the Etruscan style *c.*1772 and decorated and furnished rooms in this taste in eight houses, of which Osterley provides the most celebrated and only surviving example. This style was based on a misconception, for the ornament and furniture were not Etruscan at all, but were taken from Greek urns and vases found in northern Italy. The taste was briefly fashionable and is commemorated in the name 'Etruria' given by Josiah Wedgwood, the great potter, to his new works in Staffordshire in 1769. Contrast in colours, not imitation of form, was the basis of the style. Chiefly black, terracotta and white were used, resembling the colours on the vases and urns. The Etruscan chair from Osterley illustrated here is painted greenish-grey, with black and terracotta decoration; it is one of a set of eight which Adam designed in March, 1776. The ornament on the chair backs is closely related to that of the wall against which they stand.

The Etruscan chair is only one of a wide variety of chair designs which gained a European reputation for English designers in the Adam period. Neo-classical chairs at this time display a new lightness of form, based particularly on round and oval backs and their variations of shield and heart shapes, which are either upholstered or filled with splats and bars of great delicacy, and painted, carved, gilded or inlaid. Legs are straight and tapered, and either round or square in section. Rear legs are notably splayed—a feature of English chairs not found on French counterparts. The front seat rail is shaped, often in serpentine form. These features can be seen in the above carved, gilded and upholstered chair which forms one of a set designed by Adam in 1777 for Osterley. It has unusual back supports in the form of winged sphinxes, though Adam occasionally employed this motif elsewhere, as on the cornice of a bed and on a mirror, also at Osterley.

ARMCHAIR; CARVED AND GILT, UPHOLSTERED IN
GOBELINS TAPESTRY
c.1776. Osterley

CHAIR; LYRE-BACK, CARVED MAHOGANY
Adam design, c. 1770. Osterley

The Tapestry Room at Osterley has a famous set of chairs and a sofa upholstered in Gobelins tapestry to match the wall-hangings, but in this case the chairs are more strongly French in inspiration. There is nothing to connect their design with Adam. The tapestries were woven by Jacques Neilson (whose name can be found on them) in 1775–6, and the chairs were probably made in 1776. It is thought that they were executed by English crafts-men to a French design, thus providing an interesting basis of comparison between the two countries. These differences are subtle ones, but the round seat and round fluted legs are typically French, as is the somewhat heavier treatment of the frame-work. On the other hand, the splayed rear legs are characteristically English. If, as some experts consider, the oval-back chair was a French invention, and there is certainly evidence for this, English designers soon put their own interpreta-tion upon it, as the Adam-designed example, discussed above, clearly shows.

Whatever controversy there may be about the origin of the oval-back chair, there can be none about that of the lyre-back. It is undisputedly an English invention, and represents a major contribution to Euro-pean chair design. It later became very popular in France. Above is a mahogany example which is still in the Eating Room at Osterley. It follows an undated design by Adam, but seems to have been made c.1770. The lyre-shaped splat is bordered by carved acanthus leaves and is sur-mounted by an anthemion with acanthus scrolls. The uprights and cresting rail are fluted, the former having foliate decoration above the seat, and the latter an oval patera in the centre. The fluted seat rail has a thin gilt metal border just below the leather upholstery. Horace Walpole visited Osterley in 1773 and wrote that the lyre-back chairs 'make charming harmony'. The house has no less than three large sets of this type of chair, each set representing a subtle variation of this classical form.

ARMCHAIR; LYRE-BACK, ROSEWOOD VENEER
Probably designed by John Linnell, *c*.1770

ARMCHAIR; GOTHIC ARCADING IN BACK, CARVED
MAHOGANY
c.1775

The Eating Room chairs at Osterley are ranged against the wall as they were in the 18th century. The anthemion and abutting scrolls at the top of the lyre are repeated in a similar motif in the plaster-work decoration of the wall panels above. The centre of the room is left clear. These chairs were probably made by John Linnell, who was also almost certainly responsible for the famous lyre-back chairs in the Library at Osterley, one of which is shown above. These are veneered with rosewood and are inlaid with satinwood husks and Vitruvian scrolls; the splat is also of satinwood. The medallion above the lyre and the swags on the legs are of ormolu. The cane seat has squab cushions covered with green leather. These superb examples were probably made *c*.1770, and resemble drawings by Linnell now in the Victoria and Albert Museum. There is no evidence to connect them at all with Adam; in fact they demonstrate the arrangement whereby some furniture was the architect's responsibility and the rest the cabinet-maker's.

This chair is a reminder that the Gothic style persisted in spite of the all-conquering march of neo-classicism. Indeed, one of Adam's earliest designs, dated 1761, had been a Gothic armchair for the chapel at Alnwick Castle, Northumberland, though it was not executed until *c*.1777-80. The mahogany example above, *c*.1775 has nothing to do with Adam, but shows how the neo-classical style was translated into Gothic forms and decoration. The Gothic arcading includes paterae (see p. 104). The front legs reveal the final traces of the cabriole form which was being replaced by the tapered versions favoured in the Adam style. Carved paterae again decorate the tops of the front legs and the centre of the curved front seat rail. There are touches of the Rococo in the curved framework of the back, showing that this style contributed something to the delicacy of neo-classical forms and decoration.

ARMCHAIR; OVAL–BACK, CARVED MAHOGANY WITH
PRINCE OF WALES'S FEATHERS
*c.*1775
(*See also colour photograph 21*)

CHAIR; 'LADDER–BACK', CARVED MAHOGANY
*c.*1775

The appeal of the oval-back chair lies principally in the attractive filling of varied finely carved or inlaid classical ornaments in the back. Anthemions, draperies, wheat-ears, urns, husks, are all found in endless combinations and yet all carefully related to the structural lines of the chair. In the above mahogany example, which was made *c.*1775, the graceful carved draperies are surmounted by the Prince of Wales's feathers. This is clear proof that this motif was in use before the publication of Hepplewhite's *Guide* of 1788 (p. 119) which is often considered to have introduced it. It will be noted that the frame of the back has been 'channelled', i.e., grooved, a common treatment in chairs of this kind. In this instance the frame, like the seat rails, has been fluted. The rest of the chair has all the typical features of the neo-classical era. Note the inlaid paterae on the knee blocks, the centre of the front seat rail and in the oval frame.

The 'ladder-back' chair is of ancient origin, for turned chairs with horizontal turned spindles in the back appear in medieval illuminated manuscripts. The modified form of chair with flat splats or rails connecting the uprights became popular as a cottage type at the end of the Stuart period (*c.*1700). About the middle of the 18th century it merged into the fashionable world, and the above example, made in mahogany *c.*1775, shows how it was affected by neo-classical taste. This chair also retains vestiges of the Rococo in its carved cresting, the serpentine-shaped and pierced back splats, and the cabriole legs. As has been seen in the case of the Gothic chair of about the same date (p. 111), the curve of the cabriole is hardly perceptible, and the feet of plinth form are borrowed from the new taste, as are the carved anthemions in the centres of the pierced splats. The rustic version of the ladder-back, with its simple, traditional lines, was due to re-appear into fashion in late Victorian times (p. 182).

PLATE III

7. Casket, marquetry of brass, copper, pewter, mother-of-pearl, etc., lacquered brass mounts. German, c.1725–50.

8. Jewel Casket, pictorial marquetry of various woods; brass mounts. South German, early 18th century.

9. Writing Cabinet, deal veneered with walnut and inlaid with various woods and bone. German (Mainz), dated 1738.

PLATE IV

10. Commode, veneered with casuarina wood, tulip wood and holly; gilt bronze mounts. French, Louis XV, *c.*1745–50.

11. Commode veneered with panels of Japanese lacquer; gilt bronze mounts. French, Rococo taste, Louis XV, *c.*1755–65.

12. Pedestal Secretaire, veneered with various woods and decorated with floral marquetry. French, Louis XV.

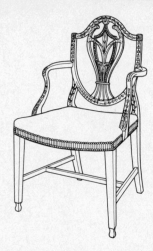

ARMCHAIR; SHIELD–BACK, CARVED MAHOGANY
c.1775–80

KIMBOLTON CABINET
Designed by Adam, 1771. Made by Ince and
Mayhew

The shield-back is one of the most celebrated of all English chair designs. Although, again, it is commonly thought to have been introduced by Hepplewhite's *Guide* (1788), that pattern book did no more than popularise a form which had already been developed, as this mahogany example of c.1775–80 demonstrates. The shield shape is an inherently simple and satisfying form. In the above example the simplicity of outline is preserved, yet the decoration, though unobtrusive, is of consummate skill. The central motif in the back splat is a vase with beaded ornament. The shield frame has a continuous carved husk which extends down the uprights to the seat rail and is also found on the arm supports which are now set back along the side rails. The arm rests are 'dished', i.e., flattened and set at a slight angle for more comfortable support. The two rows of brass studs on the stuff-over seat add final touches of quiet refinement.

This fine cabinet is a display piece—hence its shallow depth and lack of doors—which was made to show eleven *pietre dure* panels acquired from Italy for the Duchess of Manchester at Kimbolton Castle, Huntingdonshire. Recent research has revealed some interesting information on the methods employed in the production of fine furniture of this kind in the Georgian period. The cabinet was designed by Robert Adam for the Duchess in 1771, but thereafter his connection with the piece ceased. The cabinet was made to his altered design by Ince and Mayhew, the prominent London firm who have already been referred to as authors of the *Universal System of Household Furniture*, 1759 (p. 92). They were responsible for the general framework and the beautiful neo-classical marquetry. The ormolu mounts—the capitals and bases of the pilasters and the tiny frets round the framework—were supplied by Boulton and Fothergill of the Soho Works, Birmingham. This Kimbolton cabinet, of splendid quality, is now in the Victoria and Albert Museum.

'DIANA AND MINERVA' COMMODE; SATINWOOD
Supplied by Chippendale to Harewood House, 1773

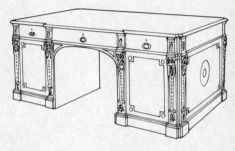

LIBRARY TABLE
Probably supplied by Chippendale to Harewood
House, c.1770

It has already been noted that Chippendale's career did not end with the demise of the Rococo and in fact his best work was done in the neo-classical style; and that so far from his furniture being merely executions of Adam's designs, it was mainly produced from his own designs. Harewood House, Yorkshire, where Chippendale was active between 1769 and 1777, bears this out, for while some of Chippendale's bills for furniture have survived there, there are no designs or bills at all from Adam. At Harewood is Chippendale's greatest masterpiece, the famous 'Diana and Minerva' commode, so called from the representations of the two goddesses on the doors. The commode is of satinwood, with exquisite marquetry of various wood in classical taste. It was supplied in 1773, as proved from Chippendale's bill, and cost £86, the largest sum which Chippendale is known to have charged for a piece of case furniture (mirrors cost more because of the high price of the glass).

Harewood House's famous library table caught the public's attention in 1965 when it was sold for 41,000 guineas and was subsequently acquired by Temple Newsam House. This table is made of rosewood and has marquetry decoration in classical taste and fine ormolu mounts. There is no bill for it from Chippendale, whose accounts for the house are however incomplete. His total bill for work there amounted to £6,839, but his surviving accounts date only from the end of 1772, and previous bills, for £3,025 (i.e., practically half the total) are missing. No other cabinet-makers' bills for the house have ever come to light, and in 1772 Chippendale's foreman, William Reid, made dust covers for the table, following the normal procedure by firms of providing protective material for their best pieces. In view of this, it seems reasonable to credit Chippendale with the design and making of the table, which must have been produced c.1770.

SIDEBOARD TABLE, PEDESTALS, URNS AND WINE COOLER; ROSEWOOD MOUNTED WITH ORMOLU
Probably supplied by Chippendale to Harewood
House, c.1772-3

One of Adam's most famous compositions was that of sideboard table and flanking pedestal-cupboards with classical urns—a highly decorative feature at the end of the dining room. Following his initial experiments at Kedleston in 1762 (p. 107) Adam developed this arrangement in a number of houses, e.g. 20 St. James's Square, London, Saltram House, Devon, Kenwood, Middlesex, etc. The side table, with four tapered legs in front, in pairs separated by a central interval, and two at the rear, had an elegant appearance in spite of its great length. The pedestal-cupboards, though very ornamental, were essentially functional. The pedestals contained table linen or, when lined with metal and provided with a heater, were used to keep plates warm. Normally one of the surmounting urns was a knife box; the other, fitted with a metal lining and a tap, contained water for washing out glasses.

One of the most famous arrangements of this kind is at Harewood House and consists of sideboard, pedestals, urns and wine cooler. They are made of carved rosewood inlaid with other woods and are decorated with ormolu mounts of festoons of husks and a running fret of classical ornament along the frieze of the table, all of which show up beautifully against the dark background. This group of furniture, made c.1772-3, is an outstanding example of English craftsmanship. Until quite recently it was universally supposed that it was the classic instance of the Chippendale-Adam relationship. But, as has been seen, there is no evidence of any kind that Adam participated in the design of this group, or indeed of any furniture at Harewood. Moreover, many features of these pieces differ considerably from any known Adam designs. No bill for the furniture exists, but most experts today are prepared to credit it to Chippendale.

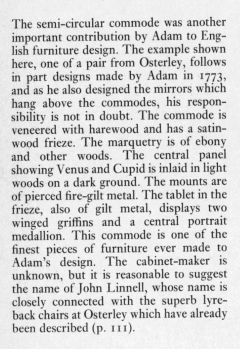

COMMODE; HAREWOOD VENEER WITH MARQUETRY OF
EBONY, ETC.
Adam design, c.1775. Osterley

COMMODE; MAHOGANY WITH MARQUETRY PANELS
By John Cobb, c.1770-5

The semi-circular commode was another important contribution by Adam to English furniture design. The example shown here, one of a pair from Osterley, follows in part designs made by Adam in 1773, and as he also designed the mirrors which hang above the commodes, his responsibility is not in doubt. The commode is veneered with harewood and has a satinwood frieze. The marquetry is of ebony and other woods. The central panel showing Venus and Cupid is inlaid in light woods on a dark ground. The mounts are of pierced fire-gilt metal. The tablet in the frieze, also of gilt metal, displays two winged griffins and a central portrait medallion. This commode is one of the finest pieces of furniture ever made to Adam's design. The cabinet-maker is unknown, but it is reasonable to suggest the name of John Linnell, whose name is closely connected with the superb lyre-back chairs at Osterley which have already been described (p. 111).

This commode, in contrast to the one just reviewed, but of about the same date (c.1770-5) has marquetry decoration of neo-classical taste on a framework which retains many Rococo elements strongly French in inspiration. It is made of mahogany with marquetry panels of satinwood and other woods. The front and sides are serpentine. The classical festoons of husks, and border of anthemions and other motifs on the *bombé* front enclose two oval panels containing marquetry of vases and flowers. The front angles, thoroughly French in conception, have ormolu mounts. This is one of a group of commodes of almost identical design made by John Cobb, who has been mentioned (p. 93) as the former partner of William Vile. After Vile's retirement, Cobb continued in business alone, specialising in high-class marquetry. Unlike many contemporary cabinet-makers, he was very successful in his business, and at his death in 1778 left a fortune of some £20,000 to his widow.

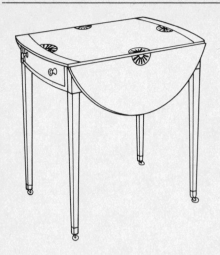

PEMBROKE TABLE; SATINWOOD, WITH MARQUETRY
DECORATION
c.1775-1800

PIER GLASS
Adam design executed in 1773 for Kenwood

One of the most charming types of small tables made in England is that known as the Pembroke table. It was introduced c.1750, but the earliest survivor appear to date from the 1760s. In the last part of the century it achieved great popularity. Its name is a mystery—possibly derived from the Earl of Pembroke, or, more simply, as Sheraton stated, from 'the lady who first gave orders for one of them'. This table is essentially a light and elegant piece with a drawer or drawers below the top, which has two hinged flaps extendable on brackets. The above example, made in the last quarter of the century, is of satin-wood and has semi-circular flaps. It is decorated with marquetry, including the top. In other versions, the tops are rectangular or serpentine, and decoration might be veneering with finely figured woods, japanning, or painting (as in Etruscan examples). When not in use, and with flaps down, Pembroke tables look very decorative against the wall.

Adam's inventive genius was perhaps at its best with mirrors. This 'pier glass in the parlour' at Kenwood is from the *Works in Architecture of Robert and James Adam*, and was executed with minor changes in 1773 when Adam was enlarging Kenwood for Lord Mansfield. Several types of mirrors were designed by Adam, who obviously considered them a most important element in his wall decoration. One kind resembled a rectangular picture frame. During the 1770s large versions of this kind were given beautiful crestings. Another kind of mirror was tripartite, divided by slender supports of griffins, sphinxes, female figures, etc., the large centre glass sometimes having an arched top. Mirrors were often closely related to the side table which stood beneath them. The oval kind, however, of the type illustrated here, was particularly attractive, setting off the delicate classical ornaments of pendant husks, griffins, anthemions, floral scrolls and urn.

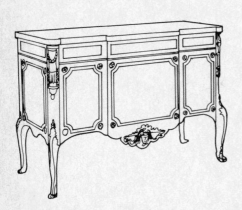

COMMODE; BREAK-FRONT
French, stamped J. F. Leleu, c.1770
(*See also colour photographs 14, 15, 16 and 17*)

COMMODE; JAPANNED IN GOLD AND SILVER ON GREEN
GROUND
Supplied by Chippendale to Nostell Priory in 1771

The advent of the *goût grec* into France in the early 1760s has already been noted (p. 103). The French in general derived inspiration from the actual forms of antiquity, the English from the ornament. In 1771 the new furnishings ordered by Madame du Barry at the Pavillon de Louveciennes for a reception for Louis XV were completely in neo-classical taste, and marked the triumph of the new style over the Rococo. Thus French neo-classicism is contemporaneous with the reign of Louis XVI (1774–93). The extravagance of the court and aristocracy in this reign, which was to precipitate the French Revolution of 1789, ushered in a period of great prosperity for the *ébénistes*, who now included some of the most famous names in French furniture-making. The above commode bears the stamp of J. F. Leleu, pupil of J. F. Oeben. There are still traces of the Rococo in the cabriole legs and apron carving. But the general rectangular form, the more restrained treatment, the break-front, the ormolu mounts and the pattern of the marquetry all proclaim the classical change.

It is interesting to compare Leleu's commode with the above English example made by Chippendale for Nostell Priory at about the same date (*c.*1770). It is japanned in gold and silver on a green ground and is part of a remarkable suite of bedroom furniture still in the house. It is authenticated from a bill of Chippendale's of 1771 in which he charges £15. 10s. for 'a very neat Commode for the Peir [sic] Japan'd Green and Gold with a dressing drawer Complete'. The centre top drawer is fitted as a dressing drawer. Chippendale's commode exhibits more advanced neo-classical features than the French one. It has a more rectangular form, the feet are fully representative of the new style and have no vestige of cabriole shape, and the angled corners are decorated with the familiar festoons of husks in ormolu. The Ionic scrolls at the top of these corners are a mannerism of Chippendale's, found on other pieces of furniture from his workshop.

CHIFFONIER; FLORAL MARQUETRY AND ORMOLU
MOUNTS
By J. H. Riesener, c.1780
(*See also colour photograph 18*)

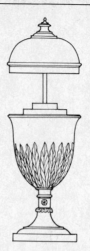

KNIFE-CASE
Design in Hepplewhite's *Guide* (1794). The top rises
on a central rod to allow space for the knives.

The greatest *ébéniste* in the Louis XVI style is beyond all doubt J. H. Riesener (1734–1806) who, like Leleu, was trained by Oeben and in fact directed Oeben's workshop after his death and married his widow in 1767. Riesener's furniture, executed with exquisite skill, has made a distinct contribution to the whole art of cabinet-making. In case furniture his forms become more definitely rectangular and upright, but in other pieces more varied forms are found. Refined delicacy is the keynote of the smaller furniture which he made, such as the writing tables and work table supplied to Queen Marie-Antoinette, whose commissions raised him to the peak of his fame. For decoration Riesener employed marquetry, particularly of floral patterns, and ormolu mounts of festoons of flowers or of classical motifs. He often modelled his own mounts. The above chiffonier, made c.1780, is typical of his work. It also shows how he made good use of beautiful veneers.

The furniture designed by Adam, or made by cabinet-makers in his style for the houses on which he was engaged—or even for houses with which he had no connection—was of course intended for wealthy patrons. Furniture of this kind was made by leading cabinet-makers. Chippendale, Ince and Mayhew, Linnell, Norman and Cobb have been referred to. Other prominent craftsmen of this period included John Bradburn, William France and William Gates, who were all royal employees. Well-known large firms were Seddon's, who in 1786 were described by a German visitor as employers of 400 workmen at their Aldersgate Street premises in London, and Gillow's of Lancaster, who established a branch in London c.1765. But the successful propagation of the neo-classical style into a form suitable for middle-class homes throughout the country, set out in designs for the practical use of smaller firms and of craftsmen generally, was the achievement of George Hepplewhite's famous pattern-book, *The Cabinet-Maker and Upholsterer's Guide*, published in 1788.

DESIGN FOR CHAIR BACK; WITH PRINCE OF WALES'S
FEATHERS
Hepplewhite's *Guide* (1794)

ARMCHAIR; SHIELD-BACK, SATINWOOD WITH PAINTED
DECORATION
Made by Seddon's, *c.*1790

Hepplewhite was an obscure cabinet-maker whose shop was situated in Cripplegate, outside the fashionable furniture-making areas of London. No piece of furniture from his premises has ever been identified. He died in 1786 and the *Guide* thus came out two years after his death. It was published by 'A. Hepplewhite and Co.', and this presumably referred to his widow, Alice, who continued the business. The *Guide*, with nearly 300 designs, was the best pattern-book which had appeared since Chippendale's *Director* and was an immediate success, being re-issued in 1789 and, in revised form, in 1794. The furniture designs, following, as the preface declares, 'the latest and most prevailing fashion', represent the refined, elegant and essentially simple furniture which was made in England from *c.*1775 until the end of the century, and which is now universally acknowledged as being in the 'Hepplewhite style'.

Hepplewhite's furniture was intended to be made in mahogany and satinwood and decorated with carving and marquetry, or else with japanning and painting ('the new and very elegant fashion'), in which case beech was normally used. The association of Hepplewhite's name with shield-back chairs has already been examined (p. 113). Painted varieties of these, the *Guide* recommends, should have cane seats and a lighter framework than mahogany chairs. These features are seen in the above elegant example, which was made *c.*1790 by the firm of Seddon, and which shows how the cane seat and slender lines of the shield, as well as the absence of stretchers, heighten the general effect of delicacy. The wood in this case is satinwood painted with floral designs and peacock's feather 'eyes'. It is significant that the third edition of the *Guide* (1794) added more designs of chairs with square backs to those already in the first edition—an indication of the effect of Sheraton's innovations (p. 135).

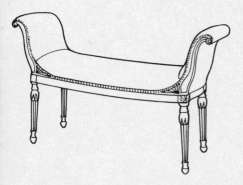

WINDOW SEAT OR STOOL ('SOPHA'), MAHOGANY
c.1785

SIDEBOARD; BOW-FRONTED, MAHOGANY
c.1785

Deep and comfortable yet elegant sofas are displayed in a number of designs in the *Guide*. A fashionable type has a curved back and sides and slender tapered legs. One design, entitled 'bar back sofa', and described as 'of modern invention', has a back composed of four shield-backs in the form more commonly included among settees. Following French fashions, the *Guide* displays a *duchesse*, a composite piece of two facing *bergère* chairs (round-backed easy chairs, described in the *Guide* as 'barjiers') with a stool in the middle, and a *confidante*, a sofa with a chair section added to each end. Other seating furniture in the *Guide* includes stools (*en suite* with chairs), window stools with two raised ends, hall chairs and a wing armchair. All these pieces have a neatness and precision of line and complete mastery of form that have prompted Siegfried Giedion (*Mechanization Takes Command*, 1948) to describe the English furniture of this period as 'timeless'.

The sideboards illustrated in the *Guide* fall into two categories. One kind, for 'spacious dining-rooms', perpetuates the arrangement introduced by Adam of a side table flanked by pedestal-cupboards and urns. The other kind, intended for smaller houses, is one of the most attractive pieces of the period and incorporates the cupboards within the table. This type has square tapered legs at each end, arranged in sets of two at the front, each pair enclosing a cupboard, and two legs at the rear. The central space contains a drawer and has a curved underframing. The front is usually of serpentine or bow form. From c.1780 smaller sideboards, normally bow-fronted, with four legs only, were introduced. According to the *Guide* the cupboards in these useful and elegant sideboards could be fitted, as they were in Adam's designs, for a number of uses—with partitions for bottles, recesses for napkins, spaces for plates or lead lining for water. The middle drawer contained the table linen.

CHEST OF DRAWERS; MAHOGANY
*c.*1770–80

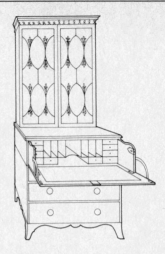

DESIGN FOR SECRETARY AND BOOKCASE
Hepplewhite's *Guide* (1794)

The *Guide* contains designs for the furniture of bedrooms and dressing-rooms, a group of domestic furniture which, apart from beds, does not figure among Adam's designs. In this group we find the distinctive and attractive Hepplewhite chest of drawers. This is often bow- or serpentine-fronted. The corners are carried down to floor level and continue into outward-curving feet, one of the most characteristic features of the period. The shaped apron forms a continuous curve with these splayed feet. The above example, made *c.*1770–80, has its top drawer fitted with a sliding mirror and with compartments for toilet requisites. Chests of drawers of good quality have oak drawer linings. The shaped drawer fronts are usually of pine veneered with mahogany, but solid mahogany is employed on straight-fronted chests, or else figured mahogany on Honduras mahogany, oak or pine. As in the above example, many chests have cross-banded borders.

Under the headings 'desk and bookcase' and 'secretary and bookcase' the *Guide* (1794) has a number of designs for elegant composite pieces in which the lower stage is either a chest of drawers or a cupboard, and the upper stage is a bookcase with glazed doors. The essential difference between the two types is that the desk has the sloping top associated with the bureau, while the secretary has a top drawer which lets down to provide the writing surface. Bracket or splayed feet are illustrated. Great attention is paid to the mahogany glazing bars of the bookcase, which are presented in varied graceful forms—classical vases and draperies, Gothic tracery, or geometrical patterns. To decorate the top, the *Guide* recommends a vase or bust placed between a scroll of foliage. A note in the *Guide* states that the cupboard beneath the secretary has 'sliding shelves for clothes, etc., like a wardrobe', showing that much writing was done in the bedroom.

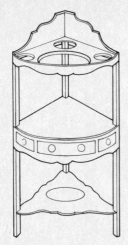

'BASON' STAND; TRIANGULAR FORM
Hepplewhite's *Guide* (1794)

WARDROBE
Hepplewhite's *Guide* (1794)

There is space here to mention only some of the many smaller pieces of furniture which appear in the *Guide*. They ally elegance and utility in a way that has never been surpassed and are among the articles most sought-after by modern collectors. Fire screens are of two kinds— pole screens of 'maps, figures, needlework, etc.', set on slender stands, and 'horse' or cheval screens swinging between two vertical supports based on curved feet. Both kinds were used to keep the great heat of the large open fires of the period from the faces of those sitting near them. Other small pieces include hanging shelves, tea trays, tea caddies, shaving tables and dressing glasses (i.e., dainty oval mirrors on a miniature stand of serpentine form with three drawers). The useful basin (or 'bason') stand, with a circular recess in the top for the bowl and a drawer below for toilet accessories, is shown above. The triangular form is useful, as it 'stands in a corner out of the way'.

Among the larger pieces was the wardrobe. The type shown here, consisting of a chest of drawers at the base and a cupboard above, had been developed in Chippen-dale's Rococo period and was so useful that it became the standard bedroom piece for the rest of the century. Naturally its decoration conformed to the varied changes of fashion. Here is Hepplewhite's design for a wardrobe which he describes as 'an article of considerable consequence'. The usual arrangement was for the chest to have three rows of drawers, two short ones in the top row and two long ones below. Beautiful mahogany veneers decorate the doors, and neo-classical motifs are seen in the two small rows of marquetry. The cupboard interiors are fitted with shelves, as clothes were laid out flat in the Georgian period and not hung. Often a strip of metal is found at the edge of one door to give protection. The characteristic Hepple-white splayed feet and shaped apron appear at the front and sides.

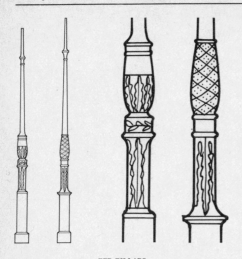

BED PILLARS
Two designs from Hepplewhite's *Guide* (1794)

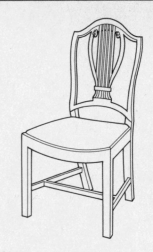

NORWEGIAN VERSION OF CHAIR IN HEPPLEWHITE
STYLE; BEECH.
End of 18th century.

Since the mid-18th century it was customary to leave the posts of beds free from hangings, and designers took the opportunity to design attractive, slender posts. These were generally fluted and tapered upwards from urn-shaped bases curved with classical leaf ornament. The *Guide* (1794) illustrates various types of posts, and also some very decorative cornices which had surmounting vases and paterae and other ornaments in classical taste. But in most surviving beds of the time it seems to have been more usual to have, instead of a cornice, a valance of frilled or pleated material concealing the wooden framework of the tester. Mention is made in the *Guide* of a press bed: this was made to fold up into a cupboard which looked exactly like a wardrobe, except that the upper drawers were false and formed part of the door, the latter being either in one piece and made to swing up and form the tester, or in two halves opening in the centre. The lower drawer could contain the bedding.

The Adam-Hepplewhite furniture style had such great influence in Denmark and Norway that 'anglomania' is the word often used in those two countries to refer to fashionable taste in the last twenty years of the century. In 1781 the Norwegian Carsten Anker was appointed director of the Royal Furniture Emporium (or Magazine) which had been established in Copenhagen in 1777 to improve standards of craftsmanship and design. Anker was a great admirer of English furniture. London-trained Danish craftsmen taught their countrymen the latest English techniques. The pattern books of Hepplewhite and Sheraton were brought in to form the basis of designs and large quantities of mahogany were imported to ensure competent execution of these designs. Native woods were also of course frequently used and the above illustration shows a Norwegian version of a Hepplewhite chair carried out in beech. Note that the legs are straight and not tapered.

6
Later
Neo-classical
c.1790-1830

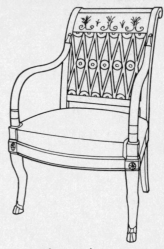

'ETRUSCAN' CHAIR
From Jacob's workshop. Similar to type made for
Rambouillet in 1787.

It was in the 1780's that English furniture was first really affected by the strict archaeological interpretation of classical forms that was to be current throughout Europe. For long the mature phase of this style was known as 'English Empire', but this term is now replaced by 'Regency', for English furniture was not just a close version of the classicism established by Napoleon's imperial rule, but had strong independent features. In the following pages we trace the beginning of the new taste with the work of Henry Holland and the subsequent development under Thomas Hope, and note the culmination of English cabinet-making skill, as superbly illustrated in the designs of Thomas Sheraton. Yet the increasing pace of industrialisation, set against the long Anglo-French wars of 1793-1815, clearly marks the coming of momentous changes in English social and economic life, and the scholarly approach to furniture design fails to be fulfilled in the commercial world.

French designers and craftsmen were the first to tackle the problems of producing furniture of classical exactitude and of devising adaptations of antique pieces to suit the requirements of their own day. Even before the French Revolution there had already been revivals of Greek, Egyptian, Pompeian and Etruscan styles in France. Etruscan chairs, for instance, had been made in 1787 for Marie-Antoinette's dairy at Rambouillet by Georges Jacob, one of the very greatest of French chair-makers. Like the English, the French confused Etruscan with Greek, but Jacob's chairs in the *style étrusque*, with scrolled backs filled with lattice work separated by paterae, and with straight tapered legs decorated with spiral fluting, had nothing in common with Adam's Etruscan chairs at Osterley (p. 109); they marked a late and austere development of the Louis XVI taste, and anticipated the Empire style by almost 20 years. Jacob made them of solid mahogany, an indication of his interest in English fashions.

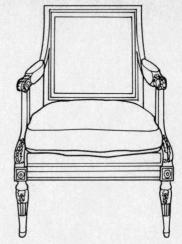

CHAIR ATTRIBUTED TO GEORGES JACOB, BUT
DESIGNED IN THE ENGLISH MANNER
Probably supplied through Henry Holland to the
Duke of Bedford in 1786

ARMCHAIR WITH CARVED AND PAINTED DECORATION
By Georges Jacob, *c.*1780–5
(*See also colour photograph 19*)

In the 1780's the latest styles in French furniture began to have a stronger than usual impact on English furniture. The reason for this was the coming of age in 1783 of George, Prince of Wales. He was given Carlton House for his official residence and at once began to furnish it with up-to-date furniture. His sympathies were strongly pro-French, in which he was supported by an influential group of Whig families. All this followed the family tradition among the royal Georges of hostility between the Prince of Wales and his father, and since in this case George III was a Tory and anti-French, the attitude of his son is easy to understand. The Prince as it happened turned out to be one of the greatest royal patrons of the arts that this country has ever known. He not only bought considerable quantities of French furniture, but also employed French craftsmen as decorators. His example was followed by the Whig coterie, who included Lord Palmerston, Lord Spencer, the Duke of Bedford and Samuel Whitbread.

When the French Revolution broke out in 1789 many French châteaux were despoiled of their contents, some of which were later sold off cheaply by the revolutionary government, and many pieces of furniture were bought by English visitors to Paris before war broke out between the two countries in 1793. Even then French influence did not cease. Some aristocrats managed to escape from France to England with articles of furniture which they often sold cheaply to English buyers. A number of French craftsmen also took refuge in England and continued to make furniture in London during the war. All this explains why there is now in England a finer collection of French furniture of the final phase of the Louis XVI style than there is in France itself. After the Prince of Wales became George IV in 1820 he continued to patronise French craftsmen until his death in 1830. There is thus a most important element of French influence, which must be taken into account in any study of late Georgian English furniture.

ORNAMENTAL STAND FOR A LAMP
Sketch by Henry Holland, c.1790

DESIGN FOR A PIER TABLE AND PIER GLASS FOR
CARLTON HOUSE
By Henry Holland, c.1785

Until 1793 the Prince of Wales spent considerable sums buying French furniture in Paris for Carlton House, employing for this purpose the two most important dealers in France, Dominique Daguerre and M. E. Lignereux. On the English side, the most influential figure in developing the new taste in interior decoration was the Prince's gifted architect, Henry Holland (1745–1806). Holland had been assistant and partner to the famous landscape gardener, Lancelot ('Capability') Brown, whose daughter he married in 1773 and through whom he gained introductions to the Prince and the Whig aristocracy. Holland carried out commissions at Carlton House, Woburn Abbey (the Duke of Bedford), Althorp (Lord Spencer), Broadlands (Lord Palmerston) and Southill (Samuel Whitbread), the last-named being his acknowledged masterpiece. Through this patronage, Holland became the pioneer of Graeco-Roman detail in English furnishing and decoration, and thus an important founder of the Regency style.

Though Holland saw much of the fashionable French furniture which was brought to England from 1783 onwards, and was in direct contact with the French craftsmen employed by the Prince and his Whig friends, he nevertheless had his own sources of information on the new taste. He himself never made the foreign tour which was normally regarded as completing an architect's training, and did not visit France until 1785. His mastery of Graeco-Roman elements came through C. H. Tatham, who was trained in his office and whom he sent, at his own expense, to Italy for three years (1794–7) to supply him with drawings of classical ornament. These drawings were published in 1799 with the title of *Etchings of Ancient Ornamental Architecture Drawn from the Originals in Rome and Other Parts of Italy*. This successful work was re-issued in 1803, 1810 and 1836, and had a German edition in 1805. Tatham also published in 1806 *Etchings Representing Fragments of Grecian and Roman Architectural Ornaments*.

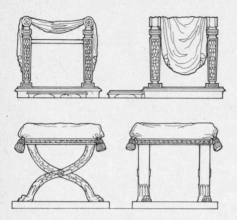

ANTIQUE SEATS
From C. H. Tatham's *Etchings*, 1799

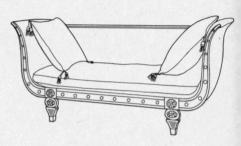

SOFA, GILTWOOD FRAME DECORATED WITH BOLT HEADS
Southill, early 19th century

Tatham's publications, it is now accepted, inspired not only accurate details of classical ornament, but also precise forms of ancient furniture which became fashionable during the Regency—circular tables mounted on three monopodia supports, lion masks with rings, X-frame stools, terminal figures supporting cabinets, chimerae, acanthus bases to tables, and so on. Tatham himself, in a letter to Holland from Italy, refers to the Grecian style 'gaining ground in England', and he was considered by contemporaries to have instituted an 'Anglo-Greek' style which in many respects was more precise than the versions then in vogue in France. Holland's exact part in designing furniture in the houses on which he was engaged is not easy to determine: he left two sketchbooks (now in the Library of the Royal Institute of British Architects), but these deal chiefly with architectural ornament. There is certainly nothing to match the collection of designs left by Robert Adam.

Expert opinion usually credits Holland with the general control of the design of the furniture in his houses. In 1796, writing to the Duke of Bedford, Holland refers to 'the endless number of drawings I have made' in connection with 'articles of furniture' and later, in 1801, we find he is paid £200 as 'commission on furniture'. At Southill, Bedfordshire, where Holland was occupied with the furnishing from 1796 until his death in 1806, there is a distinct English flavour about the furniture, which neither slavishly follows French models nor attempts a rigid archaeological version. The best examples of Holland's mature furniture style are in the Drawing Room at Southill, furnished after 1800. Here a number of well-known sofas of classical design, the largest some 9½ feet long, have their gilt frames decorated with bolt heads. The largest sofa has feet of lotus leaf form; the rest have feet which are fluted and tapered and have paterae where they join the frame.

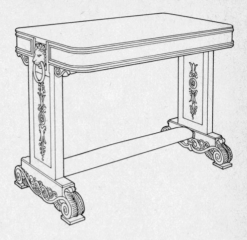

ARMCHAIR IN ANTIQUE TASTE
Southill, c.1796–9

CENTRE OR WRITING-TABLE, KINGWOOD,
ON STANDARDS
Southill, c.1812–15

The Drawing Room at Southill also contains famous carved and gilt chairs, the seat frames of which have the same bolt head decoration as the sofas. These chairs, which appear to date from the early years (c.1796–9) of Holland's association with Southill, have fluted and tapered front legs, a particularly graceful scrolling of the arms, and balanced outward-sweeping lines to the rear legs and back—features which were to be echoed on English chairs for many years. The Southill chairs are derived from classical sources and are of French inspiration, but in the treatment of the legs, and in a certain simplification of design carried out in a somewhat robust manner, there are clear signs of an English version. In the same room at Southill are a pair of armchairs which originally stood in the boudoir. These are of large proportions and have square upholstered backs and sides with carved and gilt frames. Here again, although the frames are French-inspired, their square and sturdy design is obviously English.

In the centre of the Southill Drawing Room is a fine circular monopodial table made of kingwood, on a massive triangular base which is heavily decorated with gilt carving and ormolu mounts. The gilt fluted frieze has four large gilt metal lion masks with rings in their mouths. *En suite* with this table is a carved and gilt writing or centre table with rectangular top. In this case a lion mask is found at each end, above the standard, or solid end support, which is painted green and decorated with elaborate ormolu mounts. Each standard has a cruciform base, also lavishly decorated with carved giltwood and with applied gilt metal ornament, and the standards are linked by an upholstered stretcher or foot rest. Both the circular and rectangular tables are stylistically later than the chairs and may have been made after Holland's death, during the second main period of furnishing the house, from 1808 to 1815. Standards were to become a fashionable form of table support in the early Victorian period.

J

ROSEWOOD COMMODE, MOUNTED WITH ORMOLU
Probably designed by Henry Holland, c.1800

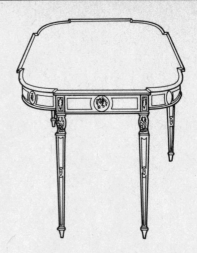

CARD TABLE
Design in Sheraton's *Drawing Book* (1791–4)

To summarise Henry Holland's contribution to English furniture design, one can say that in addition to introducing Graeco-Roman detail into England he was instrumental in blending this detail with late versions of the Louis XVI style. Much of his furniture was supplied by the London firm of Marsh and Tatham, Thomas Tatham being the brother of the C. H. Tatham from whose drawings classical detail was incorporated into the firm's furniture. In his early career Holland was undoubtedly influenced by the work of another great contemporary *ébéniste*, Adam Weisweiler. The latter seems to be the principal inspiration behind the pair of commodes (see above), with straight fronts, curved ends with open shelves, and tapered, fluted and partly gilded pillars at the corners, which Holland probably designed for Southill. These commodes are *en suite* with a shallow one of low height. Such fashionable pieces naturally took time to make their mark; for the general furniture of the time we must turn to Sheraton.

By the end of the 18th century and the first decade of the 19th, English furniture had reached its peak in both elegance of design and technical accomplishment. The prevailing style was summarised by Thomas Sheraton (1751–1806), the third of the great Georgian trinity of designers, in his *Cabinet-Maker and Upholsterer's Drawing Book*, which was published in parts between 1791 and 1794. Sheraton's story is a strange one. He was born in 1751 at Stockton-on-Tees, and after working as a cabinet-maker for some years migrated to London c.1790 and settled in Wardour Street (where a plaque today commemorates his stay). There, however, he does not seem to have had a shop of his own, and certainly no furniture by him has ever been identified. He eked out a bare living as a teacher of drawing and died in poverty in 1806. He published a useful *Cabinet Dictionary* in 1803, and in 1805 part of an unfinished *Encyclopaedia*, in which some of the designs bordered on the fantastic, suggesting a deranged mind.

PIER TABLE
Design in Sheraton's *Drawing Book* (1791–4)

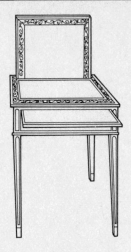

SCREEN TABLE
Design in Sheraton's *Drawing Book* (1791–4)

Sheraton's *Drawing Book* contains altogether 113 plates, covering all types of furniture and ornamental details. As his preface indicates, Sheraton seems to have obtained his ideas by making it his business 'to apply to the best workmen in different shops' to see the latest fashions. Yet there is substantial evidence that he did not merely copy what he saw, but produced designs of his own invention, and that he had a distinct gift for co-ordination. The presentation of the designs is excellent and demonstrates Sheraton's skill as a draughtsman, while the notes on the plates are sound and instructive, far fuller than those in other pattern books of the period. The author fully deserves recognition for giving posterity an admirable survey of fashions in the greatest age of English craftsmanship, and 'Sheraton' is a well-merited label for describing the particularly elegant furniture of the time. His designs cover the transition between Adam-Hepplewhite neo-classicism and the subsequent Regency style.

The *Drawing Book* had some 600 subscribers from all parts of the country and seems to have been widely influential. Its designs mark the culmination of the lightness and delicacy which had distinguished English furniture ever since the beginning of the Adam period. Sheraton's furniture has at times almost a fragile appearance, but it was superbly made by cabinet-makers of unsurpassed skill, and was strictly utilitarian. An important feature was the way in which single pieces of furniture combined the functions of two or more pieces, thus filling a special social need. Sheraton worked in a period when a sudden and accelerating increase in population put considerable pressure on living space; this trend was particularly marked in cities, above all in London, and affected the well-to-do as well as the poorer classes. There was a compelling need to limit the size of furniture and to make 'one piece of furniture serve many purposes' (T. Martin, *The Circle of the Mechanical Arts*, 1813).

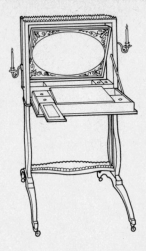

DRESSING GLASS AND WRITING-TABLE
Design in Sheraton's *Drawing Book* (1791–4)

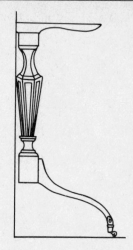

'PILLAR AND CLAW' OF A PEMBROKE TABLE
Design in Sheraton's *Drawing Book* (1791–4)

There was a notable increase in the population of England and Wales after 1750, with a very pronounced acceleration after 1780. The first official census of 1801, taken during the war with France, when many critics feared the effect of revealing such statistics to the enemy, showed a population of just over nine millions, compared with the estimated six and a half millions in 1750. Transport had not kept pace with this rise, so in the days before railways led to the development of suburbs most people had to live near their place of work. This pressure on house space is the clue to the ingeniously fitted furniture and to the number of portable pieces, easily moved about the room, or from room to room, which appear in the *Drawing Book*. In the case of larger pieces, adaptability was often the keynote, exemplified in folding bedsteads and extending dining-room tables. Modern furniture has much to learn from Sheraton's designs, with their happy combination of functionalism and simple, clear lines.

Another feature of Sheraton furniture is its employment of mechanical gadgets of all kinds. Such fitments had of course long been known in the making of furniture. Many clever devices had been fitted into Louis XVI furniture, for instance, but these were intended for wealthier patrons. Now Sheraton was occupied with their use on pieces intended for ordinary homes. The impetus came from the increasing interest in mechanisation which heralded the Industrial Revolution in England. Mechanical inventions were affecting the methods of production in several industries and attracting attention among craftsmen generally, and furniture-makers were no exception. The important development of what was then known as 'patent' furniture (whether officially patented or not) will be examined in more detail later (see pp. 162–3). It was a significant phase in furniture history, in which England, at least for a time, took the lead.

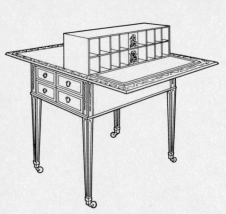

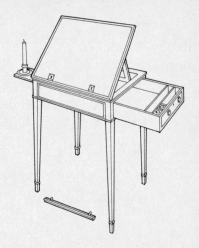

HARLEQUIN PEMBROKE TABLE
Design in Sheraton's *Drawing Book* (1791–4)

READING AND WRITING-TABLE
Design in Sheraton's *Drawing Book* (1791–4)
(*See also colour photograph 20*)

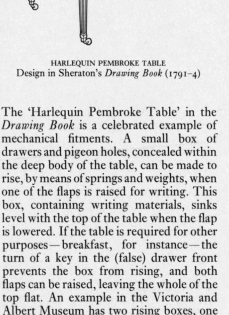

The 'Harlequin Pembroke Table' in the *Drawing Book* is a celebrated example of mechanical fitments. A small box of drawers and pigeon holes, concealed within the deep body of the table, can be made to rise, by means of springs and weights, when one of the flaps is raised for writing. This box, containing writing materials, sinks level with the top of the table when the flap is lowered. If the table is required for other purposes — breakfast, for instance — the turn of a key in the (false) drawer front prevents the box from rising, and both flaps can be raised, leaving the whole of the top flat. An example in the Victoria and Albert Museum has two rising boxes, one for writing, one for needlework. Another example, at Temple Newsam, Leeds, has an oval compartment rising from the top. The Pembroke table proper, without such additions, remained very popular, elegantly proportioned, veneered with choice woods, and decorated with marquetry or painted ornament.

Various items from Sheraton's *Drawing Book* are illustrated above. The combined reading and writing table is typical of the smaller elegant and portable pieces. Its top forms a writing board adjusted to the sitter's convenience on a ratchet fitted in the centre; a small platform for a candlestick swings out from one side; on the other side the single drawer has compartments for writing materials. Another piece — a screen table — has a pull-out writing slide and an adjustable screen at the back. A similar screen, made to rise by pressing a patera in the back, thus releasing a spring, is also found on another, somewhat larger, example of a lady's writing table, which has a recessed shelf beneath the drawer. 'The convenience of this table,' so Sheraton's text runs, 'is that a lady, when writing at it, may both receive the benefit of the fire and have her face screened from the scorching heat.' Satinwood is the recommended timber.

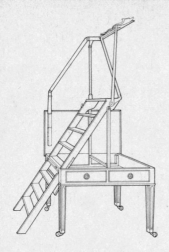

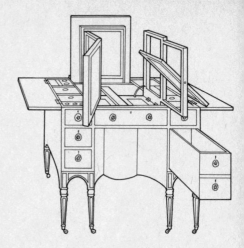

LIBRARY STEPS AND TABLE
Design in Sheraton's *Drawing Book* (1791–4)

A LADY'S DRESSING-TABLE
Design in Sheraton's *Drawing Book* (1791–4)

The 'library steps and table' illustrated in the *Drawing Book* are of a kind that became fashionable late in the 18th century. Library steps in the form of a ladder (fixed or folding) or of a chair of which the hinged seat and back swung over to form a flight of steps, had been known since the development of libraries in great houses, but they were not in general use until c.1750. The enclosing of steps within a table came later. The example shown here, one of two presented in the *Drawing Book*, is acknowledged by Sheraton to be based on those made by Robert Campbell and supplied to George III. Campbell had taken out a patent in 1774 for library steps in 'writing, library, dining and card tables'. Giving the dimensions of the table, Sheraton states that the extended steps reach a height of 5 feet 5 inches and are provided at the top with a small flap to enable the reader to make notes without bringing the book down the steps. It was claimed that the steps could be set up in half a minute.

The *Drawing Book* includes a considerable number of designs for dressing-tables. No doubt the problems of fitting out these compact pieces as fully as possible for every requirement of the toilet had a special appeal for Sheraton. In the kneehole 'Lady's Dressing Table' illustrated above, the hinged and swinging mirrors enable the sitter to view herself from every angle; as well as compartments for all articles of the toilet, the table has others for writing materials and for jewellery. The whole top folds flat when not in use. The design shows these working arrangements clearly. Another variety of dressing-table shown by Sheraton has pedestals of drawers carried down almost to floor level, and a central cupboard within the kneehole space. But the most popular table of this kind was on legs (with small drawers in the top) and had a lifting or hinged top, which disclosed small compartments and a movable toilet mirror, while the central drawer contained a basin and soap cups.

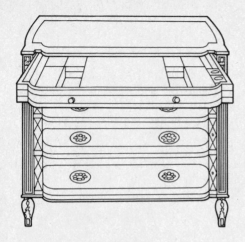

DRESSING CHEST
Design in Sheraton's *Drawing Book* (1791–4)

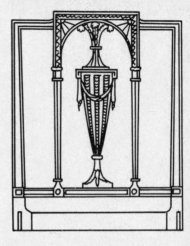

A CHAIR BACK
Design in Sheraton's *Drawing Book* (1791–4)

The elegant and compact type of dressing-tables just described went out of fashion shortly after 1800. Sheraton illustrates a 'commode dressing table' which has two side cupboards and a recessed central cupboard beneath a semi-circular kneehole and a deep top drawer. He also illustrates two 'dressing chests', which are chests of drawers, one with a bow and the other with a concave front, each with a top drawer fitted for the toilet. Sheraton's claim that this arrangement was a novel one is without foundation, for it had been known for some time. He adds that the slide commonly found on chests of drawers had been made in his examples into a shallow drawer fitted with compartments for dressing articles and with space for writing materials. Both of these dressing chests in the *Drawing Book* have their front corners projecting as columns with fluted or reeded decoration. This was a common feature on chests of drawers c.1800, the columns being sometimes spirally turned.

The chairs in the *Drawing Book* display on the whole a lightness and grace which have not been exceeded in the history of English furniture. The chairs described as 'parlour' (i.e. intended for the dining-parlour, not for the drawing-room) and as 'painted' are distinguished by the squareness of their backs. Only two shield-back forms are shown. Thus Sheraton marks the end of that phase of English chair design which began with Adam in the 1760s and which emphasised the subtle changes of round, oval, shield and similar shapes (while allowing for occasional exceptions, such as the square design of the lyre-back). In Sheraton's case, and in numerous contemporary examples, the vertical lines of the chair backs are accentuated by the original and varied arrangement of the bars which form the fillings. The *Drawing Book* illustrates how these bars could sometimes be grouped centrally into a splat and decorated with classical motifs. The top and bottom rails of the back were normally straight and narrow.

ARMCHAIR, TURNED BEECH, 'JAPANNED' IN BLACK
AND GOLD
c.1800

UPHOLSTERED DRAWING-ROOM ARMCHAIR
Design in Sheraton's *Drawing Book* (1791–4)

Sheraton's 'painted' or 'japanned' chairs, in black or colour, were usually of beech, as both this method of decoration and the material were inexpensive, an important consideration during the financial stringency imposed by the war with France, 1793–1815 (see p. 142). The chair of the Sheraton period which is illustrated here is japanned in black and gold. Its turned beech frame clearly shows its extraordinary lightness, verging on fragility; the cane seat adds to this effect. Sheraton strongly advocated the revival of cane-work for both japanned and parlour chairs. He suggested, moreover, that small cane borders round the backs of chairs would enhance their neat appearance. It will be noted that chair legs were often cylindrical in form, a shape favoured by Sheraton for all types of chairs. In this particular example, of c.1800, there is the somewhat later development of a slight outward turning of the feet, marking the beginning of the 'sabre' leg (see p. 146).

Another characteristic feature in the chair just described is the highly distinctive upward sweep of the arms to reach the back near the top; the scroll of these arms immediately above their supports (which are set back on the side rails) adds a further touch of elegance. A similar sweep of the arms is seen in the parlour chairs illustrated in the *Drawing Book*. These have straight-fronted seats, while drawing-room chairs have round or shaped seats. Both kinds could have upholstered seats, but drawing-room chairs could in some cases have their backs also covered in printed silk and their frameworks, if so desired, finished in burnished gold. Sheraton illustrates in the *Drawing Book* 'conversation chairs' which have upholstered seats and padded top rails for the sitter to rest his arms on, while facing backwards. He recommends mahogany for parlour chairs. Satinwood, which has often been associated with the Sheraton period, was in fact very rarely used for chairs in his day.

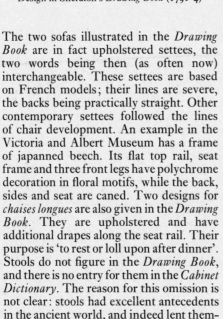

Chaise Longue
Design in Sheraton's *Drawing Book* (1791–4)

SIDEBOARD, TABLET ON CENTRAL DRAWER; BRASS
GALLERY
Design in Sheraton's *Drawing Book* (1791–4)

The two sofas illustrated in the *Drawing Book* are in fact upholstered settees, the two words being then (as often now) interchangeable. These settees are based on French models; their lines are severe, the backs being practically straight. Other contemporary settees followed the lines of chair development. An example in the Victoria and Albert Museum has a frame of japanned beech. Its flat top rail, seat frame and three front legs have polychrome decoration in floral motifs, while the back, sides and seat are caned. Two designs for *chaises longues* are also given in the *Drawing Book*. They are upholstered and have additional drapes along the seat rail. Their purpose is 'to rest or loll upon after dinner'. Stools do not figure in the *Drawing Book*, and there is no entry for them in the *Cabinet Dictionary*. The reason for this omission is not clear: stools had excellent antecedents in the ancient world, and indeed lent themselves fully to the advanced classical taste of the Regency (p. 147).

The sideboards in the *Drawing Book* in general resemble those of Hepplewhite. In one design, illustrated above, the sideboard has a straight front and curved ends, each with a deep drawer. The front of each drawer is panelled to give the effect of two shallower drawers, a usual practice at that time. Two innovations by Sheraton are the placing of a rectangular ornamented tablet in the centre of the front drawer, and the provision of a brass gallery at the back 'to set dishes against and to support a couple of candles or lamp branches in the middle'. This tablet was a device which Sheraton often employed in his designs. In contrast to the usual character of his furniture, his sideboards tend to be large in scale. Another design shows a long sideboard with a concave centre, this 'hollow front' allowing the butler to serve more freely. There is also a design for the type with flanking pedestal cupboards and urns ('vase knife cases') with the addition of a scrolled brass gallery.

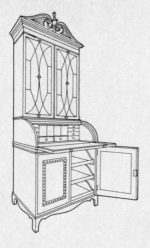

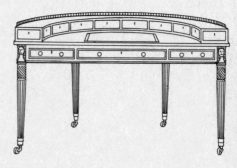

CYLINDER DESK AND BOOKCASE
Design in Sheraton's *Drawing Book* (1791–4)

'CARLTON HOUSE TABLE', ROSEWOOD, WITH BRASS
EGYPTIAN HEADS
c.1807

In 1803, according to Sheraton in his *Cabinet Dictionary*, the bureau of traditional type was 'nearly obsolete in London; at least . . . among fashionable people'. In its place various small tables, cabinets, desks and secretaries had come into use, one quite common feature being the cylinder, tambour or 'roll-top' front. The tambour was a flexible shutter composed of strips of wood glued to a canvas or linen backing, the ends running in grooves fashioned on the inside of the piece. The cylinder desk and bookcase from the *Drawing Book* illustrated here shows the cylinder rolled up to disclose the writing board, which has been pulled forward. There are drawers and pigeonholes within the cylinder, and glazed doors enclosing shelves above the desk. For this example Sheraton recommends satinwood, with green silk behind the glass, carved and gilt ornament in the 'diamonds' (in the glazing bars) and brass or wood ornaments round the top.

Among the varied writing-tables of the time a novel type, which made its appearance right at the end of the century, was the 'Carlton House table'. As is the case with other pieces of furniture, the origin of the name remains a mystery for there is no apparent connection with the Prince of Wales's residence. This table has a low superstructure of drawers and small cupboards at the back and sides of the top. A design for such a table is found in the Appendix to the *Drawing Book* where it is described as a 'lady's drawing and writing table'; this design is dated 1793. It was shortly after that date, in 1796, that the term 'Carlton House table' is first found— in Gillow's Cost Books. Sheraton's notes recommend mahogany or satinwood as the best material for the table, and suggest a brass rim round the top. Some tables of this kind have an adjustable board in the centre, rising on a rack, and it is usual to find an aperture in one of the end boxes for letters.

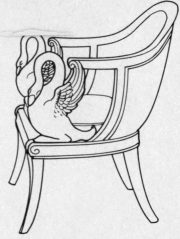

FALL-FRONT SECRETAIRE, VENEERED MAHOGANY
French; ordered by Napoleon for Saint-Cloud,
c.1804

PURPLEWOOD 'GONDOLA' CHAIR; ARM SUPPORTS IN
FORM OF SWANS
French, early 19th century

Furniture of strict classical form reached its climax in Europe under Napoleon. As he rose to supreme power on the Continent, the close similarity between his rule and that of imperial Rome—both régimes dominating and reshaping Europe and dispensing law and order—intensified the interest in antiquity. As has been seen, it was traditional in France to foster the arts and crafts so that they would redound to the credit and glory of the monarchy. Napoleon deliberately cultivated the styles of the ancient world, to produce an artistic movement which reflected his imperial rule, and his military conquests made certain that this Empire style would spread throughout Europe, though with much less impact on England. Conforming to classical rules, furniture took on rectangular forms wherever possible, with straight lines and uninterrupted surfaces. Favourite forms of decoration were inlay, and above all gilt bronze. In the latter medium, some of the finest work ever seen was produced by P. P. Thomire.

Europe had of course long been familiar with the forms of classical ornament which decorated Empire furniture, but these were now given a fresh and precise decision, and since they were to affect English furniture it will be useful here to summarise them. Antique symbolic ornaments included the trident, thunderbolt, thyrsis (a staff tipped with a pine-cone, emblem of Bacchus), and caduceus (a staff of olive or laurel bearing wings and entwined by two serpents, emblem of Mercury). Flowers and plants included the olive, laurel, palm, honeysuckle, lotus, vine, poppy, ivy and oak leaves. Among the fabled beasts of antiquity were the chimera, gryphon, dragon and sphinx. As can be expected, military features were prominent on French furniture—the victor's crown and weapons of all kinds. The eagle and swan (favourite of the Empress Josephine) were also popular. It was usual to find ornaments framed within geometrical designs of a wide range—diamond-shaped lozenges, ovals, squares and circles.

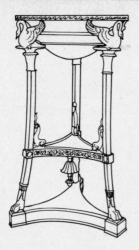

Athénienne OR TRIPOD WASH-HAND STAND IN ELM
French, after a design by Percier, *c.*1805
(*See also colour photograph* 22)

CONSOLE TABLE, VENEERED MAHOGANY; WINGED
SUPPORTS WITH EGYPTIAN HEADS
French, *c.*1804

The two most important designers in the Empire style were the architects C. Percier and P. F. L. Fontaine who were authors of a famous folio of designs, *Recueil de Décorations Intérieures*. This was first published in 1801 and re-issued in 1812, and became famous throughout Europe as the most important source of information and inspiration for the decoration of furniture and interiors. Under the Consulate (1799–1804) the two authors were given the official task of restoring the former royal residences, which had been damaged and despoiled during the Revolution. In 1804 they designed the magnificent throne for Napoleon's coronation as Emperor, and in 1805 they were designated architects of the Louvre and Tuileries. The prestige of Fontaine in particular was so great that he survived Napoleon's fall from power and became royal architect to Louis XVIII (1814–24), Charles X (1824–30) and Louis-Philippe (1830–48). The aims of Percier and Fontaine are clearly presented in their *Recueil*.

'Furniture,' declared Percier and Fontaine, 'is too closely allied to interior decoration for the architect to remain indifferent to it.' They admit the supremacy of antique forms, but are prepared to compromise with modern needs and developments, for furniture must always be functional and related to the demands of the human form: the models of the ancient world must be followed 'not blindly, but with the discrimination which modern manners, habits and materials impose'. Yet while the two authors stress the 'simple lines, pure contours and correct forms' of the ancients, they have been criticised for elaborating the part played by upholstery in interior design and for setting the fashion for the crowded rooms which were to be so characteristic of the 19th century. In spite of Anglo-French hostilities, the work of Percier and Fontaine had some repercussions in England—Percier, for instance, was a friend of Thomas Hope (p. 144), the chief figure in the archaeological approach to Regency design.

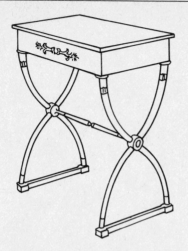

WRITING-TABLE, VENEERED MAHOGANY, X-FORM LEGS
French, similar to pieces by Jacob-Desmalter for
Napoleon, c.1810

ROSEWOOD BOOKCASE
Supplied by Marsh & Tatham in 1806 for royal
collection

The outstanding French craftsman in the Empire style was F. H. G. Jacob-Desmalter. the son of Georges Jacob. (The additional name of Desmalter came from the family's property in Burgundy.) Jacob-Desmalter was reared in the archaeological tradition and under the direction of Percier and Fontaine made furniture for Napoleon in many imperial buildings. The firm ran into financial difficulties in 1813, when the tide was turning against Napoleon and markets were lost. But a swift recovery was made, and after the final peace of 1815 the firm was commissioned by George IV for the furnishing of Windsor Castle—another remarkable tribute to the fascinating, age-old hegemony of French furniture fashions. Other distinguished French ébénistes in the Empire style included B. Molitor and C. Benneman, while a strong rival of Jacob-Desmalter was M. G. Biennais, a craftsman of great gifts who not only made fine furniture for Napoleon but was later made imperial goldsmith.

As already indicated, Sheraton's *Drawing Book* formed in general terms a bridge between the furniture of the Adam-Hepplewhite era and that of the Regency. The term 'Regency' is a convenient label for the style in vogue c.1795 to 1830, a period which considerably overlaps the political Regency of 1811–20, when the Prince of Wales acted as Prince Regent for his father. This was the time when furniture design was dominated by the search for pure classical forms. The theory behind the search was well expressed by Archibald Alison in his *Essays on the Nature and Principles of Taste*, first published in 1790 and reaching a sixth edition in 1825. After praising the forms of Grecian and Roman furniture, Alison states that 'in scarcely any of them is the winding or serpentine Form observed . . . on the contrary, the lightest and most beautiful of them are almost universally distinguished by straight or angular Lines.' The straight line thus predominated in Regency furniture as the serpentine line had in Rococo pieces half a century before.

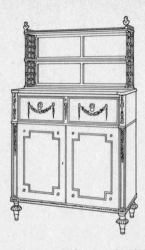

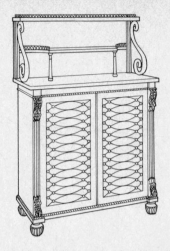

ROSEWOOD SECRETARY WITH SATINWOOD STRINGING
AND GILT BRASS MOUNTS
c.1805–10

ROSEWOOD CABINET, BRASS TRELLIS DOORS
c.1815

To conform with what designers considered to be the main feature of ancient furniture, Regency furniture tended to be of low height, with emphasis on unbroken surfaces and sharply angled corners. The long Revolutionary and Napoleonic Wars, stretching with but one short break from 1793 to 1815, imposed a severe strain on Britain's economy. The expensive procedures of marquetry and carving were therefore drastically cut down, as were the curved forms of fine late 18th-century furniture. Where a little luxury was possible, designers favoured dark, glossy and marbled woods such as rosewood (imported from Brazil and very fashionable in the Regency period), mahogany, amboyna, calamander and zebrawood. With these as background, good effect was obtained by gilt metal or brass ornament, or inlay in thin lines ('stringing') of a light wood such as holly; or, where a lighter background was found (e.g., satinwood) stringing was carried out in ebonised wood. For painted furniture, native beech was usually employed.

Brass was one of the most fashionable materials of the Regency. Sheraton had recommended its use because it was cheaper and more durable than wood. In addition to stringing, it was used for colonnettes, lion's paw feet, lion's head handles with a ring through the mouth, star-shaped bolts or beads, and for trellis work of all kinds—as galleries on tables or on the tops of cabinets, etc., and as grilles in the doors of case furniture. In the latter, brass often replaced glass or wooden panels, and had a backing of silk, in bright colours such as red or green. Brass paw feet are particularly notable features on Regency tables. There was also a fondness for striped colours in upholstery. The general low height of furniture, leaving plenty of wall space above, encouraged special attention to the hanging of pictures and mirrors. In general, there were revolutionary changes in both the forms and the decorative techniques of furniture, which were to outlast the difficult war years.

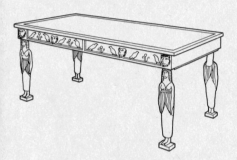

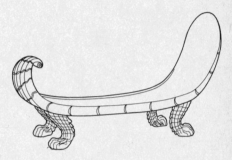

WRITING-TABLE IN EGYPTIAN TASTE
Design in Smith's *Household Furniture* (1808)

COUCH WITH CROCODILE LEGS
c.1810

Egyptian motifs are another familiar feature of Regency furniture. Emblems like the sphinx had of course long been known—witness the sphinx supports on Adam's well-known chairs at Osterley (p. 109). But until the end of the 18th century even the educated person's knowledge of Egypt went little further than what could be gleaned from a study of the Bible. In 1798, however, Egypt became the focus of interest, when Napoleon's army conquered the country, and the team of distinguished French scholars who accompanied the expedition began a detailed study of Egyptian antiquities. In the same year Nelson's brilliant victory over the French fleet at the Nile brought Napoleon's expedition to an abrupt end and led to a popular craze in England for anything that smacked, however remotely, of Egypt. This Egyptian vogue reached its height in England in the early 19th century. Leading English designers were, of course, concerned with the scholarly aspects of the style.

Meanwhile, D. V. Denon, the leader of Napoleon's team of *savants* (and later to be Director-General of French museums) published in 1802 a book on the results of his researches—*Voyage dans la Basse and la Haute Egypte*. This was soon available in an English translation, and English furniture began to incorporate the Egyptian decorative forms seen in the book. Thomas Chippendale the younger used Egyptian motifs on furniture which he made for Stourhead, Wiltshire, in 1804–5. Egyptian heads, winged discs, sphinxes, stars, hieroglyphics and above all the lotus leaf ('the lily of the Nile') were among favoured emblems. On quality furniture this ornament adhered closely to antique precedent, but elsewhere the style rapidly got out of hand. It was satirised by Miss Mitford in *Our Village* (1824–32)—'. . . the library Egyptian, all covered with hieroglyphics and swarming with furniture crocodiles and sphinxes. Only think of a crocodile couch and a sphinx sofa!'

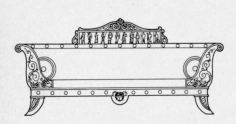

COUCH
Design in Thomas Hope's *Household Furniture*
(1807)

CENTRE TABLE
Design in Hope's *Household Furniture*
1807

The strict classical taste of English Regency furniture found its evangelist in Thomas Hope (1769–1831), whose book of designs, *Household Furniture and Interior Decoration*, published in 1807, became the bible of the new creed. Unlike other famous Georgian designers, Hope was not a craftsman or architect, but a wealthy connoisseur and scholar and a friend of Percier (p. 140). He had travelled widely in Mediterranean lands to get original material for his designs. His book embodied sketches of his own furniture for his London home in Duchess Street, which he wished to make a show-piece (a 'temple of art') of the new taste. He wished, too, to correct misrepresentations of this classical purity which had arisen in the commercial world, and which he called in his introduction 'extravagant caricatures, such as of late have begun to start up in every corner of the capital'. Furniture which was later removed from Duchess Street to Hope's country house, Deepdene, Surrey, was eventually auctioned in 1917 and dispersed.

Some pieces of furniture made from Hope's designs have fortunately been preserved. Among them is the well-known circular table (monopodium) in full classical taste now in the Victoria and Albert Museum. It is made of mahogany and is inlaid with ebony and silver, and its tripod pedestal ends on lion's paw feet. The design corresponds with plate 39 in *Household Furniture*. Another circular table in the Museum, made from plate 2 in Hope's book, is for library use. It is veneered with rosewood, its top covered with leather, and is supported on four lion monopodia which rest on a flat base with concave sides. Circular tables were fashionable during the Regency. Not only were they of classical inspiration, but also in the dining-room they helped to solve the often ticklish problem, when guests were present, of whom to put at the head of the table. Usually of circular form too were the popular loo tables, designed for the game of cards originally known as 'lanterloo', but used as convenient general tables.

'EGYPTIAN' CHAIR
Design in Smith's *Household Furniture* (1808)

DRESSING–TABLE
Design in Smith's *Household Furniture* (1808)

It will be noted that the term 'monopodium' refers both to the circular table supported on a single solid pedestal base, and to the ornamental head and leg of an animal (usually a lion) forming a decorative support. The latter device became a very popular Regency feature and appears on case furniture such as sideboards and bookcases. Illustrated above are monopodia employed as the legs of a chair, taken from a design dated 1804 which was published as plate 56, in George Smith's *A Collection of Designs for Household Furniture and Interior Decoration*, 1808. An armchair now in the Victoria and Albert Museum is based directly on Smith's design. It is carved in relief and painted black with decorative detail picked out in gilding; the whole is in the fashionable 'Egyptian' taste, as can be seen, for instance, in the winged disc in Smith's design and in additional ornaments, such as bolt heads, in the Museum example. In this chair lion monopodia make up all four legs.

George Smith's *Household Furniture* forms the most comprehensive pattern book of the Regency period, and more than any other work of the time popularised the new taste. It was published only one year after Hope's book and drew freely from it, but fell far short of the standards set by Hope's work. Smith's designs were eclectic, for he drew also upon Sheraton and Denon and upon classical sources. Smith lacked Hope's scholarly approach, made with full understanding of classical precedents, and his designs were intended for craftsmen, who often took them up indiscriminately. Smith, who claimed in his *Household Furniture* that he was upholsterer to the Prince of Wales (though no evidence of this connection has ever been found), published in 1812 a book of antique ornaments and in 1828 *The Cabinet-Maker's and Upholsterer's Guide*, in which the point was made that the rapid changes of 20 years had rendered the designs of *Household Furniture* wholly obsolete. This was a clear heralding of the Victorian era.

K

TRAFALGAR PARLOUR CHAIR, SABRE LEGS, ROPE
MOULDING ON TOP RAIL
c.1805

REGENCY ELBOW CHAIR, SABRE LEGS
c.1810

Illustrated above is one of the most delightful chairs of the Regency period, and one which continues the well-established tradition of excellent English chair design. This is a distinctively new type, which took its specific name from the incorporation of naval emblems such as anchors and rope moulding in celebration of Nelson's great victory of 1805. It was based on a classical prototype, the famous Greek *klismos*, which had concave legs, front and rear, and a shallow, concave back rest. The Trafalgar chair has curving sabre (or scimitar) front legs, of oblong section and rounded edges, narrower at the front than at the back. The front rail of the seat is normally set back a little from the face of the front legs. An important and attractive feature is the continuous curving sweep of the front legs through the curved side rail to the swept-back uprights and over the top rail. The seats are usually made of cane, and have squab cushions which are fastened by tapes beneath.

The Trafalgar type was almost always intended for use as a parlour chair, i.e. in the dining parlour. It was customary to make the frame of beech and paint it black or bronze-green—this last colour being in imitation of the bronze chairs of antiquity on which Trafalgar chairs were based. There was endless variety (as with Sheraton chairs) in the simple filling of the back, which was sometimes a cane panel. The cresting took the form of a turned rail, or a shoulder board, or a curved yoke rail with its ends shaped in spiral volutes. Elbow (i.e. arm-) chairs of this type had bold downward-curving scrolls turning inwards to rest on the side rails. This kind of arm was prevalent on English chairs by *c*.1805, and was later imitated in French Empire chairs. The swept front legs and rounded knees of Trafalgar chairs also appeared later on French chairs, so that evidence points clearly to the English origin. More sophisticated examples were of mahogany, with brass decoration.

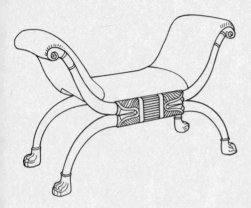

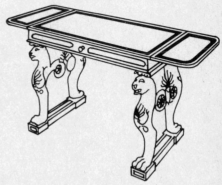

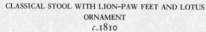

CLASSICAL STOOL WITH LION–PAW FEET AND LOTUS
ORNAMENT
c.1810

SOFA TABLE
Design in Smith's *Household Furniture* (1808)

Among other distinct types of chair of this period were the 'curule', which had crossed front legs like the ancient *sella curulis* (p. 18), and the 'curricle', a tub-shaped chair for library use. Stools became very fashionable, as they could so easily be modelled on ancient prototypes. The kind illustrated here has lion-paw feet and lotus leaf decoration where the legs meet the seat rail. (The use of lotus ornament at the junction of structural members or as a central decoration, to be seen, for instance, in the middle of stretchers, is a common Regency feature.) Another fashionable Regency piece was the Grecian couch, which had one raised end, a short arm rest and a small scroll at the foot. An example made by the firm of Gillow in 1805 has lion monopodia at the head and lion-paw feet at the foot. The frame is of beech, carved and gilt, and the upholstery has the familiar stripes (in this case of red and white) which were so much favoured during the Regency period.

Smith's *Household Furniture* contains 158 plates. Just as Hepplewhite had reduced the Adam style to the scale of ordinary furniture, so Smith translated the formalism of the designs of Hope and others to the level of the middle-class household. His designs make up in practicality what they lack in scholarly refinement. They include such useful features as window cornices and draperies, and large and small mouldings for cabinet work. He makes great (probably excessive) use of animal monopodia for chair legs and tables. His preferences are obviously for rectilinear lines, so that the Trafalgar chair does not figure among his designs. His publication certainly seems to have done much to popularise the theme of the central leaf ornament mentioned above, and the use of bolt head decoration. The illustration here is taken from plate 83 of *Household Furniture* and shows a fashionable sofa table with typical Smith touches in the lion monopodia legs.

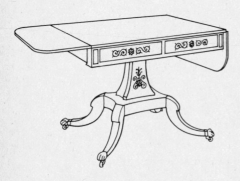

SOFA TABLE, AMBOYNA AND KINGWOOD VENEER
Made for Princess Charlotte, 1816

REGENCY SATINWOOD CABINET
Early 19th century

Smith's design does less than justice to the sofa table, another distinct product of the Regency period. This kind of table was a development of the Pembroke table, though it did not supersede it. Like the Pembroke it has two end flaps, but it has a longer rectangular top, normally extending to about 5½ feet. It is usually based either on two trestle type supports, sometimes of attractive lyre form, linked by stretchers, or on columns or a pedestal on a platform with outward curving legs. As the name implies, this table stood in front of a sofa so that ladies could use it for writing, reading or drawing. The example shown is veneered with amboyna and kingwood, and has characteristic brass inlay on the frieze, plinth and platform. This piece is of special interest as it formed one of a set of four made for the wedding in 1816 of Princess Charlotte, only daughter of George IV, to Prince Leopold. Some sofa tables were fitted with a chessboard, concealed in a sliding panel in the top.

This cabinet is an excellent example of the changes in furniture design which were introduced in the Regency. Its low height —4 ft 2½ in.—should be noted. It is made of satinwood, and has gilded and painted decoration as well as ebony stringing. The break-front form is neatly continued in the upper recessed stage, which has three cupboards enclosed by brass wire-work with a backing of green pleated silk; these cupboards are marked off by four colonnettes, which are carved and partly gilt. Between the upper and lower stages are three drawers, the central one painted with a panel of figures representing Geometry and Music. There is a glazed door to the lower central arched cupboard, which has a shelf, while the two flanking cupboards resemble those above. The short tapered feet (*en toupie*) are of French inspiration, and are here carved with gadroons. This well-designed and well-made compact piece is of very early 19th-century date.

DAVENPORT, MAHOGANY
c.1820

CIRCULAR CONVEX MIRROR, GILTWOOD FRAME AND
EBONISED MOULDINGS
c.1800

Among the pieces of writing furniture of this period the Carlton House table has already been mentioned (p. 138). The furniture supplied by Chippendale the younger to Stourhead in 1804–5 (also referred to above, p. 143) includes a famous library table with Egyptian figures. Among smaller writing-desks the Davenport now became very fashionable, and was to remain so for most of the Victorian period. This desk is said to have obtained its name (which was not, however, much used before c.1850), from a certain Captain Davenport who was a customer of Gillows in the 1790s. The above example, which is made of mahogany and is of c.1820, shows below the sloping top the typical arrangement of drawers, two small ones above and, divided by a writing slide, four larger ones below. At the other side of the desk there are corresponding dummy drawer fronts. The turned wooden knob handles of this piece were the kind in vogue in the early 19th century.

Another typical Regency piece is the circular convex mirror, a striking addition to rooms where there was plenty of wall space left by the general low height of furniture. These mirrors have gilt frames, their diameters varying from about one foot to three feet. A reeded ebonised fillet is found between frame and glass, while the frame itself is decorated with small gilt balls, the space between these becoming noticeably wider in later examples. This type of mirror remained in fashion until c.1830. Some examples have candle branches fixed on each side and a curved and gilt spread eagle above, making a most imposing crest. In contrast to circular mirrors are the rectangular chimney glasses extending the length of the chimney shelf; these are flanked by pilasters and have rows of balls in a hollow moulding in the cornice. Between cornice and glass is an upper panel decorated in various ways—with bas-reliefs, a painted picture or *verre églomisé* (painted glass backed by metal foil).

MENDLESHAM CHAIR
Early 19th century

AMERICAN SHIELD–BACK CHAIR
Based on design in Hepplewhite's *Guide*.
Probably by S. McIntire, Boston, *c.*1795

Meanwhile, against this background of fashionable changes, another country type of chair had emerged. This was the Mendlesham chair, taking its name from Mendlesham, Suffolk, where Daniel Day, a local chair-maker, is traditionally credited with its production in the early 19th century. It is related to the Windsor stick-back type and usually has the same kind of seat and turned legs. The example above shows the typical straight top rail, with the space between this and the lower cross rail filled with turned balls; the upright sticks have a narrow central splat. In some examples boxwood lines are inlaid in the upright and rails. These chairs are made of local woods, and variations of the filling of the back are found throughout East Anglia. One version, for example, has a wide, straight shoulder board, and half way between this and the seat are two narrow rails with three small balls; its legs are straight and slightly tapered, and are linked by four stretchers.

The neo-classic style was late in reaching America, owing to the quarrel between Britain and her colonies. When the War of American Independence ended in 1783, American Federal furniture (so named because there was now a federal republican government) was much influenced by the later English versions of neo-classicism represented by the works of Hepplewhite and Sheraton. Typical decorative forms of this new style—marquetry and painting, and cane work—and new woods such as satinwood, now featured in American furniture. One of the foremost craftsmen was Samuel McIntire, a woodcarver of Boston, who worked in the Hepplewhite style. He was probably responsible for the carved decoration on the shield-back chair of *c.*1795 illustrated above. The back of this chair is based directly on plate 2 of Hepplewhite's *Guide*, but there is additional decoration of carved vine leaves on the front legs. John Seymour, an immigrant English cabinet-maker, also made furniture in this style in Boston.

AMERICAN CHAIR, SHERATON TYPE, MAHOGANY
By Duncan Phyfe, New York, 1807

CARD TABLE, MAHOGANY WITH METAL ENRICHMENTS
By C. H. Lannuier, New York, c.1815

The most famous American cabinet-maker of this period is Duncan Phyfe (1768–1854), a Scottish immigrant whose workshop in New York, opened by 1795, did not cease operating until 1847. Phyfe's furniture marks the transition from the final vestiges of earlier English neo-classicism to the establishment of the Graeco-Roman phase (known in America as the 'Empire' style). But Phyfe's work was no mere copying of European elements; his interpretations were highly individualistic, to the point of creation of a truly personal style. The chair illustrated above was made by Phyfe in 1807 and shows its debt to Sheraton and early Regency designs. Of mahogany, it has reeded mouldings—much favoured by Phyfe—on uprights, arms and sabre legs. After 1810 Phyfe's work reflected the archaeological interpretation of the Regency. Some excellent examples of his furniture in this taste can be seen in the Greek Revival Dining Room in the American Museum, Claverton, Bath.

English influence in America was, however, being challenged at the same time by French. This challenge came from the many French craftsmen who emigrated to New York after the outbreak of the French Revolution and who in time introduced the French 'Empire' style. The chief influence in this respect was C. H. Lannuier, who emigrated to New York in 1803 and was active there until his death in 1819. As might be expected, his furniture, more elaborate than Phyfe's, made much use of gilt metal mounts, which were imported from France. Typical of Lannuier's work is the card table shown above, which is made of mahogany inlaid with brass and decorated with gilt bronze mounts; the legs and winged chimera are painted black, and are partly gilt. New York was particularly open to French influence, but even here, and certainly in the other main American furniture-making centres, the primary impulses in design still came from England. The designs of Hope and Smith were closely followed in America.

7
Victorian
c.1830-1914

UPHOLSTERED CHAIR
*c.*1845

The furniture of Victoria's reign (1837–1901, a period which can be extended to cover 1830–1914) must be studied against the background of the Industrial Revolution, which brought about momentous changes in the social and economic life of the country. England was the birthplace of the Industrial Revolution, and as the first industrial state experienced the effects of the upheaval before anyone else. The pace of industrialisation had been quickening since 1750, but it was not until after the advent of the railway system, c.1830, that Britain can be said to have become 'the workshop of the world'. Furniture designers had to cater for a changing society, in which a vastly expanding market, different types of patrons, and the availability of new materials had rapidly altered the conditions in which furniture had been made for centuries. In general terms, one can see a clear division between commercial producers dealing with the mass market, and pioneer designers seeking suitable styles for the new structure of society.

Contrary to widely-held belief, Victorian furniture was not made by machine but continued (until at least the very end of the reign) to be mainly produced by traditional hand methods. Indeed, in furniture of good quality the standard of craftsmanship compared favourably with that of the Georgian period, and the Victorian craftsman had a considerably wider choice of fine woods, which now arrived from newly-tapped areas in Canada, Australia, New Zealand and Africa. Machinery had been used since the 1790s for such primary processes as sawing, planing and moulding, but it did not control the design of furniture, as it was to do in the 20th century. There were, however, two important innovations. The invention of carving machinery, particularly that of Thomas Jordan in 1845, led to the production of much repetitive carved ornament, while veneering machinery encouraged the practice in cheaper furniture of covering shoddy carcases with glossy veneers, giving 'veneer' its modern pejorative sense.

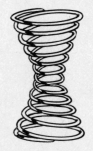

EASY CHAIR WITH BUTTONED UPHOLSTERY
From Loudon's *Encyclopaedia*, 1833

COILED SPRING FOR UPHOLSTERY
Similar to Pratt's patent, 1828; from Loudon's
Encyclopaedia, 1833

One important new concept in the design of early Victorian furniture was that of comfort. There had of course been comfortable pieces of furniture long before; to go no further back than 1700, there is the traditional English wing chair, designed for ease, while the Rococo, as has been seen, added much comfort to seat furniture through its skilful adaptation of the framework. Victorian comfort was something different. It was deliberately sought for and was applied to furniture in a much more general way. Full advantage was taken of the cheap upholstery materials which—to take but one example—poured from the Yorkshire woollen mills and which were now available in most homes. Comfort was regarded as the well-earned reward for the workers, whose skill and assiduity were producing such abundance of goods which they were fully entitled to enjoy. As late as 1864 the architect Robert Kerr put comfort as the first consideration in the house, followed by convenience for the servants, and elegance.

Although the Industrial Revolution brought social upheaval and distress to some sections of the population, it also appreciably raised the general standard of living, and more English people than ever before in our history had the opportunity of owning or renting a home of their own and of furnishing it. This was particularly so after the railways were established and the great expansion of cities occurred. Family life was stressed, and in the all-important search for comfort the home was filled with furniture to such an extent that elegance of form was of secondary consideration. Massive upholstery, for instance, thickly padded after the introduction of coiled springs (Samuel Pratt's patent, 1828), hid the outline of seating furniture, and rounded forms, of both woodwork and upholstery, regarded as essential conditions of comfort, were found in all types of furniture by 1860. Conventions which had been accepted for many generations were clearly breaking down.

GOTHIC CHAIR IN LOUDON'S *Encyclopaedia*, 1833
'This design would be a cheap one'

GRECIAN COUCH
From Loudon's *Encyclopaedia*, 1833

The formality of furniture arrangement which had been a feature of the rooms of larger houses was also being abandoned before the close of the Georgian era. Chairs, for example, were no longer set against the walls, and the interiors of rooms, instead of being left clear, were more and more cluttered up with pieces of furniture. The disorderly grouping of furniture at Osterley, where its formal disposition was previously an integral part of carefully thought-out schemes of decoration (p. 111) shocked the Franco-American visitor, Louis Simond, in 1811. He likened the apartments to 'an upholsterer's or cabinet-maker's shop'. Jane Austen's novels make reference to the new fashion—'such an overthrow of all order and neatness' (*Persuasion*, written 1815–16, published 1818). There was now a mass-market for cheaper furniture, hence the enormous increase in commercial production; probably more furniture was made in Victoria's reign than in the whole of previous English history.

The main feature of early Victorian furniture was the revival of historical styles. Here an excellent guide is the *Encyclopaedia of Cottage, Farm and Villa Architecture and Furniture* by J. C. Loudon, first published in 1833 and running into no less than 11 editions, with only minor revisions, by 1867. Loudon was an enormously hard-working and percipient writer, whose shrewd observations on the furniture of his time, with numerous illustrations, form a remarkable introduction to the Victorian period, particularly as he deals with furniture of every kind, from villa to cottage, and from state rooms to kitchens. In 1833 he names the prevailing fashionable styles as Grecian, Gothic, Elizabethan and Louis Quatorze. He is referring in this respect to villa furniture, but versions of these styles were produced for general consumption by manufacturers who freely translated them in the process, and added other historical styles of their own for good measure.

DINING CHAIR OF CARVED MAHOGANY IN GRECIAN
TASTE
Designed by P. Hardwick, 1834

'ELIZABETHAN' CHAIR WITH SPIRAL UPRIGHTS AND
CABRIOLE LEGS
A typical hybrid, c.1840

The 'Grecian or modern style' is Loudon's term for the final phase of furniture in the classical tradition; he adds that it 'is by far the most prevalent'. Much of this furniture had departed so far from the pure forms achieved in the Regency period that it merits the description coined by Peter Floud of 'sub-classical'. Good classical furniture, however, died hard, especially when designed by architects who had been trained in the authentic classical tradition. It was considered a very appropriate style for clubs and public buildings, particularly for rooms intended for men's use. The architect Philip Hardwick designed excellent furniture in this taste for Goldsmiths' Hall in 1834, while Henry Whitaker, author of the interesting pattern book, *Treasury of Designs*, 1847 (see p. 160), designed classical furniture in the mid-1840s for the Conservative Club and Osborne, Isle of Wight. Grecian furniture was well established for the early Victorian dining-room.

The Elizabethan style, which according to Loudon combined 'the Gothic with the Roman or Italian manner', was actually based on Jacobean and especially Carolean models, and not on those of the 16th century. This misconception arose, as in so many other cases, from the backward state of art history at that time. The Elizabethan style, like the Gothic, was fashionable because it was considered to reflect the sturdiness of the national character. In this respect it followed the curious theory of the period known as the 'association of ideas', by which furniture, like buildings and other objects, conjured up memories of the past. A typical Elizabethan chair had a tall back with spiral turned uprights, front legs and stretchers, a carved cresting, cane seat and upholstered panel back. Its design seems to have been first represented in 1817, in Ackermann's *Repository of Arts*, a monthly periodical published between 1809 and 1828.

ELIZABETHAN TABLE
From R. Bridgens' *Furniture with Candelabra and Interior Decoration*, 1838

CHAIR IN 'LOUIS QUATORZE' STYLE
*c.*1850

The tall chair with spirally turned decoration is sometimes given the name of the 'Abbotsford' chair, in reference to the home of Sir Walter Scott, whose romantic novels did so much to revive interest in historical styles. Spiral uprights were commonly found on other Elizabethan pieces such as pole and cheval screens. Another prominent decorative feature of the style was strapwork. This decoration is frequently found in a pattern book of 1838, *Furniture with Candelabra and Interior Decoration*, by Richard Bridgens, architect and furniture designer. This may be considered the text-book of the Elizabethan revival, for of its 60 plates (a number of which were engraved by Henry Shaw), 27 are devoted to this style, 25 to the Grecian, and 8 to the Gothic. Strapwork and carving were rapidly endorsed by the furniture trade, as critics of the style were quick to point out, because they could easily and cheaply be produced by mechanical methods.

The Louis Quatorze style—'or the florid Italian, which is characterised by curved lines and excess of curvilinear ornaments' (Loudon)—was the only early Victorian revival based on a style of the 18th century. Moreover, it was the only style which affected the actual structure of furniture and not merely its decoration. It illustrated the marked continuity of the age-old impact of French furniture on English. In France the Bourbon restoration of 1815 inevitably led to a return to the styles of the *ancien régime*, and English clients soon resumed their old practice of visiting Paris to buy the latest French furniture. What Loudon called the Louis Quatorze, however, included many elements of the Louis Quinze, and indeed the two labels were used indiscriminately by most of the trade, as also were 'Rococo' or, more simply, the 'Old French style'. This confusion persisted for a long time, though a few firms prided themselves on being able to sort the styles out.

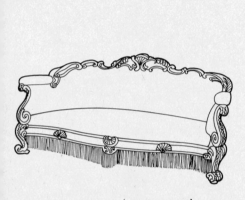

CARVED AND GILT SOFA; 'LOUIS QUATORZE' STYLE
Made for Goldsmiths' Hall, 1834

'FLY' CHAIR, BEECH, CARVED, PAINTED AND GILDED
Designed by P. Hardwick for Goldsmiths' Hall,
c.1834

The Louis Quatorze revival was established in fashion from 1825 onwards, when a number of great English houses were decorated and furnished in this style. One of the major influences was Matthew Wyatt's decoration at Belvoir Castle, which was actually carried out in Louis Quinze style, though its advocates stubbornly persisted in calling it the 'Louis Quatorze'. The first pattern book of any importance to deal with the style was Thomas King's *The Modern Style of Cabinet Work Exemplified*, first published in 1829 and re-issued, unaltered, as late as 1862 (see p. 165). King's preface states that, 'as far as possible, the English style is carefully blended with Parisian taste', and he goes on to recommend composition ornament for minute detail, as 'carving will only be required in the boldest scrolls or in the massive foliage'. Scrolls and shell ornaments were to remain a feature of this style, as well as curved frames and cabriole legs, all illustrated on this sofa made by Wilkinson's in 1834.

Loudon was scornful of the Louis Quatorze style, and some contemporary architects were equally critical of it when they gave evidence before the Select Committee of Arts and Manufactures in 1835. Its foreign origin and supposed frivolous features were alike condemned. But the style, particularly in its Louis Quinze manifestations, remained obstinately fashionable. In 1840 the Queen's decorators, H. W. and A. Arrowsmith of St. Martin's Lane, carefully distinguished, in their publication *The House Decorator and Painter's Guide*, between the 'ponderous' Louis Quatorze and the 'light and graceful' Louis Quinze. The last-named became accepted as the fashionable style for feminine rooms—boudoirs, bedrooms and drawing-rooms—for the rest of the century, and some charming furniture was made in this version. The elegant 'fly' chair illustrated here was made c.1834 by W. and C. Wilkinson to the design of the architect, Philip Hardwick, for Goldsmiths' Hall, for the room to which ladies were admitted.

BALLOON OR 'SWEEP–BACK' CHAIR, WALNUT
c.1850

DESIGN OF TABLE
From A. W. N. Pugin's *Gothic Furniture*, 1835

The Louis Quatorze style was one important factor in the development of a distinctly new type of chair in the early Victorian period. This was the balloon-back, which made its appearance in the 1830s and became the most fashionable type of chair from the mid-century until c.1870. The general tendency towards rounded forms affected not only the scrolls of Louis Quatorze chairs, but also the shoulder board (or yoke rail) of Grecian types. By 1850 the balloon-back, with or without a cross-strut at the waist, with cabriole legs for the drawing-room and turned straight legs for the dining-room, was firmly established. T. King's *Original Designs for Chairs, etc.* (c.1840) illustrates two examples described as 'sweep-backs', which seems to have been the contemporary name for balloon-backs. Lighter versions of the type, with cane seats, were known as 'fancy' or 'chamber' chairs. They were often made of birch, while mahogany or rosewood was favoured for the more formal kinds.

Gothic ornament had long been a familiar feature of English furniture. In the 1830s the Gothic style meant no more than trimming of Gothic character added to established forms. Thus chairs had ornamental tracery, buttresses, crockets and pinnacles, and applied carving, on frames which were in all other respects the same as those of Grecian chairs. Yet this style is associated with one of the most versatile designers of Victoria's reign and one who is now recognised as the first true pioneer of furniture reform in the period. This is Augustus W. N. Pugin (1812–42), the son of Augustus Pugin, an accomplished draughtsman who had fled from the French Revolution to take refuge in England. A. W. N. Pugin designed Gothic chairs for Windsor Castle at the tender age of 15—chairs which he later criticised as having fallen into the prevailing error of simply adding fanciful adornment to conventional structure. After his conversion to Roman Catholicism in 1835, he turned enthusiastically to the Middle Ages for inspiration.

STOOL
From A. W. N. Pugin's *Gothic Furniture*, 1835

ARMCHAIR, CARVED OAK
Designed by A. W. N. Pugin, c.1837

In his writings, Pugin constantly contrasted the mass-production of his own age with the craftsmanship of the Middle Ages, a period which he romanticised. For furniture, he sought inspiration in the later medieval period, and in 1835 he produced a book of drawings entitled *Gothic Furniture of the Style of the Fifteenth Century*. Unlike his contemporaries, Pugin really understood medieval craftsmanship. He praised its joinery for its straightforward, honest construction, and did not hesitate to show in his designs constructional methods, such as the pegs securing mortice and tenon joints. This was something new: to regard revealed construction as an integral part of design and as something worthwhile in itself, was alien to the cabinet-making practice of the Georgian period.

The emphasis on constructional elements amounted in Pugin's day to a revolution. The principle was followed by reformist designers of the Victorian era, and has been maintained to the present day.

Pugin's magnificent carved oak armchair illustrated above was made for Scarisbrick Hall, Lancashire, c.1837 and is a landmark in Victorian furniture design. The framework reveals full understanding of medieval forms. The carved ornament is an integral part of the construction, not merely additional; this ornament was the result of detailed study of medieval decoration and was largely based on naturalistic forms. The same masterly control is evident in a table of carved walnut which Pugin designed, with other pieces, for Abney Hall, Cheshire, in 1847. This has its top inlaid with various coloured woods. Pugin was in charge of the Medieval Court at the Great Exhibition, where his best-known piece, now in the Victoria and Albert Museum, is the fine carved and painted oak cabinet with wrought brass panels. His pioneer work, though clearly recognised today, merely heralded, and did not initiate, reform, for commercial producers continued to make 'Gothic' furniture on the old lines.

FIRESCREEN IN LOUIS QUATORZE STYLE
Carved and gilt wood, Berlin wool-work panel,
c.1845

HEAD OF A BEDSTEAD (JAMES I)
Plate 38 in H. Shaw's *Specimens of Ancient
Furniture*, 1836

In the two decades before the Great Exhibition of 1851, historical styles proliferated. One of the most detailed pattern books of the period, Henry Whitaker's *The Practical Cabinet-Maker and Upholsterer's Treasury of Designs*, 1847 (see p. 155) lists as many as seven fashionable styles: Grecian, Italian, Renaissance, Louis Quatorze, Gothic, Tudor and Elizabethan, to which '*François Premier*' is added in the text, though this style is practically identical with the Elizabethan. Many firms 'manufactured' Gothic and Elizabethan furniture by assembling genuine antique fragments such as carved panels and, with suitably adapted modern additions, presented them as authentic pieces. Loudon names London firms who indulged in this practice, and from the area in which much of it was carried on, the modern term 'Wardour Street Gothic' has been given to such furniture. The spoliation of religious houses abroad during the French Revolution provided much material of this kind.

Romantic revivals obviously appealed strongly to the early Victorians. Antique dealers began to comb England and the Continent for material to sell to the ever-growing number of collectors, among whom one of the best-known was Sir Henry Meyrick. Meyrick wrote the introduction to Henry Shaw's *Specimens of Ancient Furniture*, first published in 1836. This was a collection of drawings of furniture in private possession, from medieval to the late 17th century, and though some of the historical references were inaccurate—it is from this book that the so-called 'Glastonbury' type of chair derives its name (p. 29)—Shaw's work stimulated further interest in historical revivals and indeed helped to promote serious antiquarian research. The book had many reprints—indication of its popularity. It was undoubtedly the source of many of the details found on the so-called Elizabethan furniture of the time, while further sources of romantic inspiration were found in Sir Walter Scott's novels.

PLATE V

13 (*above*). Armchair, beech carved and gilt, made by Thomas Chippendale to design by Robert Adam. English, 1764.

14 (*above right*). Ornamental Cupboard veneered with kingwood, sycamore and various woods; gilt bronze mounts. French, Louis XVI, *c*.1775.

15 (*right*). Writing Cabinet on stand, veneered with Japanese lacquer of high quality; lacquered brass mounts. French, Louis XVI, late 18th century.

16 (*below*). Games Box decorated with marquetry, and with gilt bronze mounts. French, Louis XVI, *c*.1775.

PLATE VI

17. Commode, veneered with mahogany and lighter-coloured wood; gilt bronze mounts. French, Louis XVI, *c*.1780. Stamped Riesener.

18. Cabinet veneered with ebony and with panel of Japanese lacquer; lacquered brass mounts. French, Louis XVI, *c*.1780.

PAPIER MÂCHÉ PEDESTAL TABLE
By Jennens and Bettridge, Birmingham. *c.*1850

The inventive genius of the nation which pioneered the Industrial Revolution was founded on a spirit of enquiry and a willingness to experiment. These admirable qualities became apparent in furniture-making—not always, it is true, with the happiest aesthetic results, as the Great Exhibition was to prove. Metal, marble, stone and even coal were used for furniture. There was a vogue for mosaic work in British marbles. Metal furniture is shown in Loudon's *Encyclopaedia*. Brass bedsteads became common as the Victorian era progressed. The main factor in their popularity was the unhygienic nature of the old wooden four-posters, which, as Sheraton had already indicated, harboured vermin. Their manufacture became centred in Birmingham, which was also the chief centre for the production of papier mâché furniture. Birmingham, indeed, exemplified the rise of provincial furniture-making in the 19th century, as a serious challenge to London's traditional pre-eminence.

Papier mâché was not new to the Victorian period, for it had been well known in the 18th century and had been used by Vile and Cobb. Its production, however, was rapidly expanded in the 19th century. In the 1820s Jennens and Bettridge of Birmingham began to make papier mâché furniture, and soon became the most famous firm in this field; they almost always stamped their pieces. Chairs, sofas and tables were among the chief objects which they made, though there was also a whole range of smaller articles such as trays, letter racks and tea caddies (which were the main products of many other firms in the industry, chiefly in the Birmingham area). The furniture of Jennens and Bettridge was usually painted black and decorated with bright flowers, and it is important to note here, to avoid confusion, that 'japanning' in Birmingham at this time was a general term for papier mâché work and not (as elsewhere) for imitation lacquer.

FOOT OF BEDSTEAD; PAPIER MÂCHÉ WITH BRASS
MOUNTS
c.1850

DAWE'S 'RECLINING CHAIR FOR AN INVALID'
From Loudon's *Encyclopaedia*, 1833

In 1825 Jennens and Bettridge patented their famous pearl-shell inlay, and this became a very fashionable form of decoration. Furniture made in the 1850s and 1860s with this decoration included cabinets, chiffoniers, bookcases, and bedsteads, though for these larger pieces it was necessary to strengthen the papier mâché with a framework of wood or metal. This is the case with the bedstead in the Victoria and Albert Museum. Its head and foot boards are of papier mâché, but their substructure is of iron. But one interesting development was the production of chairs of bergère form, which were moulded in a way that is now achieved with modern materials by machinery. Such chairs were rare examples of papier mâché being used with real understanding of its qualities, and not merely as an imitation of wood or metal. There is an excellent collection of Victorian papier mâché furniture of all kinds, and of smaller articles, at Kensington Palace.

In another direction also, one which is full of interest though so far its study has been much neglected, early Victorian furniture clearly forecast the developments of the 20th century. This was in the production of 'patent' furniture, a comprehensive term which covered not only mechanically equipped furniture registered at the Patent Office, of the kind to which Sheraton devoted so much attention, but also special fitments for furniture, such as castors, metal tubes, upholstery springs and jointing devices. By the end of 1800 a total of only 37 such patents had been registered since the 17th century, but this total had risen to 220 by the end of 1850. Such was the interest in this kind of furniture and furnishings that 'patent' became a fashionable and widely abused label, rather like the word 'contemporary' in the mid-20th century. It was often applied indiscriminately to any piece of furniture with a new gadget or attachment.

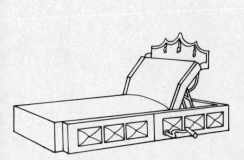

'POCOCK'S PATENT BOETHEMA OR RISING MATTRESS'
From Pocock's trade card, early 19th century

'POCOCK'S PATENT LIBRARY OR OFFICE TABLE'
From Pocock's trade card, early 19th century

At its best, 'patent' furniture effected a harmonious marriage between cabinet-making of the highest skill and precision engineering that was then the most advanced in the world. The accuracy of the metal fittings had to be matched by the accuracy of the woodwork. There was no room for fancy trimmings. A number of patents were taken out for expanding tables which used ingenious arrangements of tubes, pulleys worked on rack and pinion, lazy tongs, etc., and in most instances these devices work as smoothly today as when they were first made. At the beginning of the century some outstanding firms specialised in the production of this kind of furniture, two of the best-known being Morgan and Sanders, and Pocock. These firms flourished for two or three decades, pioneers in a field in which England took the leading part until, c.1850, functional simplicity succumbed to elaborate ornamentation. For this decline the blighting effect of the Great Exhibition can be held responsible.

There was also at this time a great interest in furniture and upholstery which was designed for invalids and which could be easily adapted for domestic use. The impetus here came from the long French wars early in the century and the need to care for the wounded and invalid service men. After the peace of 1815 interest was sustained through the great improvement which took place in medical care and hospital management. A number of patents were taken out for raising the framework of a bed without disturbing its occupant. The firm of Pocock adapted this principle for mattresses and sofas, and also made movable tops to desks—on the type sometimes known as a 'shipmaster's desk'—so that the user could work standing up if he wished. It would be impossible to detail here all the ways in which such methods could be applied. They worthily continued Sheraton's work in designing practical and versatile furniture. Intriguing sketches of such furniture appear in advertisements issued by Pocock's firm.

THE 'ANGEL COT', BRASS
By Winfield of Birmingham. Great Exhibition, 1851

ARMCHAIR, BOG-YEW
By Arthur Jones, Dublin; from sketch in
*Art-Journal Illustrated Catalogue of the Great
Exhibition*, 1851

The 1851 Great Exhibition of Industry of All Nations, held in Hyde Park in the 'Crystal Palace', had the most laudable object of putting on view, for the first time, the industrial and other products of nations from all parts of the world to demonstrate clearly the need for peaceful international co-operation. Unfortunately, so far as furniture was concerned, it inevitably encouraged exhibitionism. Historical styles seemed to be attempting to outdo each other in proliferation of ornament. Sumptuous and intricate carving of considerable skill was particularly evident, no doubt because the hand-carver was intent on showing how much more involved his work was, compared with anything the new carving machines could do. Much of this carving was of an anecdotal or narrative character—highly romanticised historical scenes, or, in the case of sideboards, emblems connected with eating, such as fruit, game, cereals and the like.

This armchair, made of bog-yew, was much admired by visitors to the Great Exhibition. It was the work of Arthur Jones of Dublin, who exhibited altogether some twenty pieces of carved furniture, for which he gained an 'Honourable Mention'. The chair has retained some traces of Louis XVI outline, much debased by the elaborate carving of the framework and lion's paw feet. At the cresting are busts of ancient Irish warriors supporting the 'ancient arms of Ireland'. Additional anecdotal features are the two Irish wolf-hounds which make up the arms of the chair, one in action (with 'fierce when provoked' carved on its collar), the other recumbent ('gentle when stroked'). The skill of the carver is considerable, and his work was particularly acclaimed in 1851 because bogwood is extremely difficult to work. A fantastically elaborate wine cooler by Jones in the same material was another celebrated exhibit; this piece was crowned by a figure of Hibernia.

THE 'DAY DREAMER', ARMCHAIR IN PAPIER MÂCHÉ
By Jennens and Bettridge. Great Exhibition, 1851

Escritoire IN LOUIS QUINZE STYLE, SATINWOOD
Made by Holland & Sons, 1868

It is important to remember that the furniture of the Great Exhibition was by no means typical of its time. Much that has been written in past years on Victorian furniture used the illustrations in the Exhibition catalogue as if they were truly representative, but this was not so. Inevitably even the best firms exhibited exaggerated, eye-catching furniture. Simple pieces such as the Thonet chairs (p. 169), shown in England in 1851 for the first time, escaped notice, while wildly elaborate bog-oak carved pieces attracted particular attention. There was a great deal of contemporary criticism of the poor taste of the exhibits, and later Exhibitions, like that in London in 1862, were deliberately arranged to foster better standards of design. Some of the 1851 exhibits went to absurd lengths and excited derision, among them the 'Day Dreamer', a papier mâché armchair by Jennens and Bettridge, decorated with various symbols of repose.

Another misleading impression that might result from the study of English furniture between 1830 and 1860 is that stylistic changes occurred with bewildering rapidity, one succeeding the other in a ceaseless search for novelty. In fact the many styles remained in fashion for a long time together, as there was a strong streak of conservatism among the Victorians. This is seen in the extraordinary long life of some pattern books. The many re-issues, practically unchanged, of Loudon's *Encyclopaedia* of 1833 have been noted (p. 154). Thomas King's *The Modern Style of Cabinet Work Exemplified* of 1829 was reprinted as late as 1862 without alteration. Late in Victoria's reign firms' catalogues were still illustrating furniture in the historical revivals of half a century before. French 18th-century styles were particularly persistent; the Paris Exhibition of 1855 renewed widespread admiration for French furniture, and English firms employed French designers and craftsmen.

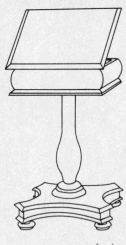

TEAPOY, PAPIER MÂCHÉ
c.1850

PRIE-DIEU CHAIR, PAPIER MÂCHÉ
c.1850

The teapoy was a very fashionable part of the equipment of early Victorian parlours. Originally this piece, in spite of its name, had nothing at all to do with tea. It was a small three-legged table or stand, or any tripod, and derived its name from a Hindu word meaning three-legged. Smith's *Household Furniture*, 1808, shows the teapoy as a small table with a flat rectangular top supported on a central column above a tripod or circular base. It was used for refreshments in drawing-rooms 'to prevent the company rising from their seats'. Through an understandable misconception, the teapoy became associated with tea, and during the 1820s the table top was replaced by a shallow box fitted with small compartments and glass bowls. Thus the piece was now a tea chest or tea caddy on a stand, and was made in a variety of woods—rosewood, mahogany, walnut, etc. Above is illustrated a papier mâché example of the type current in the 1850s, supported on a base with four feet.

Another distinctly Victorian contribution to chair design was the prie-dieu. This was a kneeling chair, the result of the Victorian custom of family prayers. It had a high back, a flat cresting rail or arm rest, and a low seat. The back legs were splayed and the front ones were turned, or were sometimes of dwarf cabriole form. Some prie-dieus were made of papier mâché, others had the spiral turned uprights of the Elizabethan style. Often the padded back, arm rest and seat were covered—like so much other seating furniture in the period 1830–60—with the very popular Berlin wool-work. This upholstery has designs copied on to square-meshed canvas with coloured wools from patterns that had been coloured by hand on squared paper. The work could easily be done at home, as it did not require any particular skill—hence its popularity. This kind of needlework was also used for screens and pictures. A variation using beads, silk and chenille was known as German embroidery.

DAVENPORT WITH SUPPORTING COLUMNS, SATINWOOD
WITH ROSEWOOD BANDING
c.1840

SIDEBOARD WITH SEMICIRCULAR MIRROR, WALNUT
c.1860

Davenports, the desks which had made their appearance during the Regency (see p. 149), firmly established themselves during the Victorian period. Loudon (who calls them 'Devenports'), describes them in 1833 as 'drawing room writing cabinets used by ladies'. He illustrates one which has a sliding flap at the top at each side for papers, candles, etc., and, at the right-hand side, a long narrow drawer which swings forward when it is pulled out, forming a convenient receptacle for pens, ink, wafers, etc. All this, of course, was additional to the drawers at one side (with false drawer fronts to match on the opposite side), and small drawers and pigeon holes within the space beneath the sloping lid. Some types had a pull-out writing drawer. Mid-Victorian Davenports were made with the desk projecting beyond the pedestal, as shown in the above illustration, and supported on columns or carved cabrioles. Many variations of this pleasant and useful piece are to be found.

The development of the early Victorian sideboard provides perhaps the best example of the progress towards rounded forms in furniture which is so typical of the period. The pedestal type of sideboard with flanking cupboards, a central open space and a low wooden board at the back, remained fashionable until the 1830s. The current historical revivals affected the decoration in their own characteristic ways; the Louis Quatorze type, for instance, had scrolled carving on the backboard, door panels and frieze. Two major changes occurred in the 1840s. The first was the development of mirrors in the back, usually in sets of three, the central and larger mirror being flanked by two smaller ones above the pedestals; by 1860 this arrangement had become a single semicircular mirror. The second major change affected, though somewhat more slowly, the body of the sideboard, which acquired a central cupboard and convex side cupboards or shelves. This style, richly carved, was in vogue until c.1900.

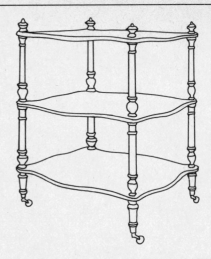

CHIFFONIER, MAHOGANY
c.1850

WHATNOT, VENEERED WALNUT, TURNED CORNER POSTS
c.1860

'Chiffonier' is a word of mixed meaning. In France it was applied originally to either a tall chest of drawers or to a small set of drawers which sometimes had a writing lid. English chiffoniers of Regency type were shelved low cupboards for books. Loudon's *Encyclopaedia*, however, illustrates one (described as a 'chiffonier pier table'), which is a cupboard surmounted by a shelf supported by brackets. It was made to stand between windows, and the door panels could be silvered plate glass or pleated silk. Loudon recommends these pieces as 'most useful objects for families who cannot afford to go to the expense of pier or console tables'. The Victorian chiffonier indeed became virtually a smaller version of the sideboard. Above is illustrated an example of c.1850, its shelved backboard having scrolled bracket supports. Like sideboards, chiffoniers of c.1860 had rounded fronts and a D-shaped mirror back, often with convex shelves at the ends.

The whatnot (a contemporary term) is a piece of furniture which will always be associated with the Victorian home. It is a portable stand consisting of tiers of open shelves, usually rectangular in plan, supported by turned posts at the corners. Such stands were in fact known well before the beginning of Victoria's reign. References to them appear in Gillows' records as early as 1790, and a very elegant pair of c.1800, made of rosewood and mounted with ormolu, are at Southill and are contemporary with Henry Holland's rebuilding of the house (see p. 128). In Victorian drawing-rooms the whatnot proved most useful as a stand for the endless trifles and curiosities so much admired at the time. It stood on feet or on a solid base and sometimes had a drawer or drawers at the bottom. Later examples have spirally twisted corner columns, and the tiers sometimes have borders, either solid or pierced with elaborate fret work. Triangular-shaped whatnots were intended for corners.

BACK OF BENTWOOD CHAIR
Made by Thonet, 1850

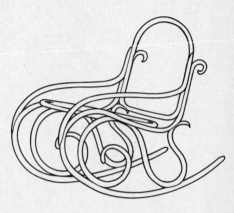

LATE VICTORIAN BENTWOOD ROCKING CHAIR

Late 20th-century furniture styles and processes were clearly heralded over a century before their time in the famous bentwood chairs manufactured by the firm of Thonet. The founder of the firm, Michael Thonet (1796–1871), was born in Prussian territory at Boppard on the Rhine, where he began his career as a cabinet-maker. Later he moved to Vienna, where he established a world-wide reputation. As early as 1830 he was experimenting with lamination—gluing thick veneer strips together after bending them in moulds under heat. He then went on to develop (and patent) the method of bending rods and struts under steam, the foundation of bentwood furniture. It was this system which made his fortune. In 1851 Thonet furniture was shown at the Great Exhibition. In 1853 the firm was made over to Thonet's five sons, though Thonet himself remained in control; hence the label 'Gebrüder Thonet' which is found beneath the frame of genuine Thonet pieces sought by collectors.

Participation in numerous international exhibitions, a vast export trade (the first exports of chairs to South America took place in 1855) and the adoption of machinery all made the Thonet firm widely known and established it as the greatest mass-producer of furniture that the world had seen. Yet the end product remained amazingly simple, light and strong, as well as cheap. The secret of the success of the chairs lies in the ingenuity with which the bentwood curves were built up to form backs and uprights. Equal ingenuity was applied to the arrangement of the underframing, arms and rear supports of the famous rocking chairs. Ordinary chairs could be packed in sections and assembled with the aid of a few screws, for the bentwood frame was strong enough to eliminate normal forms of jointing. Vast numbers of Thonet chairs were imported into England and used in homes, shops, hotels and offices. The firm's products were much copied when their patents expired.

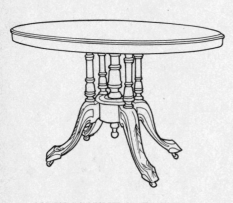

LOO TABLE SUPPORTED ON FIVE COLUMNS
*c.*1860

WINDSOR CHAIR, 'WHEEL–BACK' TYPE
*c.*1850

The circular loo table, taking its name from the popular card game and inherited from the Regency period (p. 144), was a very familiar resident in Victorian drawing-rooms. Loudon praised these tables as 'unexceptionable in point of taste', and the examples illustrated in his *Encyclopaedia* of 1833 have pillar or pedestal supports resting on triangular bases with paw or claw feet. By 1850 the solid base was giving way to curved legs flowing upwards to support the column. It was now also becoming fashionable to enrich the tops with inlaid and other decoration, instead of, as formerly, leaving them plain. More distinctive changes occurred in the central support, which now split up into a group of four or five smaller columns, as shown in the example of *c.*1860 which is illustrated above. The fine woods and mounts found on surviving loo tables of this time show how highly they were regarded. Many simpler examples also seem to have been made, as their designs appear in the chaper pattern books.

Students of the origins of the Modern Movement (p. 195) are naturally interested in 19th-century English vernacular furniture, the simple functional pieces of traditional form. References to the elegant utilitarian furniture of the Hepplewhite-Sheraton era, the practical patent furniture of 1800–50 and the joinery with revealed construction of Pugin and Morris all bear on this modern conception of functional design. Victorian Windsor chairs continued the development of this traditional 'stick-back' form. Early in the 19th century the manufacture of Windsor chairs became centred at High Wycombe, Buckinghamshire, the abundance of beech woods in that area and the ready access to the vast London market, being two important factors in this centralisation. Turners, known as 'bodgers', worked in the beech woods preparing the legs and spindles for the chairs, which were assembled in the town; the finished chairs, sold without paint or stain, were called 'White Wycombes'.

WINDSOR CHAIR, 'SMOKER'S BOW' TYPE
*c.*1870

WINDSOR LATH–BACK KITCHEN CHAIR
*c.*1860

The most popular Victorian brand of Windsor chair was the 'smoker's bow'. Its low back and arms formed a continuous semicircle, broadening out in the centre of the back and supported from the seat by turned spindles; the turned legs were splayed. Many of these comfortable, sturdy and cheap chairs survive today; they were originally intended for cottages, smaller suburban houses, public smoking rooms and institutions and clubs of every kind. A very common kitchen Windsor had a broad, slightly curved yoke supported by wide laths or spindles. By 1870 an amazing variety of Windsor chairs were produced, designed for every type of room and domestic activity (or inactivity). The trade card of one High Wycombe firm, that of Edwin Skull, is crowded with illustrations of well over a hundred different types. This card, of *c.*1870, is a remarkable tribute to the amazing vitality and adaptability of a traditional rural chair which remains essentially functional, yet loses nothing in elegance and simplicity.

Another sturdy member of the Windsor family was the lath-back. This chair had four or five vertical, slightly curved laths socketed between the seat and the top rail, flanked by stout uprights. The top rail took the form of a broad curved shoulder board, recalling Regency types. Lath-backs did fine service as kitchen chairs after the 1820s. The curved arms, broadening into round, flat ends, were supported on turned members socketed into the side of the seat at a short distance from its front edge. For the simple functional kind of furniture so close to the English vernacular tradition, the contents of the kitchen in the Victorian home are well worth study. In addition to the various types of Windsor and Thonet chairs, one could find ladder-backs and original Morris 'Sussex' chairs, tables of massive, simple construction, and dressers which, though much modified in the process of time, could claim descent from the court cupboard of Tudor days. Such furniture was to inspire progressive designers after 1880.

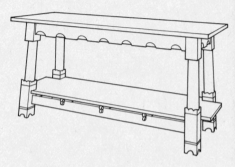

'ST. GEORGE' CABINET
Designed by Philip Webb and painted by
William Morris, 1861

OAK TABLE
Designed by Philip Webb, c.1865–70, with revealed
construction

In spite of the persistence of historical styles, it is generally true that after c.1860 furniture styles by pioneer designers were more and more based on current theoretical considerations, and comfort gradually became of secondary importance. One young visitor to the Crystal Palace in 1851 who refused to go inside to see the Exhibition because everything was 'wonderfully ugly' was destined to become the most famous reformer of all. This was William Morris (1834–96), who after Oxford (where he went with the intention of entering the Church) took up architecture and devoted his life to combating the ugliness of industrial England. For this purpose he founded in 1861, with the co-operation of friends, a firm c. (later known as 'Morris & Co.') to produce articles of fine craftsmanship for the masses. In 1862 the firm came before the public as exhibitors at the International Exhibition in London and gained an award for their tapestries, etc., 'in the style of the middle ages'.

Morris himself was not particularly interested in furniture, and apart from some attempts in his early career did not design any. But under the general direction of its chief furniture designer, Philip Webb, the firm produced two classes of furniture, 'state' pieces, the more expensive items sometimes with panels painted by Morris and his close friend, the artist Edward Burne-Jones, and 'workaday' furniture, the cheaper and simpler kind. In each case Webb was inspired by Morris's belief that medieval craftsmanship represented the true dignity of labour and reflected (as Pugin had believed) the love and satisfaction of the craftsman in his work. Morris was a great propagandist. In his numerous writings—essays, poems and novels—and in his speeches, particularly when later he took up socialism, he made his ideas familiar to a wide public. 'Have nothing in your house that you do not know to be useful or believe to be beautiful' was one of his best-known sayings.

'SUSSEX' CHAIR
Made by Morris and Co. from c.1865

CABINET WITH CANOPY
Designed by Philip Webb, c.1865. Doors painted by
William De Morgan

It is Morris & Co.'s 'workaday' furniture which attracts most attention today. Webb designed oak furniture inspired by early Gothic joinery, of rugged construction, in which the joints, as in Pugin's designs, were plainly revealed. The well-known table (seen opposite), for instance, shows the pegs as part of the construction. One of the firm's greatest successes was the 'Sussex' chair, based on a traditional cottage type and produced in great numbers after c.1865. This brought into fashion the vernacular turned chair with rush seat, made of beech and stained dark green. This simple type of chair has to be set against the general tendency of the 1860s to foster elaborate decoration, for its impact to be appreciated. Also successfully adapted from another Sussex chair was an upholstered armchair with adjustable back and turned decoration which the firm made from c.1866; this has become known as the 'Morris' chair both in England and in the United States, where it was very popular (see p. 193).

It took some twenty years before Morris's message bore fruit in the Arts and Crafts Movement of the 1880s (p. 179). While the value of his teaching is freely acknowledged today, his work has not escaped criticism. His aim of producing cheap, well-made and beautiful articles for the masses proved impracticable. Hence his continued production of 'state' furniture to cater for what he described in his socialist speeches as 'the swinish luxury of the rich'. After Philip Webb's retirement c.1890 from his position as Morris & Co.'s principal furniture designer, his successor, George Jack, designed some highly decorated furniture which was far removed from the simple cottage-type output of the firm's earlier days (p. 181). It is not true to say that Morris was a life-long opponent of machinery, for his firm made considerable use of machinery through outside companies for a number of their products. But his general denunciation of the evils of mechanisation helped to postpone serious consideration of machine-made furniture.

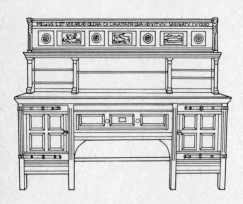

'PET SIDEBOARD', OAK AND CARVED BOXWOOD PANELS
Designed by B. Talbert, 1871

DETAIL OF THE 'PET SIDEBOARD', SHOWING HINGE

In the 1860s, following the 1862 Exhibition in London, at which the English furniture was considered to reflect much progress in design and skill, 'Art Furniture Manufacturers' employed designers to apply 'art' to furniture as an ornamental addition, and though this led to the usual debased commercial production, there was a great deal of interesting work by progressive designers. Perhaps the outstanding figure in this movement is Bruce Talbert (1838–81), who may be considered the first English professional designer to gain a national reputation. In 1867 he published *Gothic Forms Applied to Furniture*, in which he strongly recommended furniture in the Early English style (of the 12th and 13th centuries) for 'its great breadth and simplicity' and for its 'construction honestly shown'. He designed furniture of generally massive and sturdy form, using framed construction and rich, flat surface decoration. Above is shown his most famous piece of furniture.

Above is shown a detail from the 'Pet Sideboard', made by Gillows to Talbert's design for the International Exhibition, London, 1871. It is of oak, and has carved boxwood panels which set the fashion for this sort of decoration. Talbert sometimes used low relief metal panels and inlaid geometrical patterns, and the detailed sketch above shows yet another Talbert mannerism—the bold Gothic strap hinges, which were again widely copied by cabinet-makers. Talbert whole-heartedly advocated revealed construction and strongly criticised the 'false construction' of contemporary cabinet-making for its fondness for glue, which 'leads to veneering and veneering to polish'. He designed furniture for a number of leading firms, including Holland & Sons, but surprisingly little of his furniture has been traced. Yet he undoubtedly influenced the notable output of commercial Gothic of the 1870s. In his later career his work showed Jacobean influence, signs of which are apparent in the 'Pet Sideboard'.

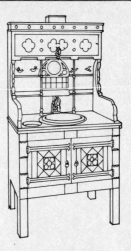

BOOKCASE
From a design in Eastlake's *Hints on Household Taste*, 1868

WASHSTAND, PAINTED AND GILT
Designed by William Burges, 1880
(*See also colour photograph 23*)

The most important propagandist of Art Furniture was Charles Lock Eastlake (1836–1906), whose *Hints on Household Taste*, first published in 1868, advocated a return to cheap, simple furniture of practically undecorated construction. Like the other progressive designers of his time, Eastlake was an enthusiast for Early English art ('it is the spirit and principle of early manufacture which I desire to see revived'). Chests of drawers, bookcases, cabinets, sideboards, chiffoniers and chests were prominent among the designs in his book, which reached a fourth (English) edition in 1878. It had a considerable influence on middle-class circles, particularly in America, where the descriptive term 'Eastlake style' became current. The above sketch of a library bookcase from *Hints on Household Taste* exemplifies the plain rectangular furniture which Eastlake sponsored, and which was a simplified version of the reformed furniture of Talbert and others.

Another progressive furniture designer whose work attracts considerable attention today is the architect William Burges (1827–81). An early Gothic enthusiast, his furniture displays a massiveness that sprang from his detailed researches into medieval architecture. It has a bold and simple structure, effect being obtained not from carving, but from painted and gilt decoration and insets of various materials. It also makes full use of architectural features. Burges worked for wealthy patrons and was not a commercial designer. Nevertheless, his designs were brought to the notice of a wide public through exhibitions and his many lectures and writings. His furniture and interior decoration can be seen at Castell Coch, Glamorgan, which he re-created for Lord Bute from 1875. The well-known washstand illustrated above was designed for Burges's own London house in 1880. It has carved decoration, painted and gilt, with mirrors and bronze and marble fittings.

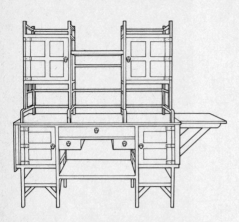

SIDEBOARD, EBONISED WOOD AND SILVER-PLATED
FITTINGS
Designed by E. W. Godwin, c.1867

CHAIR, EBONISED OAK
Designed by E. W. Godwin, c.1880

Burges was one of the first English architects of the 19th century to become interested in Japanese design, after noting the medieval character of the Japanese furniture on show at the 1862 Exhibition. But it was Burges's friend, the architect E. W. Godwin (1833–86) who made the first important adaptations of Japanese elements and became one of the most original and interesting furniture designers of the whole Victorian era. Godwin, unlike Burges, was a prolific commercial designer, and was employed by a number of leading firms, including Gillows, William Watt, W. A. Smee and Collinson & Lock. He was a close friend of the artist J. A. M. Whistler, for whom he designed the White House, Chelsea, and with whom he collaborated at the Paris Exhibition, 1878. His many writings in architectural journals and his numerous note books and sketches, which are now collected in the Victoria and Albert Museum, reveal the principles of his designs.

Godwin drew inspiration from many sources—Egyptian, Greek, Gothic and Renaissance, as well as Japanese—but his eclecticism differed fundamentally from that of contemporaries in that he never reproduced exactly any historical style. He wrote in Watt's catalogue of 1877 that he aimed at 'a modern treatment of certain well-known and admired styles rather than a mere reproduction of old forms'. He may indeed be considered the first Victorian designer to be concerned primarily with function and not with style. Writing in 1876, he reveals that his motives were originally based on considerations of economy, for he designed furniture in ebonised deal for his London rooms in 1867 and 'there were no mouldings, no ornamental work and no carving. . . . Such effect as I wanted I endeavoured to gain . . . by the grouping of solid and void and by more or less broken outline.' The examples of furniture above, all made to Godwin's design, show how his principles were put into practice.

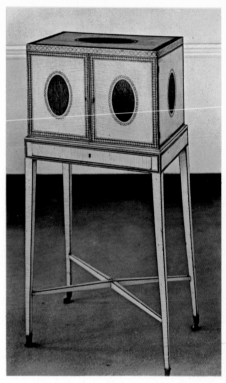

PLATE VII

19. Armchair, carved and gilt wood; modern
upholstery. French, Louis XVI, c.1785–90
(Attributed to J. B. C. Sené).

20. Writing Cabinet, satinwood,
Sheraton period. English, c.1785.

21. Two oval-back chairs,
mahogany, in neo-classical
taste. English, c.1785.

PLATE VIII

22. Armchair, inlaid decoration of anthemion and scrolls. French, Empire style, *c*.1820.

23. Washstand painted red and gold with inset panels. English, designed by William Burges, *c*.1867.

24 (*below*). Armchair, carved walnut (upholstery renewed in original pattern). French. Designed and made by L. Majorelle in Art Nouveau style, 1900.

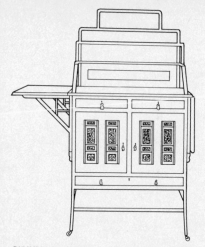

CABINET, WALNUT AND CARVED BOXWOOD PANELS
Designed by E. W. Godwin, c.1876

CABINET, EBONISED WOOD AND PAINTED PANEL
Designed by T. E. Collcutt, 1871

The sideboard opposite shows Godwin's grouping of solid and void. It is made of ebonised wood and was produced by William Watt, c.1867. Its Japanese character is emphasised by the inset panels of embossed Japanese leather paper; the only other decoration is provided by the strikingly simple silver plated fittings with pierced keyhole motif. Simple and decorative through its functionalism, this sideboard must rank as one of the most progressive pieces of Victorian furniture. The chair with elongated uprights and partly upholstered back was made by Watt c.1880. Its material is ebonised oak. Though generally considered to be in Godwin's Japanese style, this chair has legs inspired by examples on Greek chairs, as depicted on vases. The cabinet seen above is of walnut with Japanese carved box wood panels and carved ivory handles in the form of monkeys. Its neat and simple design contrasts strongly with the elaboration of so much contemporary furniture. Godwin's designs were considerably plagiarised.

Godwin's functional designs were admired abroad, particularly in Germany and Austria. Hermann Muthesius, appointed to the German Embassy in London in 1896 to report on English design, praised the progressive character of Godwin's rectilinear furniture. Ebonised furniture, following Godwin's lead, became very fashionable, and is prominently featured in the *Art at Home* series of small books published in the late 1870s with the aim of keeping middle-class readers in touch with current trends. Many features of the Art Furniture of the 1870s are shown in the much admired cabinet, illustrated above, which was designed by T. E. Collcutt (1840–1924) for the London International Exhibition, 1871. As well as being made of ebonised wood, it has painted panels, slender turned supports, a coved canopy, inlaid decoration and abundance of shelves—the prototype of numerous versions which were to be found in Victorian homes in the last quarter of the century.

M

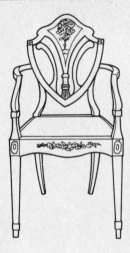

ARMCHAIR IN HEPPLEWHITE STYLE, SATINWOOD
Made by Wright and Mansfield, c.1880

CABINET DECORATED WITH MARQUETRY IN FRENCH
TASTE
By Hollands & Sons, 1868

The Art Furniture period also saw the revival of 18th-century styles, which were often executed with great skill and indeed with the declared intention by some firms of demonstrating that the craftsmanship of their workers was as good as that of the previous century. Needless to say, collectors must be on their guard against furniture of this kind, as some of the reproductions are so well done that even experts have been deceived. In the course of the century or more since they were made, such pieces have mellowed and have acquired the patina of age. The armchair illustrated above, made of satinwood and painted in colours, is in full Hepplewhite style but was actually made by the London firm of Wright & Mansfield c.1880. This firm was awarded a medal at the Paris Exhibition of 1867 for a magnificent cabinet in the Adam style—the first exhibition award to an English firm for furniture in 18th-century taste. From that date there was a vogue for Georgian reproductions.

Late 18th-century French styles were also revived at this time and among the most successful English firms specialising in this kind of furniture were Holland & Sons, who drew on French sources in great detail for some of their pieces. The above illustration shows a cabinet made by this firm in 1868, decorated with gilt mounts and marquetry panels in Louis Quinze style. Another prominent firm making reproduction furniture was Edwards & Roberts, whose products, of excellent quality, are themselves becoming collector's pieces. Most high-class firms engaged in this line labelled their furniture, for it was never their intention to mislead clients. Trouble arises, of course, if the labels are removed and the pieces passed off as genuine, as has happened in the past. What Wright & Mansfield's success in 1867 had done was to restore Georgian furniture to 'respectability' after so many years of hostile criticism by Victorian designers and consequent neglect by makers.

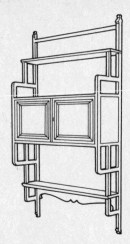

HANGING CUPBOARD
From R. Edis, *Decoration and Furniture of Town Houses*, 1881

MAHOGANY CHAIR
Designed by Mackmurdo for the Century Guild
c.1882, has early Art Nouveau features

Among the variety of styles which were fashionable in the last third or so of the century one which was very successful commercially was known as the 'Free Renaissance' style. It was based on French and Italian furniture of the 16th century and was no doubt a reflection of the general interest at that time in the art and architecture of the Renaissance. In fact, there was much of architectural character in the shelves, niches, brackets and cupboards found in contemporary wardrobes, sideboards, cabinets and overmantels, all decorated with inlaid or carved Renaissance ornament. The abundance of shelves in Collcutt's cabinet of 1871 has been noted (p. 177) and the term 'bracket and overmantel' has been used to describe the style. Its propagandist was Robert Edis who in 1881 published *Decoration and Furniture of Town Houses*. Typical of the 'Free Renaissance' furniture advocated in this book was this illustration of a 'hanging cupboard' made by Jackson and Graham of London.

The Arts and Crafts Movement of the 1880s, in which one can see the inspiration of Morris's teaching, sprang from various guilds and societies which were formed by architects, designers and craftsmen with the aim of combining good design and honest craftsmanship with social reform. The pioneer group of the Movement was the Century Guild, founded in 1882 by the architect, A. H. Mackmurdo (1851–1942), to restore the crafts 'to their right place beside painting and sculpture'. The Century Guild's furniture, as was the case with its other craftwork, was the result of a co-operative effort by craftsmen and designers, so that it is very difficult to distinguish the individuals responsible for the final product. Other groups quickly followed the Century Guild: the St. George's Art Society in 1883, the Art Workers' Guild in 1884 and two in 1888—the Arts and Crafts Exhibition Society (from which the whole Movement took its name) and C. R. Ashbee's Guild and School of Handicraft.

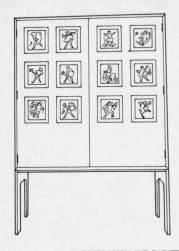

CABINET WITH INLAID DECORATION AND PAINTED
PANELS
Designed by L. F. Day, 1888

ROSEWOOD CABINET INLAID WITH ENGRAVED IVORY
By Stephen Webb, c.1890

The work of the Arts and Crafts Movement became known through special exhibitions which were arranged by members in 1888, 1889, 1890, 1893, 1896 and 1899. Discerning patrons thus became aware of the Movement's ideals and high standards of craftsmanship. But the impact on the general public was very slow. There was no clearly defined Arts and Crafts style. For one thing, designers and craftsmen freely sought inspiration from all past styles; for another, furniture exhibited by members often incorporated decorative work by a group of craftsmen in stained glass, ivory and brass—to take but random examples— and this led to much variety, not to a central, well-developed theme. The furniture was also too expensive to reach a wide market. The well-known cabinet illustrated here is typical of much early work of the Movement. Designed by Lewis F. Day, it was exhibited at the first Arts and Crafts Exhibition in 1888. It is made of oak inlaid with ebony and satinwood; the panels are painted with signs of the zodiac.

There was always a certain amount of exchange between the Arts and Crafts Movement and the commercial world. Some fine furniture in 'Free Renaissance' style was made by the prominent London firm of Collinson and Lock who had made Collcutt's cabinet for the 1871 Exhibition and absorbed the business of Jackson and Graham in 1885. Some of their pieces now attract much attention for the superb quality of their inlaid decoration in engraved ivory. This was executed by Stephen Webb (not related to Philip Webb) who was a member of both the Art Workers' Guild from 1897 to 1902 and of the Arts and Crafts Exhibition Society, and who was employed by Collinson and Lock c.1885–97. The rosewood cabinet shown above was made by the firm c.1890. The decoration, designed and made by Webb, is based on Italian intarsia work 'in the manner of the late Renaissance'. It is ranked by some experts as probably the finest work of the kind ever executed by an English craftsman.

ESCRITOIRE AND STAND, DECORATED WITH MARQUETRY
Designed by G. Jack and made by Morris & Co.,
1893

MAHOGANY WRITING CABINET WITH MARQUETRY
DECORATION
Designed by E. Gimson, 1890

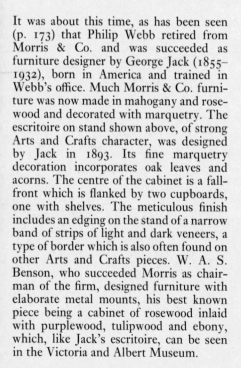

It was about this time, as has been seen (p. 173) that Philip Webb retired from Morris & Co. and was succeeded as furniture designer by George Jack (1855–1932), born in America and trained in Webb's office. Much Morris & Co. furniture was now made in mahogany and rosewood and decorated with marquetry. The escritoire on stand shown above, of strong Arts and Crafts character, was designed by Jack in 1893. Its fine marquetry decoration incorporates oak leaves and acorns. The centre of the cabinet is a fallfront which is flanked by two cupboards, one with shelves. The meticulous finish includes an edging on the stand of a narrow band of strips of light and dark veneers, a type of border which is also often found on other Arts and Crafts pieces. W. A. S. Benson, who succeeded Morris as chairman of the firm, designed furniture with elaborate metal mounts, his best known piece being a cabinet of rosewood inlaid with purplewood, tulipwood and ebony, which, like Jack's escritoire, can be seen in the Victoria and Albert Museum.

While there certainly seemed to be a gulf in the 1880s between Morris's declared principles and some of the products of his Company, the vernacular tradition of the firm's earlier days was preserved by the Arts and Crafts Movement through the emergence of the Cotswold School, and in this Morris's personal influence was paramount. The pioneers in this new development were three architects, Ernest Gimson (1864–1919) and the Barnsley brothers, Sidney and Ernest. Gimson, destined to be the leading figure of the Cotswold School, had met Morris in Leicester in 1884 and on his advice was articled to the architect J. D. Sedding, whose offices were next door to Morris's main London showrooms. In 1890 Gimson and the Barnsleys, with another architect, W. R. Lethaby, formed Kenton & Co. to make and exhibit furniture. The writing cabinet on stand illustrated above was designed by Gimson and shown at the Arts and Crafts Exhibition in 1890.

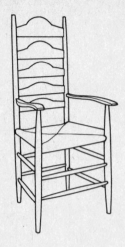

LADDER–BACK CHAIR, ASH, WITH RUSH SEAT
Designed by E. Gimson, c.1888

OAK WARDROBE
Designed by E. Gimson, c.1906

The mahogany cabinet shown overleaf is decorated with marquetry of English flowers in various woods. The handles are of steel. This piece captures the traditional form of early writing cabinets with its stand and fall-front, but does so without mere duplication, and shows admirable restraint and fine craftsmanship. When Kenton and Co. were dissolved in 1892 through lack of capital, Gimson and the Barnsleys, inspired by Morris's teaching, moved out to the Cotswolds, an area by-passed by the Industrial Revolution and one where the traditional crafts still flourished. Gimson had already mastered the techniques of rush-seated chair-making under the guidance of Philip Clisset, a Herefordshire craftsman. Shown above is a ladder-back chair designed by Gimson c.1888, at this early stage in his career. It is of turned ash but again is no replica; it is a beautifully made and finely proportioned version on traditional lines.

Gimson and the Barnsleys set up a workshop at Pinbury, Gloucestershire, in 1894 and for some years Gimson was mainly concerned with architecture and plaster-work, designing some furniture, particularly the turned ash chairs. The Barnsleys meanwhile made a great deal of furniture, many of their designs serving as a basis for later productions. In 1903 the three settled permanently in large workshops at Daneway House, Sapperton, having in 1901 engaged as their foreman Peter Waals, a skilled Dutch cabinet-maker. Thereafter, while Ernest Barnsley returned to architectural practice, and Sidney Barnsley worked independently in his own workshop, although in close contact with Gimson, Gimson himself, with a group of highly skilled craftsmen, concentrated on furniture and other crafts. He excelled as a designer. He did not make furniture himself (except for the turned chairs and a few simple pieces) but used his craftsmen's skills to interpret and modify his designs.

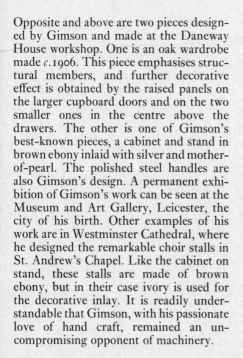

CABINET ON STAND, BROWN EBONY INLAID WITH
MOTHER-OF-PEARL
Designed by Gimson, 1908

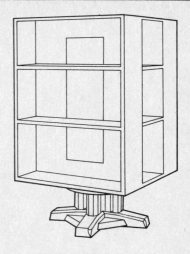

REVOLVING BOOKCASE, WALNUT
Designed and made by Sidney Barnsley, 1913
(For description see p. 184)

Opposite and above are two pieces designed by Gimson and made at the Daneway House workshop. One is an oak wardrobe made *c*.1906. This piece emphasises structural members, and further decorative effect is obtained by the raised panels on the larger cupboard doors and on the two smaller ones in the centre above the drawers. The other is one of Gimson's best-known pieces, a cabinet and stand in brown ebony inlaid with silver and mother-of-pearl. The polished steel handles are also Gimson's design. A permanent exhibition of Gimson's work can be seen at the Museum and Art Gallery, Leicester, the city of his birth. Other examples of his work are in Westminster Cathedral, where he designed the remarkable choir stalls in St. Andrew's Chapel. Like the cabinet on stand, these stalls are made of brown ebony, but in their case ivory is used for the decorative inlay. It is readily understandable that Gimson, with his passionate love of hand craft, remained an uncompromising opponent of machinery.

Gimson had an intimate knowledge and understanding of craft processes and a wonderful feeling and respect for materials. His great contribution to the development of English furniture has been to perpetuate the early ideals of Morris when they had been largely discarded by his contemporaries, and to ensure the survival of hand crafts of the highest quality. He by no means confined his designs to simple rustic pieces, as is often supposed, even though the English rural tradition remained a great source of inspiration for him. He chose his woods with extreme care and contrasted light and medium ones—walnut, elm, oak and yew—with the dark ebony and rosewood employed as panels or inlay. He also used a variety of materials for inlay—ivory, bone, pearl and silver. Revealed construction, carefully controlled, could form part of the decoration, one favourite method being the decorative use of dovetails at the corners of cabinets, cupboards and similar pieces.

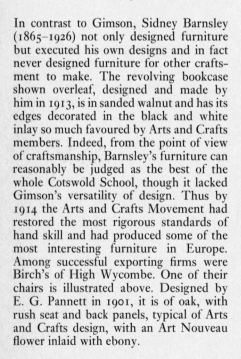

ARMCHAIR, OAK WITH EBONY INLAY
Designed by E. G. Pannett and made by William
Birch, 1901

SIDEBOARD, OAK WITH INLAY IN VARIOUS WOOD
Designed by W. R. Lethaby, c.1900

In contrast to Gimson, Sidney Barnsley (1865–1926) not only designed furniture but executed his own designs and in fact never designed furniture for other craftsment to make. The revolving bookcase shown overleaf, designed and made by him in 1913, is in sanded walnut and has its edges decorated in the black and white inlay so much favoured by Arts and Crafts members. Indeed, from the point of view of craftsmanship, Barnsley's furniture can reasonably be judged as the best of the whole Cotswold School, though it lacked Gimson's versatility of design. Thus by 1914 the Arts and Crafts Movement had restored the most rigorous standards of hand skill and had produced some of the most interesting furniture in Europe. Among successful exporting firms were Birch's of High Wycombe. One of their chairs is illustrated above. Designed by E. G. Pannett in 1901, it is of oak, with rush seat and back panels, typical of Arts and Crafts design, with an Art Nouveau flower inlaid with ebony.

W. R. Lethaby, the architect friend of Gimson and the Barnsleys did not go with them to the Cotswolds at the dissolution of Kenton & Co. (p. 182), but remained in London, where he became Joint Principal of the new Central School of Arts and Crafts in 1894 and the first Professor of Design at the Royal College of Art in 1900. He was also intimately associated with William Morris and Philip Webb and was a founder-member of the Art Workers' Guild in 1884 (becoming its Master in 1911). His influence as a designer in many fields was considerable and was acknowledged when he became President of the Arts and Crafts Exhibition Society. His most famous piece of furniture, in full Arts and Crafts tradition, is the sideboard shown above, which he designed for Melsetter House, Orkneys, c.1900. It is made of oak inlaid with ebony, sycamore and bleached mahogany. The inlay on the cupboard doors is directly inspired by Morris's pattern designs. This sideboard can now be seen in the Victoria and Albert Museum.

SATINWOOD SCREEN
Designed by A. H. Mackmurdo, c.1886

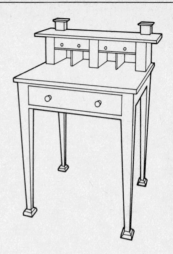

OAK DESK
Designed for the Century Guild by A. H.
Mackmurdo, c.1886

Contemporary with the Arts and Crafts Movement and in many ways closely linked with it was Art Nouveau. This was the only style of the 19th century which was not based on a historical precedent, for it represented a deliberate effort to find an art form which would ignore the past in readiness for the coming 20th century. Its ornament was inspired by sinuous curves and waving shapes taken from plants, waves and flame-like shapes, developed into languid forms which expressed a new sense of abandon. This new style spread throughout Europe and America and was known by various names, in Germany, for instance, as *Jugendstil*, in Austria as *Sezession*, and in Italy as *Stile Inglese*, or more commonly, *Stile Liberty*, after Liberty & Co. of London, specialists in products in the new style. 'Art Nouveau' became the generally adopted term when Samuel Bing opened his famous shop under this name in Paris in 1895. But 'Stile Liberty' illustrates the influential part played by English designers in the new movement.

Among the early Art Nouveau pioneers was A. H. Mackmurdo, the founder of the Arts and Crafts Movement. The chair which he designed for the Century Guild c.1882 (see p. 179) can be ranked as one of the very first examples of Art Nouveau in applied art, for the brilliantly original back has undulating flame- or tendril-like curves. These curves can also be seen on the embroidered silk panels of the screen with satinwood frame (illustrated above) which Mackmurdo designed for the Century Guild c.1886. His furniture generally, however, retains a certain basic conservatism of form in which such curves are only ornamental; he usually achieves a simple structural elegance which is typified in the attractive small oak desk (shown above) which was designed for the Century Guild c.1886. Here the Art Nouveau feature is the flat-capped uprights standing clear of the back of the desk. These extended members are a well-known mannerism of Art Nouveau furniture.

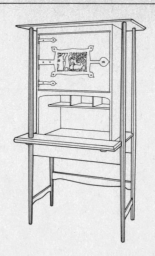

SATINWOOD SETTLE
Designed by A. H. Mackmurdo in 1886 for
Pownall Hall, Cheshire

WRITING DESK, OAK, WITH COPPER HINGES
Designed by C. F. A. Voysey, 1896

The emphasis on verticality in the desk overleaf echoes Mackmurdo's design for the Century Guild's stand at the Liverpool International Exhibition in 1886. This had thin tapering posts extending upwards to end in flat ('mortar-board') tops. Mackmurdo's fundamental simplicity of design comes out again in the satinwood settle (above) which he designed for the Century Guild in 1886 for Pownall Hall, Cheshire. It was probably made by E. Goodall & Co. of Manchester who are known to have made other pieces to Mackmurdo's designs. The settle reflects the co-operation beloved by Arts and Crafts members, for the fabric was made by Herbert Horne and the brass repoussé panelling by Bernard Creswick. A representative selection of Mackmurdo's furniture, illustrating his love of simple lines and careful proportions, can be seen at the William Morris Gallery, Walthamstow, London. The Century Guild was disbanded c.1888, but its craftsmen continued to work in close co-operation.

Probably the best example of the close relationship which existed between the Arts and Crafts Movement and Art Nouveau is provided by the furniture of C. F. A. Voysey (1857–1941). On the Continent Voysey was the most admired and the most widely imitated of all the English designers of Art Nouveau. Yet his furniture has the simple functional lines which are in full accord with English vernacular tradition. Voysey, trained as an architect, began c.1882, on the advice of Mackmurdo, to design wallpapers and textiles. He joined the Art Workers' Guild in 1884, ultimately becoming its Master in 1924. He first exhibited furniture at the Arts and Crafts Exhibition in 1893, showing a sideboard which, combining sinuous curves with simple traditional forms, attracted much attention abroad. A reviewer of the Paris Exhibition of 1900 wrote that Voysey was 'the prophet of that school of artistic expression which finds its outlet . . . in utterance of its own thoughts in its own vernacular'.

OAK CHAIR
Designed by C. F. A. Voysey, 1899

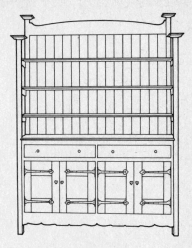

SIDEBOARD, OAK WITH BRASS HINGES
Designed by C. F. A. Voysey, c.1900

Among the characteristic features of Voysey's furniture may be noted the stress on verticals, especially in attenuated members of chairs and tables; the use of plain unvarnished wood, particularly oak; and heart-shaped metal hinges of elaborate form. The writing desk seen opposite, effectively illustrating these features, was made to Voysey's design in 1896 by W. H. Tingey. Its slender legs continue upwards in detached columns to support the flat cornice, while an interesting effect is obtained by the gap between the uprights and cabinet. Heart shapes, this time in the form of pierced ornament, can be seen in the splat of the oak chair (above) which was designed by Voysey in 1899. This ornament, and the extended uprights, are the only concessions to Art Nouveau on what is a fine version of English vernacular chair design, with simple underframing and rush seat of familiar pattern. This simplicity was the result of deep calculation, requiring, as Voysey himself said, 'perfection in all details'.

While foreign designers continued to regard Voysey as the very fountainhead of Art Nouveau, his designs remained a very personal and English interpretation. He disliked the revivals of the 19th century and stressed the value of simple traditional craftsmanship. In 1893 he said: 'Let us begin by discarding the mass of useless ornaments and banishing the millinery that degrades our furniture and fittings. Eschew all imitations and have each thing the best of its sort.' The sideboard shown here was designed by Voysey c.1900, with characteristic square finials and heart-shaped terminals to the hinges. It is clear that Mackmurdo was the greatest single influence on Voysey's style. Voysey carried his principles into interior decoration and was the first architect to make a successful attack upon the cluttered-up Victorian interior. The Orchard, Chorley Wood, Hertfordshire, designed by Voysey in 1900, is a model of the new interior simplicity which he introduced.

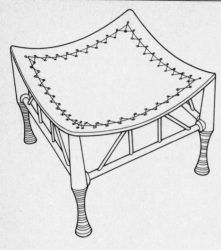

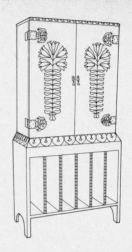

'EGYPTIAN' STOOL, MAHOGANY
Made by Liberty & Co., c.1884

MUSIC CABINET
Designed by M. H. Baillie Scott, 1898

Liberty's of Regent Street, London, rapidly established a reputation as leading specialists in the production of Art Nouveau furniture, and many of their products were exported. But their furniture showed a considerable range of styles. Much of it was obviously influenced by Voysey's work and many Liberty pieces resembled his sideboard (c.1900, overleaf). The firm also sold furniture of rustic type made by such craftsmen as William Birch of High Wycombe. Of completely different character was the imported Japanese, Egyptian and Moorish furniture which first made Liberty's reputation when they began business in 1875 as an 'Oriental Warehouse'. This branch of the firm's activities influenced their own interpretation of the contemporary Egyptian revival, and of the production of furniture based on ancient Egyptian models. One successful example was the mahogany stool shown above, with turned legs, stretchers and struts, and a leather seat. Another stool, the 'Thebes', had three curved legs and solid seat.

Another important English contributor to the development of European Art Nouveau was M. H. Baillie Scott (1865–1945), architect and designer. Baillie Scott built and furnished a considerable number of houses on the Continent—in Switzerland, Poland, Germany and Russia—and in the U.S.A., as well as throughout the British Isles. He had a devoted following in Germany, where he was commissioned in 1898 by the Grand Duke of Hesse to decorate the New Palace, Darmstadt. It is here that his best-known furniture is found, made to his design by the Guild of Handicraft. With sound construction thus assured, Baillie Scott placed great stress on good proportions. His pieces are basically simple but rely for their effect on lavish decoration in colour and relief, with inlay in coloured woods and in other materials such as pewter, pearl and ivory. The music cabinet of 1898 shown above, from Darmstadt, is of oak with coloured inlays and metal relief, and is an excellent example of his special approach to design.

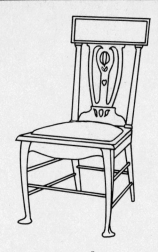

CHAIR OF 1899
A commercial adaptation of Art Nouveau

OAK CHAIR
Designed by C. R. Mackintosh, c.1900

As can be seen from a study of the furniture of Voysey, Mackmurdo, Baillie Scott and others, the best designers of Art Nouveau furniture were able to draw upon the considerable resources of skill created by the Arts and Crafts Movement. For this reason much Art Nouveau furniture is very well made and decorated and has attracted many collectors in recent years. But it must be admitted that ordinary commercial manufacture was often a caricature of the style. Aiming at novelty, and misunderstanding the aims and ideals of good designers, many firms turned out flimsy pieces in the so-called 'Quaint' style, with pseudo-Art Nouveau motifs, often in cheap woods stained to resemble the unstained oak of the best pieces. The chair illustrated above is a commercial adaptation of Voysey's designs and was published in the trade journal, *The Cabinet Maker and Art Furnisher*, in 1899. It is an illustration of the now familiar theme of an attempt to satisfy an undiscriminating market.

The most spectacular designer of Art Nouveau furniture, and one whose name is most commonly associated with the style, is Charles Rennie Mackintosh (1868–1928), the Scottish architect. Like Robert Adam, Mackintosh was concerned with the complete unity of design of his buildings and rooms, down to the last detail. Thus his furniture must always be related to its context, for in isolation it has often an eccentric appearance. His principal furnishings were designed for the Glasgow School of Art (from 1897), Miss Cranston's tearooms, Glasgow (1897–1910) and a number of private houses. He is particularly remembered for his tall-backed chairs. The example shown here, of oak, with upholstered seat, was designed c.1900 and exhibited at the Sezession Exhibition in 1900 in Vienna, where Mackintosh enjoyed a very high reputation. The chair back in this example is four and a half feet high. Other chairs designed by him often reached a height of five feet. This exaggerated elongation is typical of his work.

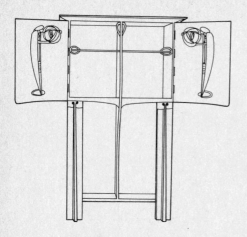

CABINET OF WHITE ENAMELLED WOOD WITH
COLOURED GLASS INLAY
Designed by Mackintosh, c.1902

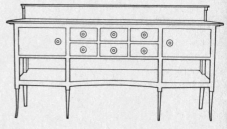

SIDEBOARD, BIRCHWOOD STAINED BLACK
Designed by G. Walton, c.1903

Mackintosh's furniture made less impact on England, where his followers were dubbed the 'Spook School'. Some of his decorative schemes, however, are of great interest. He often favoured a predominantly white setting, forming an elegant background to his furniture which was painted to match. On this furniture he strove to balance slender elongated forms with curved and coloured motifs. On the example illustrated here—a cabinet designed c.1902 and exhibited at the Turin Exhibition of that year—the white enamelled wood has decoration of coloured opaque glass. But Mackintosh failed to forge with the Arts and Crafts movement that close link which benefited so many other designers in sound construction and functional efficiency. In many instances he sacrificed construction to effect. By 1900, too, Art Nouveau had lost its momentum in England. Mackintosh's furniture was regarded as exaggerated and too abstract, even though at the same time it achieved considerable acclaim abroad.

The furniture of George Walton (1867–1933), a contemporary of Mackintosh and a fellow-Scot, also has Art Nouveau features, but is far more restrained than Mackintosh's and is both elegant and practical. Walton was a man of considerable business experience. He set up his own decorating firm in Glasgow in 1888 and also exhibited at the Arts and Crafts Exhibition in 1890. He was employed by Kodaks and designed shop fronts and interiors, with furniture, for them in many foreign cities as well as in London, and in addition designed and decorated a number of houses. The sideboard shown above was made of birch stained black to his design c.1903. The mannerisms of Mackintosh and his school are here brought under control with the elegant effect reminiscent of the furniture of the Hepplewhite-Sheraton era. A feature of Walton's furniture is the delicate outward tapering of the legs at the bottom, a characteristic also of the chairs which he designed.

PRIE-DIEU IN GOTHIC (*troubadour*) STYLE
French, c.1840

SECTION OF BOOKCASE
By Leistler of Vienna, Great Exhibition, London,
1851

This is an opportune time for a glance back at the export trade of English furniture in the Victorian period. References have been made to the interest abroad in English furniture towards the end of that period. The traditional influence of French furniture on English has also been noted, particularly in the revivals of French styles of the 18th century. In the earlier part of the 19th century French influence was strong in many parts of Europe as a result of Napoleon's conquests, for France's already established cultural leadership was emphasised even more by her military and political supremacy. Thus the Empire style was readily accepted in the countries most directly under French control, a number of which were ruled by Napoleon's relatives—Italy, for instance, where classical ornament was doubly welcome, Spain, Scandinavia, the Netherlands, Germany and Austria. French influence outlived Napoleon in many areas, but after 1815 Europe in general was affected by the same kinds of revivals that affected England.

France herself experienced a medieval revival which resulted in a picturesque version of Gothic taste known as *troubadour*, an example of which is seen in the prie-dieu of c.1840 shown left above. For a time between c.1815 and 1848 Germany produced a relatively simple middle-class style known as *Biedermeier* which found some favour outside Germany, but this was increasingly challenged by Rococo, Renaissance and Romantic revivals which resulted in the familiar eclecticism. Foreign firms which exhibited in London in 1851 showed, with a few exceptions, of which Thonet's is a shining example, the same love of elaborate ornament which characterised English commercial production. The great firm of Leistler of Vienna, whose furniture was described by the Exhibition's *Illustrated Catalogue* as 'one of the principal points of attraction', exhibited a number of pieces in Renaissance taste, including their well-known bookcase, part of which is shown here.

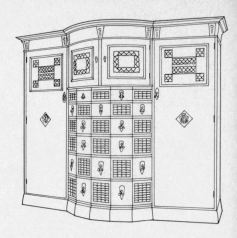

LATE VICTORIAN ARMCHAIR
Heavily upholstered, of general commercial type

WARDROBE, OAK INLAID WITH PEWTER AND EBONY
Designed by Ambrose Heal, exhibited Paris, 1900

The internationalism of furniture styles would not at first sight appear to offer particular scope for English exports. But in fact the overseas trade in English furniture, which, as we have seen, was already substantial in the 18th century, increased enormously in the 19th. Apart from the sustained interest in English furniture in foreign countries, there were now great new markets in the expanding colonial empire. Australia, New Zealand, South Africa, Canada and India all wanted furniture from home for their settlers. After 1850 the first two in particular were busy building Victorian cities and stocking their houses with the products of the homeland. From the 1860's there was a quite extraordinary rise in the value of these furniture exports, which in 1885 reached a grand total just short of £650,000. Much of the furniture sent to British settlements was of stock commercial type with an emphasis on comfort, represented by the upholstered armchair illustrated above.

The most significant trend in the export trade, however, occurred in the last quarter of the century, with the remarkable upsurge of interest throughout Europe and the United States in English furniture design. The fine quality of the furniture produced by the best English firms commanded respect abroad in its own right. Writing in 1876, H. J. Pollen (in *British Manufacturing Industries*) stated that London firms were supplying furniture to 'foreign potentates in every corner of the world'—Holland & Sons, for instance, to the Emperor of Austria, and Jackson and Graham to the Khedive of Egypt. But to professional designers, architects and others with special interest in furniture, the work of English reformers represented the most progressive ideas in the world. It was bold and experimental, solving many of the problems raised by the new industrial society. International exhibitions in Europe and America played an important part in spreading knowledge of these latest English developments.

'DRAWING ROOM CHEFFONIER'
From Eastlake's *Hints*, first U.S.A. edition, 1872

THE 'MORRIS' CHAIR
In widespread use in the U.S.A. after *c.*1866

Cultural links with the United States remained strong. From the 1820's America experienced the revivals of historical styles then current in England—Gothic, Elizabethan, Renaissance, etc.—as well as those of the French *ancien régime*. The great success in America of Eastlake's *Hints on Household Taste* in the 1870's has been noted (page 175). Indeed, America can boast an Eastlake style in furniture, which never took root to the same extent in England. The relative simplicity of Eastlake's designs and his advocacy of oak, durable and cheap, obviously made a strong appeal to Americans. The above illustration of a 'drawing room cheffonier', taken from the first American edition (1872) of Eastlake's *Hints*, is typical of much of the furniture made in America. The style became even more widespread towards the close of the century and seems to have inspired many early 20th-century American designers. 'Eastlake furniture', however, was to represent only part of England's influence in America.

Mention has already been made (page 173) of the armchair with adjustable back which Morris & Co. made from *c.*1866 and which became fashionable in the United States. This type had bobbin turned decoration and is still known throughout America simply as 'the Morris chair'. At the Philadelphia Centennial Exposition of 1876, held to celebrate the centenary of the Declaration of Independence, many of the furniture exhibits, both English and American, were a medley of the styles—Elizabethan, Jacobean and Classic—which were at that time popular commercial productions in England. After the Exposition there was a notable revival in America of colonial (or 'centennial') styles. Thus in the late 19th century American firms frequently advertised furniture in Jacobean, Queen Anne and Chippendale styles, together with Eastlake pieces and Morris chairs. Imports of furniture from England rose during the same period; in 1890 their value reached a total of over £48,000.

N

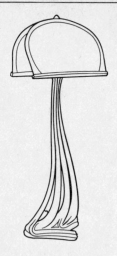

MUSIC STAND, ELM
By A. Charpentier, Paris, 1901
(*See also colour photograph 24*)

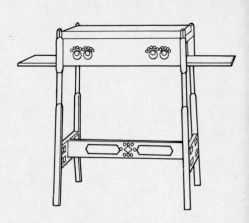

TEA TABLE, OAK INLAID WITH EBONY AND IVORY.
Designed by the Dutch architect, de Bazel, *c*.1905

It was on the Continent that English furniture design made perhaps its most significant impact towards the end of the Victorian period, and reference has been made in this connection to the influence of men like Voysey, Mackmurdo and Baillie Scott. They were widely known abroad through exhibitions and illustrations of their furniture in numerous art magazines. English furniture in Art Nouveau style, with its simpler lines and firmer sense of proportion, was radically different from its continental counterpart. The music stand shown above, for instance, could never be taken for an English piece. Its sinuous elegance is typically French. It was made in 1901 by A. Charpentier, who —not surprisingly—excelled as a sculptor. Yet France at this time imported large quantities of English furniture—in 1885, for example, to the value of no less than £72,000. In that year France was the largest single market in Europe for English furniture, which reached all parts of the Continent.

As can be expected from the long history of close cultural relationship between the Dutch and the English, Holland was foremost among continental countries in showing interest in the developments of English furniture in the late 19th century. In 1899 Dutch imports of English furniture amounted to £17,500. William Morris had considerable influence among those Dutch designers who had grown tired of the exuberant eclecticism which after 1850 succeeded the quiet and well-mannered *Biedermeier* style. They were particularly attracted by the work of the Arts and Crafts Movement in their attempts to get back to good design and honest craftsmanship. Outstanding among these reformers was the architect, K. P. D. de Bazel, whose mature work reflected the aims of the Morris school. Above is illustrated a tea table, of oak inlaid with ebony and ivory, which was made to his design *c*.1905. In complete contrast to Holland, Belgium succumbed to the fullest expression of Art Nouveau. (See p. 196.)

8
Modern – 1914 to present day

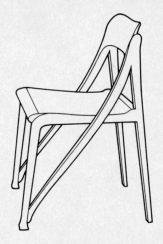

CHAIR FOR A MUSIC ROOM
Designed by R. Riemerschmid, *c*.1899

Industrial design is the keynote to the furniture of the 20th century, that is, the design of furniture for production by machinery, with the employment, where necessary, of the wide variety of new materials and of new constructional techniques created by the technological age. This new approach has been given the name of the Modern Movement, which covers the whole field of production, notably architecture and interior decoration, affected by this revolution in design. Though England played a significant part in the development of the Movement at its beginning, attention has for long been focused on foreign designers, among whom those of the German Bauhaus have been outstanding. The ideas and influence of these designers will be examined in detail. Recently, however, the validity of the rôle of the Bauhaus approach has been questioned in some quarters, and increasing attention is being paid to vernacular design, the intuitive adaptation to function.

It is ironical that the pioneer work of English furniture designers, which was so much admired on the Continent in the thirty years or so before 1914, should have encouraged foreigners to become the first successful practitioners of industrial design. The reluctance of leading English designers, with some exceptions, to turn to the idea of machine production lost England the lead in the Modern Movement. Hermann Muthesius, who had come to England to report on English design (page 177) returned to Germany in 1903 delighted and impressed with what he had seen. He noted particularly the willingness of English furniture designers to recognise the appeal of functional form and to attack meaningless historical revivals, while English engineers were effectively using in new ways the raw materials of industry—glass, cast iron, concrete and steel. He saw in these developments the key to future progress, and found a receptive audience for his ideas in his own country.

CABINET, MAHOGANY
Designed by W. Gropius, 1913

CHAIR
Designed by H. van de Velde, 1900

Muthesius was in control of Schools of Art and Crafts under the Prussian Board of Trade, and this important post enabled him to appoint men of his own way of thinking to key positions in these Schools. He also lectured and wrote widely on the theme of machine production, with decided impact on the more progressive German designers. Germany's lead in design for industry was already being taken by younger architects such as Richard Riemerschmid, whose chair, illustrated overleaf, was designed for machine production as early as 1899. In 1907 a decisive step was taken with the formation of the Deutscher Werkbund, an association of architects, craftsmen and, most significantly of all, manufacturers, who were united in their aim of improving standards of industrial design. Among the gifted designers in the early years of the Werkbund was Walter Gropius, who though primarily an architect, made interesting essays in furniture design, as the above example of 1913 shows.

Gropius became the first Director of the Bauhaus at its formation in 1919. He had succeeded Henri van de Velde as head of the Weimar School of Applied Arts. Van de Velde, a Belgian who had settled in Germany, had been inspired by Morris to turn from painting to design, becoming one of the outstanding exponents of Art Nouveau, in which he preferred abstract to natural forms. In 1895 he designed the interior of Samuel Bing's shop, L'Art Nouveau, in Paris, from which the whole movement took its name. The chair shown above was designed by him in 1900 and is fully Art Nouveau in conception. A comparison with Riemerschmid's chair of about the same time (overleaf) clearly shows the distinct difference in approach between the two schools of thought. Gropius converted the Weimar School of Applied Arts into the Bauhaus (House of Building) at the conclusion of the First World War, and made it into the greatest centre of the Modern Movement.

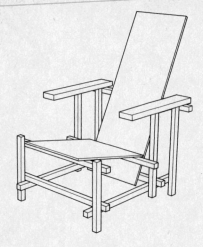

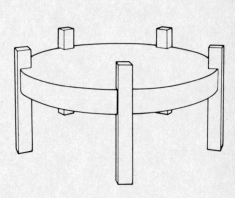

'RED-BLUE' CHAIR (RED BACK, BLUE SEAT)
Designed by G. T. Rietveld, 1917

TEA TABLE, PEARWOOD
One of the first designs of M. Breuer, 1921–22

The First World War marked a turning point in the development of modern design. It became clear in the era of European reconstruction after 1919 that Art Nouveau was no solution to the problems of large-scale machine production. As well as Germany, Holland and France also made important pioneering contributions to the Modern Movement; indeed Holland, helped by her neutrality during the war, produced one of the earliest radical movements, *De Stijl*, so called after a periodical of that name which promulgated its ideas. The furniture produced by this movement is best represented by the designs of its leading figure, G. T. Rietveld. He employed only rectangular and cubic forms, making no attempt to disguise structural elements. His famous chair designed in 1917 (see above) is made of two pieces of unbent plywood set on square wooden members fastened with screws. It typifies the simple geometrical forms, pure and uncompromising, sought by devotees of *De Stijl*.

Many of the ideas of *De Stijl* were absorbed by the new Bauhaus when, under the direction of Gropius, it began to revolutionise the training of industrial designers. Gropius surrounded himself with a brilliant group of teachers, whose willingness to experiment in all fields made their influence felt throughout the world. All the arts and crafts were considered in essential unity, and the initial training of artists, craftsmen and designers was common to all. A considerable amount of time was devoted during training to workshop practice, in order to achieve a thorough feeling for the nature of materials, as well as for form and colour. One of the first furniture designers of the Bauhaus to attract attention was Marcel Breuer, who was put in charge of the joinery and cabinet-making workshop in 1925, after completing his course as a student. The table illustrated above is made of pearwood and was designed by Breuer in 1921–22. Like *De Stijl* furniture, it was inspired by contemporary Cubism in art.

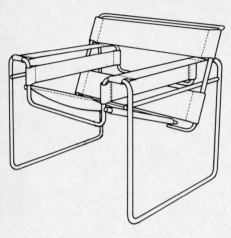

FIRST TUBULAR STEEL CHAIR
Designed by M. Breuer, 1925

FACTORY-MADE 'JACOBEAN' SIDEBOARD OF THE
INTER-WAR YEARS

Breuer, impressed by the purity of form achieved by *De Stijl* furniture, was instrumental in directing early Bauhaus design ever further towards industrial production. He began to experiment with metal furniture, which is said to have been suggested to him by the curved metal tubing of the handlebars of his bicycle. In 1925 he designed his first tubular steel chair, shown above. The chromium-plated steel tubing for the frame is composed of one continuous piece of bent metal. Canvas is employed for upholstery. The new material emphasises the structure of parallel and angular forms in a much lighter and more attractive way than Rietveld's chair. Breuer's chair, which is still in production, marks a breakthrough in furniture design. Between 1925 and 1928 (when he left the Bauhaus) Breuer produced many designs for tubular steel furniture, many of which, it is interesting to note, were mass-produced later by the Thonet firm, for so long celebrated for their bentwood furniture.

While all these interesting experiments were proceeding on the Continent, English furniture-makers failed to grasp the great opportunity offered by post-war reconstruction. In the building and furnishing boom of the 1920s, completely machine-made furniture was available for everybody for the first time. But despite the considerable progress made during the war in the mechanisation of the wood-working industry, there were no trained and experienced industrial designers. The reluctance to design for machine-made articles, engendered by the traditions of English furniture-making, now produced the worst possible results—the output, as speedily as possible, of badly-designed and badly-finished furniture, often with poor materials. Uneducated designers were matched by an uneducated public. The demand was for decorated furniture in traditional styles, made for show. Simple functional furniture was regarded as altogether too plain, and naturally manufacturers catered for the biggest market.

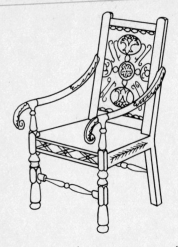

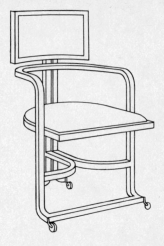

MACHINE-MADE 'CARVED OAK HALL CHAIR'
Renaissance design made in 1946

DESIGN FOR METAL CHAIR
By Frank Lloyd Wright, U.S.A., 1904

Thus the absurd position was reached of machine-made furniture dressed in traditional garb—Tudor, Jacobean, Queen Anne, etc. Sections of mass-produced carving were glued to case furniture, while power lathes turned thousands of legs in bulbous, bobbin and other forms. The machinery, in effect, instead of manufacturing the shapes which it could do so much better than any other medium, was producing debased versions of decoration and structural members which owed their forms to carefully-worked hand processes. Hire purchase helped to perpetuate the demand for these products. Examples are shown above and opposite. The 'Jacobean' sideboard has bulbous supports and applied carving of card-cut form. The 'Renaissance' chair with carved back was being advertised as late as 1946. A good case can be made for judging the mass-produced post-1919 furniture as the worst-designed in the whole history of English furniture—worse than the oft-derided revivals of the Victorian era.

It will be useful at this point to pause and sum up the general principles behind the design of furniture, as this developed during the first quarter of the 20th century in the work of the more progressive designers. The main consideration was essentially one of form. This was always abstract and no longer based on shapes from nature—either directly imitative or symbolic—and was not decorated.

The production of furniture by machinery demands relatively simple forms, sparing of material and employing as few joints as possible. The results are quantity and cheapness, making furniture available for all, but not at the expense of comfort or convenience, for modern technological processes can produce an enormous variety of both shapes and materials. All these developments by no means indicate the end of craftsmanship; much furniture is still made by hand with traditional materials and methods, and some machine-made furniture still requires finishing by hand.

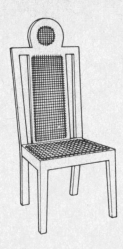

DINING CHAIR, PAINTED RED, CANE SEAT AND BACK
Designed by Roger Fry for Omega Workshops,
*c.*1914

WRITING TABLE
Typical English commercial production of 1912

The best modern hand-made furniture (unless it is a deliberate reproduction) rarely fails to conform to the accepted rules of modern design in its avoidance of ornament and symbolism. Traditional decorative methods such as carving, marquetry and gilding are completely out-of-date. They belong firmly to the past and there will surely never be any point in reviving them. The folly of superimposing cheap mechanically-contrived carved decoration on furniture becomes more and more obvious: it shows a fundamental misunderstanding of the modern approach. To many people 'abstract' furniture appears too stark and austere, even primitive, and devoid of warmth; indeed, in some instances the insistence on functionalism has resulted in furniture of this kind. Often, however, sheer conservatism causes a reluctance to appreciate new forms and materials, for it has been repeatedly shown that functional form, when controlled with discrimination, can achieve true refinement and elegance.

The developments of the 1920s, showing the need to discard outworn techniques, forms and decoration, did not mean total rejection of the lessons of the past. The emphasis on functional forms has in fact underlined the value of a study of English furniture, which has won its special place in the international field through the craftsmen's traditional use of the best available materials in a direct, straightforward way. This tradition has persisted, and can continue unbroken, through a similar use of new methods and materials. Moreover, the study of English vernacular furniture, with its simple functionalism, has been given a fresh meaning in the context of the modern age. The story of 19th century English furniture as outlined in this book shows how successive generations of English designers, from Pugin and Morris to Godwin and Voysey, were aware of the importance of functionalism and the appeal of simple forms and revealed construction.

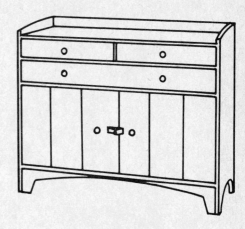

CUPBOARD, UNSTAINED OAK
Designed by Ambrose Heal, c.1905

SIDEBOARD, OAK
Designed by Ambrose Heal, 1906

The English tradition was fortunately kept very much alive in the 1920's in spite of the vast output of atrociously designed factory furniture which threatened to sweep the market entirely, and, also the great attention focused on the important innovations of foreign designers. Gimson, (see pp. 181–3) had made a valuable contribution to English furniture by his preservation of hand work, though he failed to turn his attention to the possibility of machine production. His work did not cease at his death in 1919. The legacy of the whole Arts and Crafts Movement has been retained, and among the gifted (and growing) number of designers who have continued this tradition two outstanding figures are worth detailed study, for they preserved a remarkable continuity with the past and also successfully took up designing furniture for production by machine. They are Sir Ambrose Heal (1872–1959) and Sir Gordon Russell (born 1892).

Ambrose Heal was the great-grandson of the founder of the famous firm, which, originally established in 1810, has been in Tottenham Court Road, London, since 1840. A fresh stage was reached when the firm issued its first *Catalogue of Plain Oak Furniture* in 1898, one of its specialities being the well-known wooden bedsteads which began to replace the ubiquitous Victorian brass beds. The young Heal spent three years (1890–3) training in a cabinet-maker's workshop before entering the family business. He met members of the Art Workers' Guild, including Lethaby and Voysey, and as an enthusiastic member of the Arts and Crafts Movement he exhibited at the Paris Exhibition of 1900, gaining a silver medal for a bedroom suite. One piece of this suite has already been illustrated (page 192). The sure control of design manifest in this exhibition furniture was directed towards the production of simple, well-made pieces, of which the sideboard in natural oak, shown above, is a fine example.

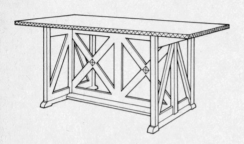

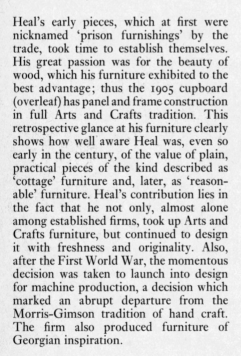

DINING TABLE
Painted black and other colours. Designed by
Ambrose Heal, 1916

CHEST OF DRAWERS, CHESTNUT
Designed by Ambrose Heal and made by
Heal & Son, 1926

Heal's early pieces, which at first were nicknamed 'prison furnishings' by the trade, took time to establish themselves. His great passion was for the beauty of wood, which his furniture exhibited to the best advantage; thus the 1905 cupboard (overleaf) has panel and frame construction in full Arts and Crafts tradition. This retrospective glance at his furniture clearly shows how well aware Heal was, even so early in the century, of the value of plain, practical pieces of the kind described as 'cottage' furniture and, later, as 'reasonable' furniture. Heal's contribution lies in the fact that he not only, almost alone among established firms, took up Arts and Crafts furniture, but continued to design it with freshness and originality. Also, after the First World War, the momentous decision was taken to launch into design for machine production, a decision which marked an abrupt departure from the Morris-Gimson tradition of hand craft. The firm also produced furniture of Georgian inspiration.

Heal's firm now produced both hand-made and machine-made furniture, all the pieces, irrespective of the method of manufacture, being designed with great skill and care. With ever-improving mechanised methods this fine furniture could be sold at reasonable prices. The nursery chest of drawers illustrated here was designed by Ambrose Heal and made by Heal & Son, Ltd. in 1926, for factory production. It is made of chestnut and, while still strongly reminiscent of Arts and Crafts taste, shows how smoothly some of the furniture of this type can, under wise guidance, pass into mass production. Heal—who became chairman of the firm in 1913, was knighted in 1933 and retired in 1953—immensely extended the scope of the firm's business, not only in the provision of craftsman-made and factory-produced furniture, but also in the making of almost all kinds of household equipment. No student of the development of English furniture should miss the opportunity of visiting Heal's premises.

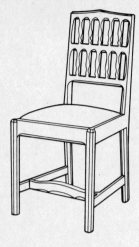

CHAIR, OAK
Designed by G. Russell, 1925

WRITING CABINET, CHERRYWOOD
Designed by G. Russell, 1926

Gordon Russell, the other dominant figure in English furniture design since the inter-war years, has had a career quite different from that of Ambrose Heal, which is described in his fascinating autobiography, *Designer's Trade* (1968). Russell was the son of the owner of the Lygon Arms, Broadway, Worcestershire, and acquired his early skill in cabinet-making by repair-ing the antique furniture in his father's hotel. After service in the First World War he decided to devote himself to furniture design, continuing the tradition of Gimson (see pp. 181–3), who had died in 1919. This was a natural development, for Broadway was not far from Gimson's Daneway House workshops and was thus in an area where the spirit of William Morris was very much alive. Russell's furniture of the early 1920's was thus strongly inspired by Gimson's. It was shown at a number of exhibitions and a gold medal was awarded at the Paris Exhibition of 1925 for a walnut cabinet inlaid with various woods.

These early pieces were almost entirely in English woods, which were left in their natural colours and included oak, walnut, yew, laburnum, cherry, chestnut, box and cedar. Two Russell pieces of 1925–26 are shown here. The chair in solid brown oak was first made in 1925. The unusual back has two rows of chamfered arches and the front stretcher is shaped; the drop-in seat is covered with hide. The writing cabinet is in cherrywood with handles of ebony and laburnum. It was made in 1926, the year in which Russell was elected a member of the Art Workers' Guild. Fine decorative effect has been obtained by the arrangement of the handles round the small central cupboard of the upper stage, and by the spirally-grooved and curved stretchers of the stand. This cabinet, which recalls those of the late Stuart period (e.g. p. 60), was obviously inspired by the similar piece designed by Gimson and made at the Daneway House work-shops in 1908 (page 183). Thus Gimson's work was carried directly into the 1920s.

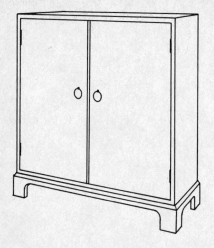

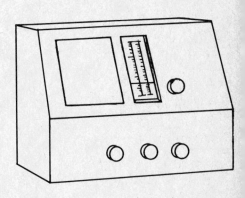

CUPBOARD, CUBAN MAHOGANY, DOOR OF VENEERED
BLOCKBOARD
Designed by G. Russell, 1925

RADIO CABINET (MURPHY)
Designed by R. D. Russell in the 1930's

All this furniture was made in the work-shops at Broadway where, in the mid-1920s, when the work of the most progressive foreign designers was beginning to attract more and more attention in England, the first tentative essays with machinery were made, but only for preparing timber for the craftsmen, who then completed their individual pieces. During this time also two events occurred which were to be of vital importance: R. D. Russell, Gordon Russell's brother, completed his training as an architect and began to turn his considerable talents to designing furniture; and W. H. Russell (no relation) joined the firm as a young but highly-skilled cabinet-maker, and was later to become the firm's chief designer. Thus the challenging problems of styles and production methods could be tackled with the aid of two talented specialists with very different backgrounds. In 1929 the decision was taken to open showrooms in London, in Wigmore Street, and to expand the retail side of the business.

1930 witnessed a major change in Russell's manufacturing methods. He turned to mass production of wireless cabinets for Murphy's radio factory. Although the radio set was an increasingly popular feature in English homes, nobody had yet produced properly designed cabinets; they were either 'period' reproductions or boxes with fretwork decoration. Russell saw the problem of design as very similar to that created by the development of clock-making in the late Stuart period, and just as the cabinet-makers then produced bracket (table) and long-case clocks (p. 59), which formed fitting and attractive cases for the fine precision work of the movements, so now, in 1930, R. D. Russell began to design a series of cabinets as precise and appropriate for their purpose as the intricate pieces of engineering within them. These wooden radio cabinets were then the best of their kind to be found anywhere in the world. They made the firm's name and at the same time gave it a clearer insight into the meaning of real engineering precision.

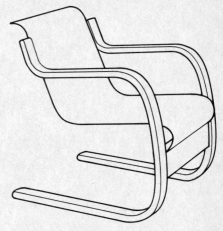

SIDEBOARD, WALNUT
Designed by Christopher Heal, *c*.1935

CANTILEVERED CHAIR, SEAT OF BENT PLYWOOD,
FRAME OF LAMINATED BIRCH
Designed by A. Aalto, 1935

Thus in the 1930s the Modern Movement in English furniture can be said to have got under way. Nobody has done more than Heal and Russell in establishing the profession of the industrial furniture designer in England. Their work is all the more significant because in their transition to factory production they retained firm links with the past; there was no sudden or complete break. Both designers also preserved the highest stands of hand craft. For this reason they have a special place in English furniture history, as important as that of the great figures of the Georgian period. A visit to Russell's Broadway show-rooms and to the factory which has developed behind the original workshop is as informative as a visit to Heal's shop in Tottenham Court Road. Russell does not sell machine-made furniture direct to the public (though commissions for hand work on an individual basis are executed), but markets it through a few selected firms, including Heal's.

A potent foreign source of inspiration for English furniture design is Scandinavia. One of the earliest figures was the Finnish architect, Alvar Aalto. The great forests of his native country enabled him to use timber widely for his buildings and their contents. His main contribution to furniture design came from his use of bent plywood in 1932; in that year he designed a chair in which the seat and back were formed from one piece of bent plywood supported on a tubular steel frame—clearly taken from Breuer's Bauhaus experiments (p. 198). Plywood, built up from an uneven number of veneers glued together in such a way that the grain of any one veneer is at right angles to the next, has immense strength and can be bent to curved shapes. This material is by no means a new one; varieties of plywood were found in the 18th century, and it was processed and applied to furniture by Thonet in the 1830s. As in so many other materials, it is the application which is novel.

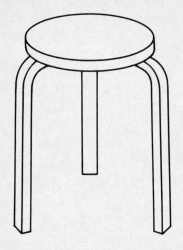

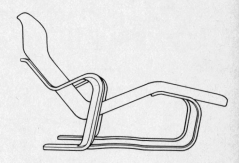

STOOL, SOLID LEGS AND LAMINATED CURVES
Designed by A. Aalto, 1938

LONG CHAIR, LAMINATED WOOD AND BENT PLYWOOD
Designed by M. Breuer, 1936, for the London firm,
Isokon

Aalto's innovation was certainly a dramatic one. He soon abandoned metal supports in favour of timber construction throughout. He also used laminated wood, formed from layers which are thicker than ply and which have their grain running in the same, not the opposite, direction. The cantilevered chair illustrated overleaf shows how the great strength and resilience of laminated wood has been utilised in the curved side supports which make up the arms and front legs, with a basic support which obviates the need for rear legs. Aalto's favourite wood is Finnish birch. Its natural spring is fully exploited in these new uses, which have produced chairs of completely new form. Another unusual construction is employed for solid legs on stools, chairs, cabinets, desks, etc. Saw cuts are made through one end of these legs, which are steamed; a glued veneer is inserted in each cut, enabling the bending to be carried out. This gives immense strength to the curved supports.

Aalto's great success as a designer springs from his imaginative application of industrial processes to timber, the most traditional of all furniture materials. The warm, glowing colour of Finnish birch, its smooth, silky texture and lovely grain all add attraction to his furniture. The pieces remain eminently functional; the stool, for instance, is one of a series designed for stacking. It also demonstrates the free borrowing of ideas which has always been a feature of European furniture. Thus Aalto owed his use of the cantilever principle to the Bauhaus pioneers. In the same way Breuer, the inventor of tubular steel furniture, has been influenced by Aalto's designs. Breuer left the Bauhaus and came to London, where in 1936 he designed the celebrated long chair (above) for the firm of Isokon. The ingenious arrangement of the frame, base and arm rests from sections of laminated wood, and of the back and seat from bent plywood, shows perfect understanding of materials and processes.

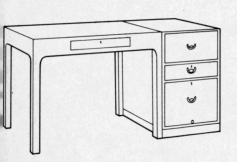

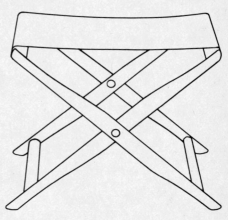

DESK WITH PEDESTAL DRAWER UNIT, MAHOGANY
Designed by K. Klint, 1933

FOLDING STOOL, ASH WITH SAILCLOTH SEAT
Designed by K. Klint, in the 1930's

The impact of Aalto's furniture in the European field is clear enough from the foregoing account. At the same time as his influence was making itself felt, another Scandinavian country, Denmark, was also attracting attention in applying industrial methods to the production of furniture. As Danish design has much in common with that of progressive designers in England, it is well worth particular study. The outstanding pioneer was Kaare Klint (1888–1954) whose approach was quite different from that of other contemporary designers. He did not reject the past or deliberately seek novel forms, but adopted the policy of renovating traditional methods, forms and materials in a way which suited modern conditions. This has meant cutting out stylistic trimmings to get down to basic forms and to produce pure (or 'timeless') designs in which traditionalism is happily united to function. The enormous importance which vernacular furniture can play in this approach can be readily appreciated.

With his emphasis on functional forms Klint gave Danish furniture a reputation for graceful simplicity combined with comfort which it has retained until the present. He was much influenced by late 18th-century English furniture. English visitors to Denmark are soon aware of the amount of furniture in Hepplewhite and Sheraton styles which can be seen in antique shops, museums and private houses. Such pieces were either imported from England, or were Danish-made, based on English models. Klint was also inspired by the furniture of other countries and periods, by the Orient, for example, and by ancient Egypt, but it was his interest in the classic period, when there were close links between English and Danish furniture, and his determination to preserve the legacy of hand craft, which had important subsequent repercussions on both Danish and English design. Nothing could be simpler, or more ancient in its inspiration, than the folding stool designed by Klint (above).

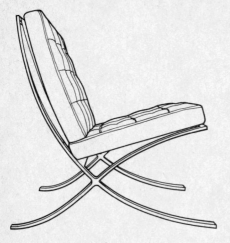

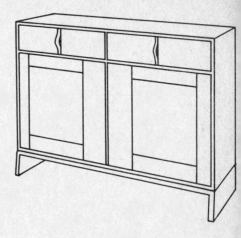

THE 'BARCELONA' CHAIR, STEEL FRAME
Designed by Mies van der Rohe, 1929

SIDEBOARD, OAK
Designed by Edward Barnsley, c.1933

With Hitler's advent to power in Germany in 1933 the Bauhaus was closed after only 14 years of existence. The Nazis regarded its work as decadent, especially as some of its most gifted designers were Jewish. But though fewer than 500 graduates were trained at the Bauhaus, its influence has been immense, not less because many of its leading figures took refuge abroad, there to carry on their mission. Gropius left the Bauhaus in 1928. Its director in its last three years was Mies van der Rohe, who was responsible for perhaps its greatest furniture masterpiece. This was the 'Barcelona' chair, so called because it was shown at the International Exhibition, Barcelona, in 1929. Its framework is composed of slender steel bars crossing to form a graceful pattern and combining great strength with extreme delicacy. Welted leather cushions form the back and seat, supported on leather straps. Here engineering precision, allied to the most advanced techniques, produces a chair of classic simplicity.

In broad terms three strands in English furniture-making can be seen emerging in the inter-war years: the depressingly low standard of most mass-produced furniture, the enlightened efforts of the pioneer industrial designers, and the survival of hand craft. While Heal and Russell and their followers preserved so much of the hand work of Arts and Crafts tradition, but were also preparing to tackle the problems of machine production, a number of skilled craftsmen continued to design and make furniture by hand on the lines laid down by Gimson. Foremost among these is Edward Barnsley (b.1900) the son of Gimson's friend, Sidney Barnsley, and thus a direct connection with the Cotswold School. At Froxfield, near Petersfield, Hampshire, Edward Barnsley established a workshop in the early 1920s on the Gimson model, and there, with a small group of assistants and the use of some machinery, he has produced individual pieces of the highest quality.

WARDROBE, OAK, WITH EBONY AND HOLLY INLAY
Designed by Peter Waals
*c.*1920

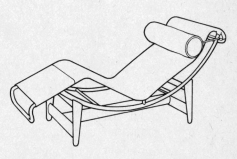

ADJUSTABLE *chaise longue*, CHROMIUM-PLATED STEEL
Designed by Le Corbusier, 1927

In more recent years, as will be indicated later, Edward Barnsley's furniture has changed considerably since his early days. His attitude to machinery is the very reasonable one of regarding it as a most useful adjunct to the workshop so long as it is not allowed to alter the highly individual character of the craftsman's final piece. Gimson's work was also continued by his chief cabinet-maker and foreman, Peter Waals (1870–1937, page 182), who after Gimson's death set up his own workshops at nearby Chalford and produced work to Gimson's own designs as well as original furniture of his own. The wardrobe illustrated above was executed at the Chalford workshops as a protest, in Waals's own words, against 'the dull flat surfaces of modern furniture'. In an effort to improve design standards among craft teachers, Waals was appointed design adviser to Loughborough Training College in 1935. He was succeeded in this post in 1937 by Edward Barnsley.

Another celebrated architect-designer of the 1920s and 1930s whose ideas had a decided impact on English designers was Le Corbusier, Swiss-born, but living and working in France. Following his description of a house as 'a machine for living in', he considered design to be as much a social as a technical problem, and reduced furniture (which he called 'equipment') to a few standardised forms which could be equally well used in all his interiors. Shelves (either open or of enclosed cabinet form), tables and chairs were his three categories, each containing a number of variations. His work was obviously influenced by the Bauhaus, as can be seen in his *chaise longue* above. First made in 1927, this has a chromium-plated steel frame adjustable to various angles. This notion of adjustability and versatility was an essential feature of Le Corbusier's furniture, always considered within his architectural framework. His immense prestige ensured close consideration in England for his furniture.

SIDEBOARD, MAHOGANY WITH IVORY PLASTIC HANDLES
War-time utility furniture

UTILITY WINDSOR CHAIR

The Second World War (1939–45) gave England a great opportunity of inaugurating a new era of progressive furniture design. This was the introduction of 'utility' furniture. Furniture became very scarce during the war. Many furniture firms, including the largest, were switched to the production of war materials, particularly aircraft parts. Bombing destroyed much furniture in private houses and shops, and just when it was essential to supply bombed-out people speedily with homes and furniture, there was a great shortage of timber, primarily needed for war purposes. The government's solution was to set up a committee to advise on specifications for 'utility furniture of good sound construction in simple but agreeable designs for sale at reasonable prices'. Gordon Russell was among the designers appointed on the committee. The result was a range of furniture available for all, competently designed and devoid of the capricious trimmings of so much pre-war production.

Utility furniture had clean lines and good proportions, its simplicity masking the considerable thought and painstaking preparation that went into its design. The sideboard illustrated here successfully embodies those very principles which were so much admired in the late Georgian period. Such furniture it would be true to say would have been available before the war only in the more expensive shops. At the same time, Windsor chairs made a triumphant return to fashion, exemplifying their ageless qualities and providing simple and useful pieces at a very reasonable price. They were particularly useful because their seats were made of their traditional timber, elm, which was not as easily workable as other woods for general purposes. Experiments were also made with utility metal furniture, and much standardised furniture of interesting design was produced for schools. The public has become accustomed to sets of stacking chairs since these proved their use during the war.

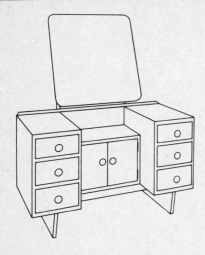

UTILITY DRESSING-TABLE, OAK

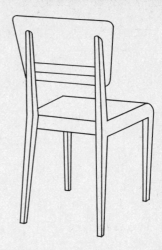

CHAIR, PARTLY SOLID WOOD, PARTLY PLYWOOD
Designed by Christopher Heal, 1946

Other utility experiments included painted furniture—a table, for instance, employing two colours, one for the top, the other for the legs. In the dressing-table shown above, made in oak, the simple proportions are enhanced by the use of trusses for supports, a feature often found in Gimson's work. But it must be noted that utility furniture did not solve the problem of mass-production, as it was manufactured by smaller firms with limited resources. The label 'utility' was perhaps unfortunate. It was connected in the public's mind with war-time restrictions and making-do with what was available (generally the second-best). The post-war years therefore brought the inevitable reaction. Many manufacturers returned to the production of 'traditional' decorated furniture on the plea that their customers found utility pieces too austere, and in fact some of the first furniture to come off the production lines after 1945 was labelled 'non-utility'.

It is understandable that with the coming of peace nobody in the furniture industry supported the continuation of government control over design. Yet the war-time utility experiments clearly made a valuable contribution to the development of well-designed furniture. The wide scope of the scheme, covering the whole country, introduced more people than ever before to the basic principles of good design. The trade had also seen the result of the efforts of a group of the country's outstanding designers and had become aware of the wider issues involved. During the war there had been a big increase in the general development of new materials, some of which could be applied to furniture. Above all, the chief legacy of the war has been the Council of Industrial Design, originally established in 1944. Gordon Russell became its director in 1947, was knighted in 1955 and retired from it in 1960. His work for the Council marked the summit of his career.

'ANTELOPE' CHAIR, WIRE AND LAMINATED PLYWOOD
Designed by Ernest Race, 1951

STACKING CHAIR IN POLYPROPYLENE
Designed by Robin Day for Hille, London, 1960s

The Council of Industrial Design has a permanent display at the Design Centre, Haymarket, London, and a visit there is essential again for anyone who wishes to see the latest essays in furniture design. Indeed, the large number of visitors who are attracted to the Centre every year is a good sign of the generally awakened public interest in the problems of machine production. One of the most interesting of the younger designers to emerge after the war was Ernest Race. The 'Antelope' chair shown above was designed by him for the Festival of Britain, 1951. A happy combination of lightness with economy of materials is achieved by the framework of wire and the seat of laminated plywood. Partly as a result of his experiences while working in the aircraft industry during the war, Race has designed some adventurous and exciting furniture, using a variety of modern materials, including steel mesh, cast aluminium and resin-bonded laminated wood.

The last half-century has seen extraordinary changes in the materials and processes of furniture-making, with consequent developments in furniture; in some instances the established forms of centuries seem to have been abandoned altogether. Metals and plastics of all kinds, fibre glass, etc., are being used extensively for furniture. Plastics in particular can form pleasing shapes which are difficult to produce in other materials. The chair illustrated above is made of a plastic (polypropylene) which was first produced in Britain by a process known as injection-moulding. There are also now available various timber materials. Plywoods are familiar enough. Two others, among many, are blockboard (a core of wood strips about one inch wide, sandwiched between veneers) and chipboard (wood chips bonded under pressure with resin glues), both of which do not split or warp, are light and strong, are ideal for large, unbroken surfaces, and can, of course, be decorated with veneers.

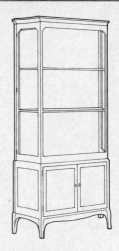

SIDEBOARD
Designed by Gordon Russell, 1950

CHINA CABINET, ROSEWOOD INLAID WITH HOLLY
Designed by Edward Barnsley, 1958

The plastic chair seen opposite, by Robin Day, is an excellent example of the way in which English designers have been able to strike out on their own in the application of new technological processes to furniture. In other fields of design the same kind of sturdy independence and enterprise can be seen. Consider, for instance, the Russell-designed, machine-made sideboard of 1950 illustrated here. Its simple, graceful form and attractive decoration are on traditional lines. The repeated pattern on the front is obtained by cutting it through a dark coloured veneer which is then applied to the carcase so that the lighter coloured wood beneath shows through. Unit furniture is another line which has been much developed in recent years. This can be bought piece by piece, to be arranged as the purchaser wishes, added to, and re-assembled quite easily in another room or even another house. Special units have been designed to bridge the corners of a room—usually awkward places to fill.

We have seen how, in spite of all the changes in furniture-making since the 1920s, English furniture has preserved a remarkable continuity. Hand-made furniture has strongly survived into the modern world. The china cabinet shown above, made of rosewood inlaid with holly, was designed by Edward Barnsley in 1958. It is one of the finest pieces of furniture made in this century, well able to hold its own with the best examples of the Georgian period. History has shown how this continuity emerges after periods of re-adjustment. The last fifty years have many similarities with the fifty years that followed the Restoration of 1660—the introduction into the English scene of new techniques, materials and processes of foreign development (even the influence of refugees is apparent in both periods), the same ferment of ideas, and a particular English contribution in developing furniture related to a new scientific instrument (clocks in one instance, radio sets in the other—see pp. 59 and 204).

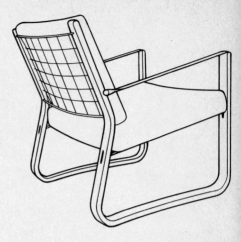

SOFA, UPHOLSTERED OVER LATEX AND POLYETHER FOAMS
Designed and made by G-Plan, 1965

ARMCHAIR, LAMINATED FRAME, STEEL MESH SEAT
AND BACK

The comparison between the two periods cannot be carried too far, but just as by about 1700 English craftsmen had absorbed the foreign influences and developed them with great efficiency along traditional lines, so much the same process is apparent now. Critics are beginning seriously to question whether the Modern Movement, so much the creation of the Bauhaus, provides the real answer to present-day design problems. Some indeed see the Modern Movement in these terms as simply another style, taking its place with the Gothic, the Classical and the Rococo. Bauhaus designs, it is claimed, were dominated by Cubism (now outmoded) were too often searching for mere novelty, and were too abstract, ignoring national characteristics and traditions. Attention is swinging back to vernacular forms. These have the simplicity and gracefulness which are sought in modern furniture, and they are by their very nature easily adapted to machine production, embodying, not discarding, tradition.

Thus the study of the history of English furniture can be of value and interest for the light which it throws on social conditions, for the opportunity which it gives us to appraise the reactions of successive generations of craftsmen to the challenge of social changes, and for guiding us to an appreciation of fine craftsmanship. Certain basic principles remain and hold the key to the present however much styles, techniques, materials and decoration have changed over the centuries. The reader's reactions may be tested finally by observation of a chair, that most fundamental piece of furniture. The example shown above gained the Design Centre award in 1966. It was made by Race Furniture Ltd., the firm established by the gifted Ernest Race, who died in 1964. The laminated framework is made of resin-bonded beech veneers, the arms are composed of two strips of dyed hide, and the back and seat are of steel mesh and are upholstered with fabric-covered foam cushions.

Select Bibliography

General
Edwards, R., *Shorter Dictionary of English Furniture*, London, 1969
Fastnedge, R., *English Furniture Styles*, London, 1969
Gloag, J., *A Short Dictionary of Furniture*, London, 1952
Hayward, H. (Ed.), *World Furniture*, London, 1969
Joy, E. T., *Country Life Book of English Furniture*, London, 1964
Macquoid, P. and Edwards, R., *Dictionary of English Furniture*,
London, 1924, revised edition, 1954

Special Studies
Aslin, E., *Nineteenth Century English Furniture*, London, 1962
Coleridge, A., *Chippendale Furniture*, London, 1968
Connoisseur Period Guides; *Tudor to Early Victorian*, London, 1956–8
Edwards, R. and Jourdain, M., *Georgian Cabinet-Makers*, London, 1944
Fastnedge, R., *Sheraton Furniture*, London, 1962
Harris, E., *The Furniture of Robert Adam*, London, 1963
Harris, J., *Regency Furniture Designs*, London, 1961
Joy, E. T., *Chippendale*, London, 1971
Musgrave, C., *Regency Furniture*, London, 1961
Ormsbee, T. H., *The Story of American Furniture*, New York, 1934
Watson, F. J. B., *Wallace Collection Catalogue*, London, 1956

Design Books
Selected reprints of Chippendale, Hepplewhite and Sheraton designs
published by Tiranti. Full reprints by Dover Publications Inc., New York

Modern Furniture
Giedion, S., *Mechanization Takes Command* (Part V), London, 1948
Moody, E., *Modern Furniture*, London, 1966
Pevsner, N., *Pioneers of Modern Design*, London, 1970
Schaefer, H., *The Roots of Modern Design*, London, 1970

Victoria and Albert Museum
English Chairs; Short History of English Furniture, booklets on Tables,
Commodes, etc.

Index

Index

Index

Index

226